THE STORY OF THE

IRON COLUMN

...

We fought and we won; we spread our ideas and we were heard.

We watched the golden wheat grow and our band of fighters grew alongside it.

They flocked to our Iron Column because they were iron-willed, and our struggle was and will be as hard as iron.

We are rebels and we keep the banner of rebellion flying high.

We fight in the war and in the revolution: on the front, in the vanguard, our weapon is muscle; in the rearguard of the city, our weapon is the mind.

Some hate us, while others love us.

But the 'others' are the workers, who see us as the faithful guardians of revolutionary principles.

The bureaucracy that sprouted out of the revolution hates us, because we unmasked it and held the real pariahs up to the light of day.

But we do not care about their hate.

What matters to us is that the factory and the field are on our side, and on the side of the revolution.

...

THE STORY OF THE

IRON COLUMN

by ABEL PAZ
translated by Paul Sharkey

Militant Anarchism
in the Spanish Civil War

The Story of the Iron Column: Militant Anarchism in the Spanish Civil War
© Abel Paz, translation © 2011 Paul Sharkey

This edition © 2011 Kate Sharpley Library and AK Press (Oakland, Edinburgh, Baltimore)
ISBN: 978-1-84935-064-8 | eBook ISBN: 978-1-84935-065-5
Library of Congress Control Number: 2011920480

Kate Sharpley Library
BM Hurricane, London, WC1N 3XX, UK
PMB 820, 2425 Channing Way, Berkeley, CA 94704, USA
www.katesharpleylibrary.net

AK Press   AK Press
674-A 23rd Street   PO Box 12766
Oakland, CA 94612   Edinburgh, EH8 9YE
USA   Scotland
www.akpress.org   www.akuk.com
akpress@akpress.org   ak@akedin.demon.co.uk

The above addresses would be delighted to provide you with the latest AK Press distribution catalog, which features the several thousand books, pamphlets, zines, audio and video products, and stylish apparel published and/or distributed by AK Press. Alternatively, visit our websites for the complete catalog, latest news, and secure ordering:

www.akpress.org | www.akuk.com | www.revolutionbythebook.akpress.org.

Printed in Canada on acid-free, recycled paper with union labor.
Special thanks to John Barker for Indexing.
"Eyewitness in Barcelona" (© George Orwell) used by permission of Bill Hamilton as the Literary Executor of the Estate of the Late Sonia Brownell Orwell.

Contents

By Way of Historical Introduction

The months leading up to the fascist uprising of 19 July 1936 passed with dizzying speed, changing the political panorama at each moment. General elections were held on 16 February. Two coalitions converged on the ballot-boxes: the left-wing Popular Front and the right-wing Confederación Española de Derechas Autónomas (Spanish Confederation of Autonomous Rightists—CEDA). The election results gave a majority to the left-wing bloc, and within that bloc the Partido Socialista Obrero Español (Spanish Socialist Workers' Party—PSOE) faction got the most of the votes, thereby earning it the largest number of seats in parliament.

Following the PSOE within the Popular Front, in number of votes won was the alliance that revolved around the figure of Manuel Azaña; in other words, the republicans. The Partido Comunista de España (Communist Party of Spain—PCE) constituted a minority of thirty thousand adherents and fourteen deputies, which in no way reflected its political strength. The latter derived from concessions previously granted by the PSOE during the pre-election negotiations.

The election results entitled the PSOE to form the government, but the tug of war between Largo Caballero and Indalecio Prieto over who would lead that government ultimately tipped the balance in favor of the republican bloc, headed by Manuel Azaña. The president of the Republic, ex-monarchist Niceto Alcalá Zamora, urged Portela Valladares to expedite the transfer of power.

On 18 February, Azaña formed a government drawn from the republican parties. CEDA leader Jose María Gil Robles retired from the political scene under pressure from General Franco, the army chief of staff for the outgoing right-wing government, after Franco failed to convince Portela Valladares to declare a state of war. But Gil Robles's disappearance did not mean that he was accepting defeat; rather, it meant that he accepted that it would be General Franco and the rest of the conspirators who would determine the speed at which the planned military uprising against the Popular Front would proceed.

Prior to the elections, the National Committee of the Confederación Nacional del Trabajo (National Confederation of Labour—CNT) issued an appeal on 14 February in which it denounced the military conspiracy and alerted the working class to take steps to resist it. Given the almost prophetic nature of this appeal, we reprint it here in its entirety:

> PROLETARIANS! On a war footing against the monarchist and fascist conspiracy! Day by day the suspicion is growing that rightist elements are ready to provoke military intervention. This is public knowledge due to the left-wing newspapers, which are constantly issuing warnings of the once secret, now blatant, intrigues being hatched by the reactionaries in the barracks and in the civilian and ecclesiastical precincts of the counter-revolution ... Morocco seems to be the epicentre of the conspiracy. Insurrection has been deferred, pending the outcome of the elections. They are to implement their preventive plan if there's a leftist victory at the polls. *We are not the defenders of the republic, but we will do unstinting battle with fascism, committing all of our forces to rout the historical executioners of the Spanish proletariat.* Furthermore, we have no hesitation in recommending that, wherever the legionnaires of tyranny launch armed insurrection, an understanding be speedily reached with antifascist groups, with vigorous precautions being taken to ensure that the defensive contribution of the masses may lead to the real social revolution and libertarian communism. Let everyone be vigilant. Should the conspirators open fire and should their fascist rebellion be defeated in its first stages, then the act of opposition must be pursued to its utmost consequences *without tolerating attempts by the liberal bourgeoisie and its Marxist allies to hold back the course of events.* Once hostilities begin in earnest, and irrespective of who initiates them, democracy will perish between two fires because it is irrelevant and has no place on the field of battle. If, on the other hand, the battle is tough, that recommendation will be redundant, for no one will stop until such time as one side or the other has been eliminated; and during the peoples' victory its democratic illusions would be dispelled. Should it be otherwise, the nightmare of dictatorship will annihilate us. Either fascism or social revolution. The defeat of fascism is the duty of the

whole proletariat and all lovers of freedom, weapons in hand, yet the most profound preoccupation of members of this Confederation is that revolution should be social and libertarian. If we are to be the greatest source of inspiration of the masses, if they are to initiate libertarian practices and create an unbreachable bulwark against the authoritarian instincts of the whites and the reds alike, we must display intelligence and *unity of thought and action*. From now until the reopening of parliament, if the danger persists then militants ought to meet frequently in each locality in the normal way and keep in touch with the confederal committees so that the latter are informed about the course of events.

Albeit in irregular fashion, a will to fight must be displayed. Anything is better than our remaining on the fence and our incredulity leading to our extermination and repression by the dark hordes... Let others shoulder the humiliation of failing to understand current circumstances and of having disdained their place in the coming battle. Once again: eyes peeled, comrades! It is better to move prematurely with courage than to have cause to lament our inactivity.

The National Committee
Zaragoza, 14 February 1936

The government turned a deaf ear to what the CNT—along with a number of leftist newspapers and certain republican servicemen—was publicly denouncing. The government limited itself to a minor reshuffling of generals, but as the clamour grew in intensity, the minister of war was forced to make his position public on 18 March:

Certain rumours that seem to insistently circulate around the state of mind of the army's officers and other ranks have come to the attention of the minister of war. These rumours, which can of course be dismissed as false and lacking any foundation, nevertheless tend to maintain public unease, sow animosity towards the military and undermine—if not destroy—discipline, which is the very foundation of the army. The minister of war is honoured to announce that all of the officers and other ranks of the Spanish army, from the highest ranks to the lowest, abide by the limits of the strictest discipline, and is prepared at any moment to carry out its duties to the letter and—needless to say—conform to the dispositions of the lawfully constituted government.

Meanwhile, the conglomerated rightists (military, church, bourgeoisie, nobility and landowners) were making their plans and sharpening their knives. Outside, the streets were a hotbed of agitation. The revolutionary process was maturing, particularly among the peasantry.

In March, unable to wait any longer, farm workers from the CNT and the Unión General de Trabajadores (General Workers' Union—UGT) struck by occupying the large estates in Extremadura and La Mancha. It is estimated that this peasant movement involved some eighty thousand people who, after occupying the land, organised themselves into farming cooperatives that prefigured the unleashing of agrarian collectivisation some months later. The government had the good sense to hold back the Civil Guard and instead recognise the land occupations under the provisions of the Agrarian Reform Plan.

The Falange Española, created by José Antonio Primo de Rivera in October 1933, took on the responsibility of heightening public tension by shooting at vendors of the left-wing press or at personalities of a leftist persuasion, and by setting off bombs. The object of this offensive was clear. It intended to create a state of alarm that would justify the acceptance of the military uprising in the court of public opinion, as the reaction of order to widespread disorder. Thus, Falangist gunfire became a daily occurrence in Madrid. On the other hand, although Barcelona wasn't a completely tranquil place, a climate of relative calm prevailed there.

In the upper reaches of the government, Alcalá Zamora was dismissed from his post as president of the Republic on 7 April, and on the 10th an assembly of deputies and representatives appointed Manuel Azaña as the new head of state. On the 19th of that same month, Santiago Casares Quiroga presented the new government to parliament. He himself assumed the positions of president and minister of war.

The new leader of the government, during his presentation before the Cortes, affirmed that 'the government is belligerent in the face of fascism.' The left-wing faction asked itself if this was really true. The question hung in the air, but it began to receive a response through incidents like that at Casas Viejas, which had led to the republican government being tagged the "government of the 110 deaths." Since 1931, the CNT had not been able to hold a single congress. Existing in an almost constant state of semi-legality, it simply did not have enough time to organise a sorely needed congress. After 16 February, with the CNT's unions operational and its newspapers on the streets, it thus became a matter of urgency to convene a congress, which opened in Zaragoza on 1 May 1936.

In fact, the preparation for the congress was more important than the congress itself. From the moment that it was announced and the agenda distributed to the unions, not a single Sunday passed on which the unions did not call their members together. Given that the local union halls were small, the assemblies were held in cinemas and theatres. In Catalonia, *Solidaridad Obrera* published in its pages the opinions of the members and the initial texts regarding the principal points of discussion, with texts referring to the project of libertarian communism occupying the most space. Special trains were organised from different locations around Spain, particularly from Barcelona, and thousands of workers—male and female—dyed Zaragoza an intense red and black for days on end.

On 1 May 1936, the CNT congress began. It was attended by 649 delegates representing 982 unions with a total card-carrying membership of 550,595. The opposition unions—which had broken away in 1932—attended the congress and had speaking rights, the object of which was to find a solution to the CNT's internal crisis. In addition to relations with the opposition, the agenda included important items regarding the analysis of revolutionary activities (a critique of the uprisings of January and December 1933 and October 1934) and a revolutionary alliance with the UGT. The congress also attempted to define the CNT's concept of libertarian communism, and to likewise adopt positions regarding agrarian reform, the current political and social circumstances and unemployment.

The accords adopted at this congress were publicly explained at numerous rallies and mass meetings held in the bullrings of big cities like Barcelona, Zaragoza, Madrid, etc. Nevertheless, despite the enthusiasm awakened by the congress, serious questions (raised at the twelfth session) pertaining to an analysis of the effects of the insurrectional cycle weighed heavily upon the delegates. During a private session, the National Defence Committee explained its opinion; not so much with regard to past events, but rather in reference to the outlook that would be created by the inevitable fascist uprising.

In the section of the report on libertarian communism that dealt with revolutionary defence, the congress anticipated the role that would be played by the people in arms and by the confederal defence groups, as well as the necessary action pact with the UGT. But all this would remain uncertain as long as it depended on uncertain factors. As a result, all agreed:

A. To activate the CNT-Federación Anarquista Ibérica (Iberian Anarchist Federation—FAI)-Federación Ibérica de Juventudes Libertarias (Iberian Federation of Young Libertarians—FIJL) Defence Committees or Commissions; to avoid clashes that would waste the scarce war material available; and to achieve maximum results through the most direct methods.

B. To attempt to attract socialist workers using all means, for it was clear that, without a CNT-UGT alliance, the isolation suffered by previous insurrections would be repeated.

C. That the anarchist groups (FAI), together with the CNT sections in the Protectorate of Morocco, will seek an alliance with the Moroccan nationalist forces in order to jointly defeat the military stationed there. All of this would be geared towards not only extending the revolutionary process to the Spanish protectorate, but also towards creating an alliance with socialist forces in both territories. One way or another, the rebel generals' elite army had to be stopped from crossing the Strait and disembarking on the Peninsula. Delegations at the congress from Tetuán, Ceuta and Melilla firmly committed themselves to working towards this as soon as they returned to their districts.

D. To lobby the Asociación Internacional de Trabajadores (International Workers' Association—AIT) to alert its sections so that, when the time came (and particularly in France), contacts with the Confédération Genérale du Travail (General Confederation of Labour—CGT) could be intensified with the aim of fomenting among the people a wave of sympathy for the Spanish revolution that would stop the French government from contributing aid to the potential mutineers.

The delegates who attended that private session of the congress thought that if fifty per cent of what was agreed was to meet with success or was given real form, then they would be able look to the future with optimism. The enthusiasm that the CNT congress had revived among the workers needed to be nurtured, and this led to the holding of numerous rallies and public assemblies throughout the country. As the reader will be able to appreciate, the plan outlined and explained above rested on two fundamental points: that the Defence Commissions would achieve their objectives and that a revolutionary alliance would be reached with the UGT. Regarding the first point, there were grounds for hoping that all would proceed according to plan. However, regarding the second point, pursuing a revolutionary alliance with the upper echelons of the UGT could be dismissed outright, which meant that it would be necessary to circumvent the UGT executive in order to achieve an alliance with the grassroots, as had been done with the peasants in Extremadura and La Mancha.

In socialist circles, things were not going well. The rivalry between Largo Caballero and Indalecio Prieto continued to worsen. The former—who was beginning to discover Lenin—had lapsed into a revolutionary infantilism that was being nurtured by flattery from the PCE, which was glorifying him as the 'Spanish Lenin.' He was also allowing himself to be dragged along by the advice of his friend Álvarez del Vayo, who was a PCE 'fellow traveller.' Out of this relationship came the unification of the Juventudes Socialistas (Socialist Youth—JJSS) and the Juventudes Comunistas (Communist Youth—JJCC) in order to from the Juventudes Socialistas Unificadas (Unified Socialist Youth—JSU). Santiago Carrillo, the JSU's first general secretary, had already been won over by the PCE.

Thus, Largo Caballero's position did not augur well for the call made by the CNT for a revolutionary alliance with the UGT. As was to be expected, the UGT general secretary did not even bother to respond. In the face of so many troubles and unknown factors, the delegations attending the CNT congress returned to their respective places of residence in order to fervently devote themselves to the task of putting into effect the commitments they had made to the CNT community.

For their part, the conspirators were not wasting any time, and in the month of May the coterie of generals implicated met in Madrid to apply the finishing touches to their subversive plan. They resolved to name José Sanjurjo—exiled in Portugal at the time—as overall commander, while Emilio Mola was tasked with preparing the insurrectional plan. The date of the uprising was left undetermined, although there was talk of launching it during the month of July in order to coincide on the one hand with the army's annual military manoeuvres, and on the other hand with the summer leave period for the conscript army, in which the commanders had very little confidence given its level of politicisation.

This military cabal enjoyed the support of José María Gil Robles, representing the CEDA; José Antonio Primo de Rivera, from the Falange; the aristocracy, as represented by its doyen the Duque del Alba; the church, through Luca de Tena, director of the newspaper *El Debate*; the Alfonsine and Carlist monarchists Antonio Goicoechea, Rafael Olazábal, General Barrera and J. Lizárraga; and the bankers and haute bourgeoisie, represented by Juan March.

June and part of July were a time of anxiety, in that each day the danger of a military uprising became plainer, although neither the republican government nor Minister of War, Casares Quiroga, seemed the least bit disturbed by the progress of the conspiracy. The government only paid attention to the leftist forces, particularly the CNT, which it relentlessly persecuted; suspending its newspapers— *Solidaridad Obrera* in Barcelona and *CNT* in Madrid—under any pretence at all or jailing its militants as *presos gubernativos* (governmental prisoners), which was a euphemism for the arbitrary incarceration of leading militants like Cipriano Mera or David Antona, the latter of whom was general secretary of the CNT National Committee.

During parliamentary sessions, disputes between leftist and rightist deputies were a daily occurrence. The leading figures in these melees were Gil Robles, who was always menacing; Calvo Sotelo, who constantly announced that 'the revolutionary seed had to be exterminated, even in the womb of its mother'; and 'La Pasionaria,' who won her spurs as a PCE parliamentarian.

Given the nebulous but imminent military coup, the CNT and the FAI in Barcelona, convinced that the battle that would set the pattern for events was going to be waged on Catalan soil, decided to immediately fulfil the Zaragoza congress agreements pertaining to the Defence Commissions, and a team of militants from the 'Nosotros' group—formerly the 'Los Solidarios' group—was named. One of the first activities of this Commission was to organise neighbourhood commissions and instil in their militants the idea that, if Barcelona fell into the hands of the conspirators, the battle would be as good as lost at the national level.

The main objectives pursued by the commissions were to tighten relations with the antimilitarist committees operating inside the barracks and to maintain constant watches around said barracks, the Civil Guard barracks, police stations and centres of right-wing activity. The ultimate goal was to proceed with the disarming of policemen and night watchmen and the raiding of gun shops, and to designate strategic places to serve as meeting centres in the various neighbourhoods. The plan was well-organised and well-structured, to the point that the entire city could be mobilised within an hour, with action groups showing up at locations that had been previously designated as enemy centres. By early July the established strategy was running like clockwork.

Taking into account the political tenor of the city and province of Barcelona, the local Defence Commission was certainly not exaggerating in its consideration of the CNT and the FAI to be the only forces that could effectively confront the uprising. In reality, the parties that formed the so-called Popular Front could not be relied upon. The Esquerra Republicana de Catalunya (Republican Left of Catalonia—ERC) was a petit bourgeois party whose militants—and more particularly whose regular members—were ill-suited to the kind of fight that was predicted if the army took to the streets. The 'escamots' of Estat Català had already demonstrated their combative worth [in their failed revolt] on 6 October 1934. Very little could be expected from these two groupings.

The remainder of the political groups that adhered to socialism consisted of the UGT—which had a slight presence among shop assistants—plus certain groups commanded by Joan Comorera. The only forces that the CNT could count on as allies were the few action groups from the Partido Obrero de Unificación Marxista (Workers' Party of Marxist Unification—POUM) led by Andrés Nin and Juan Andrade, whose ranks included leading militants from the Izquierda Comunista de España (Communist Left of Spain—ICE), and sections of the Bloc Obrer i Camperol (Worker-Peasant Block—BOC), which was directed by Joaquín Maurín but mainly based in the province of Lérida. In reality, these were the only forces capable of confronting a potential uprising.

The Generalitat had some four thousand Assault Guards at its disposal—spread throughout Catalonia—and the *Tercios* of the Civil Guard under the command of General Aranguren. But to what extent could the Generalitat trust the loyalty of these corps? If it took part, the Civil Guard could decide the result of the fighting. But, given its reactionary spirit, it would likely be tempted to ally with the mutineers (as it eventually did in some cases). As for the Assault Guard, whose personnel were more reliable given their recent formation, its police-type approach nevertheless made it equally dubious.

In view of all of the above, it was clear that the CNT and the FAI would have to bear the brunt of the fighting, albeit in poor conditions and with a motley collection of weapons: pistols and some rifles recovered after they had been dumped on the streets by Estat Català on 6 October 1934. Given the lack of weapons as the decisive moment approached, the Defence Commission urged Lluís Companys, the president of the autonomous government, to arm some five hundred CNT militants. But he always claimed that he 'had no weapons at his disposal.'

It was clear that Lluís Companys was not going to give a single pistol to the CNT, and this proved to be the case. Those in contact with republican authorities came to the conclusion that the republican governors and ministers were more afraid of the revolution than the military uprising.

Before concluding these brief remarks, it seems appropriate to settle several points about which most—but not all—historians keep quiet:

1. The passivity with which the republican government behaved between the months of March and June 1936, as it ignored the machinations of the seditious generals and the governors' refusal to accede to the demand for weapons, was decisive in allowing the rebels to be victorious in those major cities where the uprising emerged triumphant.

2. The conspirators and their cronies were not rising up against the republican government, but rather against the revolutionary process that had been maturing in Spain since 1931. The pretexts used by the rebels and their allies, particularly the church—such as the persecution of the clergy and the existence of a Marxist threat—were false. The PCE's political influence in Spain at that point was almost nil.

3. The reproaches and accusations against anarchism (CNT-FAI) represent the greatest falsehoods ever uttered in order to conceal

the positive role played by anarchism. For the first time in history, anarchism acted as a determining force—with positive results—in the construction of an autonomous, federalist society based on antiauthoritarianism and solidarity.

4. With regard to Catalonia, that country never had at its disposal such an ample opportunity to develop its autonomous status within the federation as it had between 19 July 1936 and 3 May 1937; on which date the Catalan government, by allying with the counterrevolution, lost all that it had gained in terms of autonomy.

5. Meanwhile, the predisposition of the French and English bourgeoisie against the Spanish revolution did not stem from 'the abuses of the mob,' but rather from the revolution of October 1934. The machinations of the Duque del Alba in England and Luca de Tena in France coincided in the purchase of the 'Dragón Rapide'[1] under the tolerant gaze of the French and English secret services. Franco was a product made in France and England, for he guaranteed the protection of the global empire (including Spain) maintained by those two countries.

A historical study that took these points into consideration would turn history on its head. No matter. I conclude by invoking Galileo Galilei's celebrated dictum: 'Eppur si muove' ('And yet it moves').

Abel Paz
Barcelona, July 2001

---

1   The Dragón Rapide was the plane that left Croydon on 11 July 1936, flying to Portugal and on to the Canaries to pick up Franco and deliver him to Morocco in time for the army revolt that month. [KSL]

Declaration (from the first edition)

There is a school of thought that suggests that books need neither forewords nor introductions, because forewords are always too self-congratulatory while introductions are at best showy displays of erudition. But in this particular instance, I believe I owe the reader some words of explanation.

I will concede that, while I was immersed in researching the life of Buenaventura Durruti, I was already attracted to the notion of writing about the Iron Column. During that time I seized every opportunity to gather information and documents relating to the Column.

I embarked upon collecting documentary evidence in anticipation of the day when I would finally have a chance to come to grips with it. But while waiting for that day to arrive, something occurred that I wish to place on record here.

While I was living abroad in Paris I had a visit from a young Spaniard who was studying at the University of Vincennes (a hotbed for the events of May 1968). He had turned to me, he said, for advice on a dissertation he was writing about the Iron Column. His interest in the matter was matched only by his sympathy for the revolutionary intransigence of the Column. I found this delightful, because in addition to relieving me of the task of writing about the Column myself and releasing me for other undertakings, it showed me that there were young people who shared my interests, not as scholars—I already knew plenty of those—but as revolutionaries.

That fellow's name was Miguel Moreno,[1] and he put in a fair bit of work on his thesis. But his militant anticapitalism eventually led to his being imprisoned, which stopped him from completing his undertaking and led to the loss of what notes he had managed to amass.

In light of that turn of events I resumed my own research and completed it in 1980, at which point I went off to look for a publisher. I met up with Eliseo Climent in Valencia and he signed a contract stating that he would publish a Catalan edition of my *Crónica Apassionada de la Columna de Ferro*, that being the original title of the work.

---

1 No connection to Néstor Romero, author of *Los incontrolados: chronique de la "Columna de hierro" (Espagne 1936–1937)* Editions Acratie, Paris, 1975. [KSL]

But two years later, in roughly the middle of 1983, he returned my translated manuscript with an accompanying letter in which he explained that financial straits had prevented him from honouring the contract. He also apologised for having to inform me that my original manuscript had somehow gone astray. When that happened I had just published the book *CNT—1939–51* through the small Hacer publishing house, and sales of its somewhat limited print run were proceeding quite well. It thus occurred to Pep Ricou and I that we should go out on a limb and publish the book which the reader now holds in his hands.

To conclude this note, let me express my gratitude to those who helped me in this undertaking. I shall not mention too many names but I will single out two from the list. First, Miguel Moreno, because I believe that he will be pleased when he learns that the Iron Column now enjoys a life of its own in print. My thanks also go to Rudolf de Jong and the library staff at the International Institute for Social History in Amsterdam for the assistance they afforded me during my time in their reading-rooms.

Finally, I thank all those directly involved with the Iron Column who either provided me with their testimony on the subject or obtained documents for me.

I do not wish to close without also offering my gratitude to a young employee at Paterna (Valencia) city hall who showed great patience while locating in the register of deaths the precise date upon which the Pellicer brothers—both leading figures in the Column—were shot, as well as the death certificates which record, with clinical cynicism, that 'death was due to internal bleeding.'

Abel Paz
Barcelona, 1 May 1984

I
Levante Confronts the Mutinous Generals

Valencia was the capital of the Third Military Region. As of 19 July 1936, its military complement consisted of two infantry brigades (the Fifth, which was based in Valencia, and the Sixth, which was based in Alicante), one artillery brigade (the Third, which was based in Valencia), four infantry regiments, two artillery regiments, two sapper regiments and the appropriate services for a division.

Also present in the Region was the Cartagena Military Command, which comprised a naval base, one infantry regiment, one artillery regiment, a flying boat base and the General Air Force Directorate. The Civil Guard had its Fifth *Tercio* stationed in Valencia, with three commands (Inner Valencia, Outer Valencia and Castellón) and a total of thirteen companies, while the Second District Carabineers were also based in the capital along with some Assault Guard units.

The military commands were vested in Generals Martínez Monje (Third Division), Gamir Ulibarri (Fifth Brigade), García Aldave (Sixth Brigade), Cavana de Val (Fourth Artillery Brigade) and Martínez Cabrera (naval base). Of these five, Martínez Monje was fiercely loyal to the Popular Front, Gamir Ulibarri and Martínez Cabrera were regarded as greatly undecided, and García Aldave and Cavana de Val were all for the uprising. The officer corps were also partial to the mutineers, with those from the Valencia garrison displaying a particular enthusiasm, and the revolt could count upon civilian support from the Valencian bourgeoisie attached to the Derecha Regional Valenciana (Valencian Regional Right—DRV) led by Luis Lucia.

The DRV's very substantial youth wing was battle-hardened and perfectly organised and officered, so much so that there is a possibility that, next to Navarre, it may well be that it was in Valencia that the forces disposed to revolt enjoyed—theoretically, of course—the widest collaboration from the civilian element. The DRV youth, who were scarce in Alicante province but numerous in the provinces of Valencia and Castellón, were the first to embrace a recourse to violence, and as a result they trained for the armed struggle.

On the other hand, it was well-known that Carlism also enjoyed strong support in some Valencian districts, especially in the Valencia-Teruel district known as the Maestrazgo, where the Comunión Tradicionalista retained a foothold and commanded some splendidly regimented and determined units. Plus, there were the small Falange Española groups.[1]

In opposition to this motley right-wing line-up was an equally hodge-podge left. Republicanism, spread by Blasco Ibáñez and Rodrigo Soriano, was firmly ensconced, as was an anticlerical current which found expression in the satirical anticlerical weekly *La Traca*.

The socialists of the PSOE enjoyed superb support in Valencia and a solid foothold in Alicante, but only middling enthusiasm in Castellón. It should be pointed out that theirs was quite a radicalised socialism, demonstrated most clearly by the working-class base in the UGT.

As for the anarcho-syndicalists, their history could be traced back to the beginnings of the First International in Spain (1869). In the years before 1936 the CNT and the FAI held firm throughout the Peninsula, even though many people had written off both organisations following the severe repression to which successive governments had subjected them.

In 1936 the CNT had solid roots in the region, especially in Valencia. At the Zaragoza National Congress of May 1936, Levante was represented by 112 unions boasting a total of 100,000 dues-paying members. Meanwhile, the FAI, which was launched in Valencia in July 1927, could at that point count on some 150 anarchists scattered throughout the region.

On 12 July 1936 the Levante region of the CNT held a reorganisation Congress (Valencia was the greatest stronghold of the moderates who had broken away from the CNT in 1933, and in the wake of the aforementioned Zaragoza unification Congress the duplicated trade unions had to be amalgamated), at which it became apparent that the CNT was lagging behind in the rural areas. A decision was thus made to step up propaganda activity, which was duly escalated

---

1   José Manuel Martínez Bande, *La Invasión de Aragón y el Desembarco en Mallorca*, 37. [Martínez Bande was a Colonel and pro-nationalist historian. KSL]

right after the fascist revolt and which led to the creation of the famous collectives, which, according to the Regional Congress held in November 1936, were admirably supported by 40,000 peasants.

Such was the politico-military profile of the Levante region on 17 July 1936, when the mercenary army of Morocco, headed by General Franco, mutinied at the instigation of General Emilio Mola.

In Barcelona the uprising took shape on 19 July 1936, with troops leaving their barracks at 5:00 a.m. By 4:00 p.m. that same day, General Goded—who led the revolt in Barcelona—had been taken prisoner, at which point the army revolt in Catalonia could be deemed over. The people in arms were in control of the streets and the situation.

On 20 July the populace stormed the Montaña barracks in Madrid, thereby foiling the uprising in the nation's capital as well.

In Valencia the barracks were not attacked until 1 August, after ten days of dramatic tension. But with the storming of the barracks, doubts were dispelled and the Levante region began to breathe more easily.

When José Manuel Martínez Bande came to assess the military situation, he offered the following summary of the reasons for the failure of the uprising in Valencia and in the Levante region:

A series of events precludes the declaration of a state of war on 18 July as had initially been agreed, thereby allowing the mob to quickly seize control of the streets and call a general strike on 20 July. On that day General González Carrasco's plan to seize command of the division falls apart, while General Martínez Monje manages to deceive his supporters with false promises: first by adopting a stance of passive neutrality before later declaring a state of war. His troops are confined to barracks, but that is as far as it goes. The climate on the outside matches this passivity, and day after day all hope of success evaporates amid the most absurd inactivity. The sappers' barracks are stormed on 29 July, the Guadalajara and Lusitania barracks on 1 August and the remainder fall on 2 August.

Castellón: The failure of the uprising in Valencia is crucial to the fate of Castellón, despite the favourable disposition of most of the army and Civil Guard officers along with the great mass of committed civilians. On 20 July, Lieutenant Colonel Peire Caballero—a great supporter of the Popular Front—manages, with indubitable daring, to override the ditherers and the irresolute, thereby neutralising them completely.

Alicante: To the particular problems faced by the uprising in this province—given the political loyalties of the bulk of the population—was added the lack of resolution on the part of General García Aldave, who waited for the state of war to be declared from Valencia. The arrival of the destroyer *José Luis Díez* on 22 July tipped the balance once and for all the following day.

Nor was a state of war proclaimed in Alcoy by the Vizcaya Regiment, whose colonel took his lead from the attitude adopted by the province's military commander. However, the officers didn't surrender until 2 August.

Murcia: Despite his well-known allegiance to the mutineers, Colonel Cabanyes—who headed the artillery regiment located there—inexplicably changed his attitude regarding the uprising, which led to the weak reaction of those officers committed to it. Thus, there was no declaration of a state of war.

The same thing happened in Cartagena, where the revolutionary masses—both from the locality and from the vessels at anchor in the port—gradually took command of the situation, which was finally resolved on 20 July. General Martínez Cabrera gave them his determined support.

Albacete: Without any proper garrison and planted in the middle of fiercely hostile territory, it nevertheless offered a sharp contrast in that it was the only centre in the Third Division where the uprising enjoyed momentary success before collapsing a few days later.[2]

---

2   Ibid., 38. Let us expand upon Martínez Bande's comment by adding a summary taken from Alicante's *El Luchador* (21–31 July 1936): 'In Albacete—which was an important railway link between Madrid and Levante—the Security Corps, some soldiers and the entire Civil Guard command mutinied, and also seized other important towns in the province. Immediately, two columns of soldiers, Assault Guards and militians set off from Alicante, Cartagena and Murcia and liberated Almansa and Hellín. Along the way they were joined by militians from nearby towns, escapees from Albacete and reinforcements arriving from Valencia. On the morning of 25 July all these forces met up in Albacete and took on the fascists with air support. The fighting in the city carried on into the evening, when the Civil Guard barracks finally surrendered. The militians then completed their military apprenticeship by mopping up the remaining fascists and Civil Guards who were swarming over the entire region. Tension was running high throughout Levante. Every town was on edge. Barricades were erected at the entrances

to every village. Passers-by were stopped, arrested and questioned. Religious objects were burned. In no time at all, all kinds of committees were set up, while militians rushed to enlist or argued about which column they would be joining.'

II
Valencia on the Edge

Once news of the military revolt broke, the CNT and the UGT called a general strike in Valencia on 19 July. Both organisations set up a Strike Committee which in effect supplanted Civil Governor Braulio Solsona, who was dismissed for being 'politically incompetent.' But parallel with the establishment of the Strike Committee, the political parties making up the Popular Front launched a second committee called the Peoples' Executive Committee, which was set up in the civil government headquarters. However, it should be stressed that the real power was still in the hands of those applying the pressure from the streets: namely, the CNT and UGT labour organisations.

Within a few days, these clearly revolutionary Committees had been joined by another committee that saw itself as the official representative of the central government. On 21 July, just before the civil governor had been driven out of Valencia, Manuel Azaña—the president of the Republic—signed a decree which established the Republican Government Delegate Council over the territory comprising the provinces of Valencia, Alicante, Castellón, Albacete, Murcia and Cuenca. At its head was Diego Martínez Barrio, the speaker of the Spanish Cortes. This was Azaña's way of restoring republican order in the Levante region, for the aim of the Delegate Council was to force the spontaneously created popular bodies to submit to its authority.

In addition to Martínez Barrio, the Delegate Council was made up of Minister of Agriculture Ruiz Funes and Ministerial Undersecretaries Carlos Esplá and Martinez Echevarría. But when these ministers arrived in Valencia and established their first contact with the People's Executive Committee, it became immediately apparent that 'too many cooks spoil the broth.' In other words, one of the groups was superfluous.

This dual power situation persisted until 6 August, on which date a formal resolution was passed whereby the representatives of the Delegate Council returned to Madrid and the Peoples' Executive Committee remained as the repository of representative functions and public order. In this way the shadow of formally lawful 'republican' authority vanished, and the established power remained as it was in practice: purely revolutionary.

In Valencia we had a governor who was the very embodiment of political ineptitude and frivolity. He was so inept that, only a few days prior to the fascist military revolt—and following the death of Calvo Sotelo[1] and the spread of alarming rumours to the effect that the mutineers were stirring—he asserted that, in the view of the Valencia authorities, there was not even a shadow of a doubt regarding the loyalty of those same military forces to the republican regime.

The first reports of the revolt reached Valencia on the morning of 18 July in the form of vague rumours. Those rumours took on more substance as the day wore on until they finally confirmed early that night. The entire night of 18 July was spent in Valencia listening to contradictory reports broadcast by the government-controlled Unión Radio and by fascist radio stations. All of Levante was mobilised at the instigation of the CNT and the UGT.

On the evening of 19 July, the Local Federation of Sindicatos Únicos (CNT) in Valencia called a revolutionary general strike which began at the stroke of midnight. A Strike Committee was appointed to oversee the strike and to come to an agreement with the sister trade union body—the UGT—regarding concerted action.

In the early hours of Sunday night there was a minor gun battle when the Dominican monastery was attacked by a group of workers from the Construction Union. This news was brought to the attention of the governor by a member of the CNT Strike Committee in order to make sure the governor knew that the working class would not countenance any act of repression on the part of the forces of public order controlled by the civil

---

1 'On 13 July, José Calvo Sotelo, the monarchist parliamentary leader and one of the most important of the civilian conspirators, was slain by leftist members of the police as a reprisal for the murder of José Castillo, a left-wing member of the republican Guardia de Asalto, the Assault Guard'. Burnett Bolloten, *The Spanish revolution*, 39. [KSL].

government. The governor's response to this warning was to call upon us to remain calm, lest the government forces be obliged to deal with any kind of abuse.

Meanwhile, the officers commanding the Valencia military garrison—ensconced inside their barracks from the very outset—were arguing over whether or not to throw in their lot with the uprising while at the same time acting in concert with the fascists who were still roaming the streets of Valencia and who had not yet been rendered powerless. The parties of the Popular Front, persuaded of the weakness and incompetence embodied in the person of the governor, decided to replace his authority with a specially appointed Revolutionary Committee. On the morning of 20 July that Committee met in one of the offices at the civil government headquarters.

The Strike Committee appointed by the Valencia CNT and made up of, among others, comrades Domingo Torres, José Pros, Juan Candel, Artiáñez, Juan Acha and Juan López was in session at the headquarters of the Local Federation when a report swept through Valencia stating that the military garrison had mutinied and was beginning to emerge from its barracks. This news, which related to a scheme hatched between the fascists operating on the streets and the military plotters, led the Strike Committee to immediately urge all CNT-mobilised personnel to set up a blockade around the barracks.

The Popular Front Revolutionary Committee had been set up in order to take the lead in the struggle for which the governor had proved incapable of making due preparations, and it was in session when the delegation from the CNT Strike Committee strode into the civil government building. Confusion reigned within those premises, and in the midst of such confusion a man loyal to the Republic—Captain Uribarry—was making the rounds. Militants from all the antifascist organisations were also there, and they were there for just one reason: to ask for guns and to place themselves at the disposal of whomever was ready to confront the army rebels.

Once we CNT delegates realised that a dangerous hesitancy was afoot, we decided to step aside and exchange impressions before deciding whether to take part in the Popular Front Executive Committee. After we had taken stock of our views, it was decided that, as the basis and precondition for our joining the Executive Committee, we had to impress upon it the necessity for immediate adoption of the following measures:

First, that steps be taken to ensure that the telephone exchange, post office, telegraph headquarters and the Unión Radio transmitter are seized by a number of Assault Guards and twice that number of militants chosen from each of the groups affiliated to the antifascist organisations.

Second, that the people of Valencia be mobilised to cordon off the garrison's barracks and to take up strategic positions in order to maintain a blockade of the same.

Third, that once the first two conditions had been met, the military commanders be informed of the antifascist authorities' decision that they should hand over their weapons to the people so that the latter could safeguard the situation.

Fourth, that in the event of a refusal to hand over weapons to the people, we proceed immediately to storm the barracks.

Fifth, that the CNT would join the Popular Front Executive Committee in an advisory capacity until such time as all of the aforementioned measures proposed by us were put into effect, at which moment we would begin acting in an executive capacity. Our suggestions were accepted.[2]

From the moment that the CNT joined the Executive Committee, thereby making it into a revolutionary popular organisation, things started to get complicated. The political parties—particularly those of the republican persuasion—did not look kindly upon the working class intervention of the CNT, and therefore made overtures towards the governor to undermine the CNT while seeking assistance from the Madrid government.

While all this scheming was going on in the civil government offices, events on the streets were beginning to synchronise with the overall situation, as workers armed with all sorts of equipment

---

2   Juan López, 'El 19 de Julio Levantino,' in *De Julio a Julio: Un Año de Lucha*, ed. CNT, 41. This is a reprint of articles published in a special edition of Valencia's *Fragua Social* (19 July 1937).

patrolled their neighbourhoods while other groups carrying shot-guns besieged and attacked churches from whose bell-towers shots had been fired at the workers. The city was starting to take on all the hallmarks of a workers' uprising.

On Tuesday 21 July, Valencia was lit up like a flame: the churches were burning. The first act of a populace that still did not know the true situation inside the barracks was directed against religious authority.[3]

Consistent with the conservative character that they had invested in the workers' defence of the Republic, the socialists made overtures to José Giral, and the Valencia civil governor's pleas to Madrid were heeded. A decision was made to send in a team of politicians led by Diego Martínez Barrio, whose tasks would include bringing the siege at the barracks to an end, disbanding the Revolutionary Committees and ultimately restoring the republican government's authority in Valencia.

> The Government Delegate Council—made up of Martínez Barrio, Ruiz Funes, Echevarría and Carlos Esplá—had arrived in Valencia, and the governor summoned us to a joint meeting between that delegation and the Executive Committee, at which the situation was reviewed. Carlos Esplá hinted at calling off the general strike, but he was not very specific about the idea until the second meeting at 4:00 a.m. The CNT did not dismiss his suggestion, but made it plain that the strike could not be called off until the people had a clearer picture of what was going on in the barracks. The government's delegate, Carlos Esplá, assured us that the garrison would stay loyal to the Republic. But in real-ity the barracks remained sealed, and inside them the wrangling continued between those who wanted to take to the streets and those who did not.
>
> On Thursday night (23 July) the Executive Committee met at the invitation of Carlos Esplá. He explained that he had decided to proceed with the dissolution of the Peoples' Executive Committee. His decision, he added, did not mean that he was rejecting the collaboration of all the political and trade union

---

3   Ibid.

groups which comprised the Executive Committee. Each party and organisation would subsequently choose a representative to liaise with him, as he would be taking charge of the civil government from that moment on.

After hearing this announcement the CNT realised that nothing more could be done there. With the exception of the Communist Party and the Republican Left, everyone agreed that matters could not possibly be left like that. The CNT let it be known that Esplá's resolution should be regarded as a suspicious and dangerous step, against which it had a duty to issue a caution.[4]

With his decision made, Carlos Esplá believed that republican power had been reestablished and that the parties and workers organisations would bow to his command, thereby serving as instruments of popular demobilisation. His analysis of the Valencia political situation might have been inspired by the manner in which problems had been resolved in Madrid, but if that was the case, he was ignorant of how things really stood in Levante and its capital. The military were still confined to their barracks, the general strike had led to a shortage of foodstuffs and those shortages were aggravated by other deficiencies resulting from the work stoppage. Carlos Esplá thought that cancelling the order to strike was all that was needed in order to bring everything back to normal, but in reality his was not a feasible solution because it did not address the urgent matter of the troops, whose attitude was akin to a sword of Damocles poised over the head of militant antifascism.

When the CNT abandoned the civil government building, they immediately met with the UGT in order to get a handle on the situation and work out some solution to the most pressing problems.

Essentially at issue was the problem that had arisen in Valencia, its province and the Levante region as a whole, and important decisions were made with the aim of channelling the energies of the masses in a constructive direction.

It was decided that preparations should be made for a gradual lifting of the strike, and it was agreed to publish a unified daily

---

4   Ibid.

newspaper bearing the title *UGT-CNT.* A plan was drawn up for tackling the supply problem in which both trade union organisations took charge of impounding all existing food stocks in order to introduce the tightest possible control and prevent any thieving and hoarding, which could create difficulties. The plan to restore normality in the city was to take effect in such a way that those unions involved in the food and allied trades would return to work, but the rest of the striking unions would remain mobilised in order to maintain control of the streets until the threat of military revolt dissipated.

The Strike Committee's agreements were shared with the Executive Committee, which, along with the elements that comprised it, continued to operate behind the back of Señor Esplá, who was the main representative of the Government Delegate Council. The Executive Committee approved the trade union plan, but when the time came to put it into effect the delegate from the government opposed it on the grounds that it was the responsibility of the city council, and not the trade union associations, to assume such functions.[5]

But in practice, the city council and the state's bureaucratic agencies, which were more or less non-existent, were incapable of reinitiating the distribution of products necessary for the upkeep of the city and the surrounding villages. They only increased the chaos so the force of circumstances led to the trade union organisations assuming the functions of distribution. Once again, the harmful role played in society by the state and its bureaucratic organs was made patently obvious.

Behind the scenes of the situation we have been describing, the troops unfathomably remained inside their barracks despite the assurances of loyalty they had given to Martínez Barrio, who kept in constant touch with the military command by telephone. It would finally be the region's villages that broke the deadlock brought on by this incomprehensible situation.

In the region's villages, the working-class and antifascist elements had mobilised, spontaneously standing guard and keeping a watch on the roads and highways. Hunting rifles and rusty

---

5 Ibid.

old handguns were the weaponry with which they stood ready to swoop down from their villages upon Valencia at a moment's notice to take on the fascists.

The presence in the harbour of the first loyal warship was another factor that helped keep the mutineers confined to barracks. The workers of El Grao, who were in control from the very beginning, established their absolute command over port traffic and began to fraternise with the sailors, maintaining constant contact with them. The seamen were ready to spring into action at the slightest hint of revolt from the troops in the Valencia garrison.

The first shipments of rifles and handguns began to arrive from Barcelona, increasing popular enthusiasm. Saturday 25 July saw publication of the first issue of the newspaper UGT-CNT, which was the organ of the United Strike Committee.[6]

The week drew to a close without a solution to Valencia's military problem. The Government Delegate Council postponed a resolution to the matter, but the People's Executive Committee—now operating independently of the Council—and the Strike Committee were both facing increasing pressure from the masses, and these two bodies decided to hold talks with the commanders of the warships at anchor in the harbour in order to determine whether the sailors were ready to cooperate with the workers in what was regarded as an inevitable fight with the troops.

> The meetings proceeded, at which point Martínez Barrio asked us for just a little confidence in his actions so that he might see them through to their conclusion, adding that if—contrary to his expectations—his initiatives failed and the Popular Front parties withdrew their support, he would pack his bags and head back to Madrid.[7]

During that week, amidst the alternating tension and calm between the Executive Committee and the Government Delegate Council, something took place which clarified the intentions of the Delegate Council: it raised a military column for dispatch against Teruel.

---

6   Ibid.
7   Ibid.

We will never forget that expedition organised to march on Teruel, which cost the lives of more than 200 militians who were executed by the Civil Guard members of the column, the composition of which failed to meet the standards recommended by the Executive Committee. The Executive Committee wanted a column made up of three militians for every Civil Guard member. Instead, they got the exact opposite. One-fourth of the column was made up of militians, while three-fourths were Civil Guard personnel. As a result, the Civil Guard murdered the militians and defected to the enemy with arms and equipment before even reaching Teruel. Those Civil Guard members then constituted the basic military complement in Teruel from that moment on.[8]

But the province could no longer abide by the situation facing its capital city. The military garrisons of Játiva, Alcoy and Alicante took the people's side on 28 and 29 July. Nevertheless, it should be pointed out that the detonator needed to unblock the situation was Sergeant Fabra from the Paterna Engineers' Regiment, who raised his men in revolt, disarmed the fascist officers and took to the streets with the aim of marching to the capital. Faced with this situation, the Executive Committee and the United Strike Committee in Valencia resolved to storm the barracks on the night of Saturday 1 August.

After attacking the barracks fifteen days into the uprising, Valencia and the surrounding region were able to regroup and organise aid to comrades fighting on the front lines. Civil Governor Braulio Solsona finally resigned. The Government Delegate Council, now completely incompatible with the People's Executive Committee, disbanded. And the Executive Committee, free at last from all the hindrances with which it once had to contend, began to organise life in Valencia along with columns of militians for the Teruel front.[9]

---

8   Ibid.
9   Ibid. As a matter of fact, as far as Spain as a whole was concerned, once Barcelona had been secured the main aim was to avert the capture of Madrid, and it is in this context that we should interpret the republican drive towards Córdoba, Granada and Málaga to stem the Francoists' advance. Teruel remained an enclave

The narrative of Juan López corresponds well to actual events, but we ultimately find ourselves with a situation similar to that which we related before, only now it pertains to the Delegate Council: the government, or its 'legal' forms, steadfastly resisted its own demise and thus managed to give continuity to its authority. General Martínez Monje, who was the previous captain-general of the region, kept his rank, but he was replaced by General Miaja (an utterly nondescript individual, but one who would acquire an undeserved international reputation thanks to the PCE propaganda campaign surrounding the defence of Madrid in November 1936). However, the presence of either Martínez Monje or Miaja at the head of a division was purely decorative, because once the barracks had been stormed, the regiments either disbanded or, in other cases, lost their military discipline upon integrating into the workers' militias.

On the other hand, the War Department of the People's Executive Committee, along with the CNT and UGT Defence Committees, assumed responsibility for the military defence of the revolution. In that context, what could possibly be done by generals who had no troops and a mandate that no one obeyed? Yield to circumstances and await better times.

Such an exceptional situation was bound to give birth to exceptional figures, like 'Pancho Villa,' [Rafael Martí] who headed the Iron Column, and Domingo Torres, who led the Torres-Benedito Column. And as far as 'military specialists' were concerned, they tended to be servicemen with the best-known republican credentials or those who had rallied with the greatest enthusiasm to the workers' cause. In this sense, the most distinguished were Colonel Arín, Captain Manuel Uribarry and Lieutenant José Benedito, who was the war delegate from the People's Executive Committee.

---

in the republican zone, and the security of Valencia was dependent on control of it, which is why the militias from Valencia mobilized for that front.

III
The Militias Push Against Teruel

In Valencia, as in Barcelona and Madrid, the working class did not allow itself to be dominated by capital, but the problem of securing local and territorial victory immediately emerged. The theory of cantonalism, along with those of the autonomists and the localists, made the most concrete sense when oriented towards federation, because autonomy without federalism had no meaning. Thus, the Spanish working class was at this time committed to struggles on a nationwide scale.

However, the bourgeois separatists aimed to open up fissures in working class solidarity, just as the Lliga Regionalista Catalana (a bourgeois fiefdom) and later the Estat Català (the hotbed of reactionary nationalism) had done in Catalonia. But little headway was made among the workers, who held firm in their battles to a defensive federal compact: this was equally true of the CNT and the UGT.

For reasons based on tradition and revolutionary history, the first thing that the CNT and UGT did was to begin organising a workers' militia capable of bringing its fighting solidarity to the nearby areas that had fallen into the hands of the military uprising. From Madrid, militians headed for the Guadarrama, Guadalajara, Toledo, etc.; from Catalonia, Aragón was the destination; and from Valencia, the Teruel front was the prime target.

In many respects, Teruel occupied a crucial position in the struggle that had just begun. It was a strategic nerve centre for communications because its main roads reached out to Sagunto and on to Valencia and Castellón; first to Montalban and Alcañiz, then to Tarragona, Zaragoza, Calamocha, Daroca, Calatayud and finally to Torrebaja, before fanning out towards Cuenca and Valencia. There was also a rail link as well as a mining link that connected Teruel with Calatayud and Sagunto, and thus with Madrid, Zaragoza, Barcelona and Valencia.

In addition to being a communications centre, Teruel enjoys natural defences in the form of the surrounding highlands and mountains: the San Justo, El Pobo, Gudar and Mora highlands to the east, and beyond that the great massif of the Maestrazgo. Between the Alfambra and Jiloca rivers rise the Palomera and Lidón highlands, and it was there that the only pass permitting communication between the front and the rearguard was situated. It was a corridor so narrow and dangerous that, in military terms, control of it was a matter of life and death for the city's defence.

Going towards Sagunto, Teruel overlooks Escandón: a highly significant and hotly disputed location, as we shall soon see. The Torrebaja area (in the Turia valley) was not significant in military terms, so the best approach was to blockade the highway at a given point in order to secure the Camarena and Jalambre hills for defence or attack purposes.

From the outset, the expansive Albarracín region was in the nationalists' hands, along with the sierra that gives it its name (the 855-metre high Sierra Alta), but its defences were assured more by its geography than by its military complement. This gave a great advantage to Teruel's defenders, because it meant that they could maintain a relaxed attitude about their northern and western flanks.

On this basis it is easily understood why the militia columns hurriedly put together in Valencia or Castellón promptly made the capture of Teruel their objective. Unfortunately, the delays in Valencia between 19 July and 2 August did the militias no favours, as it allowed the mutineers to successfully capture Teruel, organise their defences and receive reinforcements from Zaragoza.

Lieutenant Colonel Mariano García Brisolara, who commanded the Teruel military garrison, was relieved on 8 August by Colonel Antonio Civera Ayxemus, who had arrived from Zaragoza. But García Brisolara had not been idle up to that point, as he had dispatched troops to tackle the two most dangerous revolutionary zones in the province: the mining areas of Libros (south of Teruel) and Utrillas (northwest of Teruel).

The first sortie was made on 24 July when a group comprised of Assault Guards and volunteers managed to occupy Libros. But these same troops were beaten back at Utrillas despite two successive attempts to seize the mines there. The miners roused themselves to mount a counterattack that successfully repelled the attackers and gave the victors control of the Montalbán district.

The first republican column deployed against Teruel came from Castellón and was commanded by Carabineer Colonel Fernández Bujada, Captain Luis Sierra and Lieutenant Joaquín Oset Merlo, with Francisco Casas Salas—the socialist deputy for Castellón—acting as its political delegate. The column was comprised of one thousand militias, more than four hundred Civil Guards and a few Carabineers from Valencia, Castellón and Cuenca. They headed for Teruel via Sagunto, and on the night of 28 July they arrived in Barracas, a town along the main route. Before pressing on to Sarrión, the column split into two parts: one, headed by Captain Sierra and deputy Casas Salas, marched on Mora de Rubielos, which was taken without a shot fired; the other, led by Fernández Bujanda, set off for La Puebla de Valverde on 29 July.

Once the column arrived in La Puebla de Valverde on the night of 30 July, 'the Civil Guards mutinied, capturing the expedition's military and political chiefs along with many of the militias—including those who had returned from Mora—dispersing the rest and seizing all the weaponry. They then joined the nationalist forces defending the approaches to Teruel along that very route. The Bujanda expedition thus came to an end, and strongly reinforced the meagre local garrison in the process.'[1]

While this first column suffered the above setback, the anarchist Cipriano Mera and a group of militias set off from Madrid on 28 July and made haste through Guadalajara province with the objective of attacking Teruel. But upon reaching Orihuela del Tremedal a battle erupted which lasted for many hours, after which the militias had to fall back owing to the strength of the enemy forces, which were made up chiefly of Civil Guards.

There were other forays against Teruel, like the one made by the Peñalver Column, which set out from Tarragona via the Muniesa-Moyuela front on 3 August. In order to head it off, Major Aguado

---

1 José Manuel Martínez Bande, *La Invasión de Aragón y el Desembarco en Mallorca*, 92. In his *Historia del Ejército Popular de la República*, Ramón Salas adds further detail regarding events in Puebla de Valverde: 'The column of Civil Guards and militias under the command of Fernández Bujanda left Valencia on 25 July, linked up in Sagunto with another column originating in Castellón, and pressed on to Segorbe, where it was joined by militias and Civil Guards from the villages in that district. In total, there were seven hundred militias and four hundred Civil Guards. At Segorbe the column split into two details: one went to Teruel via Puebla de Valverde and the other went to Mora de Rubielos. Upon arrival in Puebla de Valverde on 30 July, the Civil Guards mounted an ambush while the column was resting, killing 72 militias and taking 47 prisoners including the expedition's leader Bujanda and his commanders Casas and Sierra, who had come from Mora for talks. The prisoners were escorted to Teruel and shot.'

left Teruel and made it as far as Vivel del Rio, but the resistance he encountered forced him to retreat and take cover back in Teruel. Thus, the Utrillas area was left in revolutionary hands. It was at this point that Colonel Antonio Civera Ayxemus arrived from Zaragoza and took charge of the defence of Teruel. The new commanding officer:

> found the front in dire straits from all points of view, even though the garrison had swollen to the size of roughly one thousand men, with four artillery pieces.
>
> Based on these forces, the colonel formed two small columns of around two hundred men each, which were led by Major Aguado and Major Pérez del Hoyo.
>
> In view of the danger posed by the enemy concentration (the Iron Column) in Sarrión, Civera decided to attack it.[2]

However, before we describe the Iron Column's first engagement, it would be better if the reader was familiar with how it had been put together and how it had left Valencia. To this end, we call upon the aid of one of its members, Roque Santamaría:

> The organisation sent our group out to the Liria district in order to organise and agitate in that area. We stayed there for a few days, and upon returning to Valencia on 1 August to report to my union—the Barbers' Union, of which I was the secretary—I found that my comrades were forming a century to join up with the Iron Column, which was being organised in Las Salesas. The people from my union who belonged to that century were all very young: less than 25 years old.
>
> While the Iron Column was being formed by the most extremist elements of the CNT and the FAI, another column (the symbol of what was then called 'confederal reformism,' a tendency that caused a schism in the CNT which was healed at its congress in Zaragoza that year) was being raised alongside it, which took the name Torres-Benedito. But it was clear to all that the Iron Column represented real anarchist extremism while the Torres-Benedito Column merely represented the 'confederal opposition'

---

2   Martínez Bande, 93.

of those who had broken away from the CNT in 1933.

The Iron Column was led by comrades from my FAI group, in particular one fellow named Segarra who went on to become commissar of the Eighty-third Mixed Brigade, which was the militarised version of the Iron Column. Later on, the Pellicer brothers joined, with Pepe especially distinguishing himself (the other brother lived somewhat in his shadow). I remember this because it cost both of them their lives later, with one being killed simply for being the other's brother. We were close friends.

I showed up with the Barbers' Union century, as was common practice among trade union members. We gave ourselves the name 'Hygiene and Cleanliness,' just like the others had done, like the 'Metalworkers,' 'Transporters,' etc.

The Iron Column was made up of peasants and industrial workers. Its basic unit was the century, which was in turn divided into groups. The peasants formed their own units with people living in the same village. Within a month of its establishment, the Iron Column had twelve thousand enlisted members, but we only had enough equipment to arm around three thousand fighters.

I should clear up the matter, later to become so controversial, of the San Miguel de los Reyes prison. The opening of the gates and the releasing of all the inmates was the doing of a small group of comrades. They arrived at the prison and demanded that the gates be thrown open. There was no resistance, so they set everybody free.

Most of the inmates were in San Miguel de los Reyes for criminal offences but there was also the odd comrade convicted for bank robbery or something like that. The opening up of the prison was prompted by principle and nothing more. It was an attempt to do away with something we regarded as a product of bourgeois rule: the inmates were victims of society and they had to be given a chance, at which point most of them joined the Iron Column, fighting and conducting themselves in an extraordinarily brave and intrepid fashion.[3]

---

3   As an example of what Roque Santamaría is talking about, the reader will find towards the end of this book an article penned by 'an uncontrollable' who had been one of those 'petty criminals.' Regarding this issue, E. Manzanera, who was a member of the Iron Column himself, writes: 'The social prisoners released when the revolt

The first eight centuries of the Iron Column left Valencia on 8 August and took the road to Sagunto in order to reach the road to Teruel, which was the front to which we had been assigned. We were on our way to a front that just days before had been the object of what can only be called treachery.

In Castellón, a militia column had been raised under the aegis of a Socialist deputy by the name of Casas. In terms of its make-up, it was a very motley column, with its membership drawn from the CNT, UGT, etc. Its theatre of operations covered a number of villages in Castellón province, up to and including Puerto de Sagunto in Valencia province.

The men of that Column arrived in a village named La Puebla de Valverde, along with the Civil Guards who formed the substance of most of the Column. Upon arrival in the village, which is located some thirty kilometres from Teruel, the advance party stopped to rest, intending to press ahead the next day. But they awoke to find the guns of their Civil Guard colleagues pointing at them. The Guards disarmed, subdued and hunted down whomever they could. Those who were captured were shot on the spot.

---

broke out lined up with the militians in a surge of fervour and enthusiasm. Much has been said, including a lot of chatter, mud-slinging and slander, with regard to these inmates of the San Miguel de los Reyes penitentiary. Upon leaving prison, many of them made their way home. But several reported to us... Two of our delegates screened them one at a time before they could join. We had implicit confidence in these comrades. They knew everyone well. As our comrades made their way through San Miguel de los Reyes, they signed up those prisoners whose upright, decent behaviour had distinguished them from others inside the prison, and this certainly proved to be a wise decision, contrary to what some cheap hacks have written. The writer's trade shouldn't be open to people who, on account of their immorality and dishonesty, fall short of the lofty standards of journalism and a life of letters. That is the truth of the matter, not the slanders and misrepresentations hurled at men who earned the respect of each and every one of us' (E. Manzanera, *Documento Histórico (La Columna de Hierro)* [published by the Kate Sharpley Library as *The Iron Column: Testament of a Revolutionary*], 14 [forty-page pamphlet, courtesy of the author]). The writer's remarks clarify how such 'nonsense and baseless rumours' could blind the likes of J. Andrade (a member of the POUM Executive Committee), who regurgitated them in an article entitled 'La Columna de Hierro,' published in the 13 March 1937 issue of *La Batalla* (J. Andrade, *La Revolución Española día a día* [Barcelona: Ed. Trazo, S.A.—Nueva Era, 1970], 187), in which we find him saying things like: 'The Iron Column was comprised of elements of a very motley social extraction... Above all, basic instincts ... [and] a rampant hunger for revenge prevailed in its ranks,' etc.

This was the front for which we were now bound, fully aware of what had occurred, having heard it from those who had successfully escaped from the trap.[4]

Initially, the Column had few weapons. The first centuries to deploy were given rifles at the artillery depot. Perhaps some twelve to fourteen centuries were armed this way. The rest had to rely on weapons that the Column had recovered from enemy hands. Regarding the question of arms, I do not think that we were on our own in being targeted for constant sabotage. The CNT's Torres-Benedito Column was in the same boat as us as far as arms and ammunition were concerned.

Our plan of action was very simple: war and revolution were synonymous. Consequently, wherever we went, revolution as we understood it was vital, and we used to announce to the populace that there would be no point in winning the war and losing the revolution and not much point in winning the revolution unless we won the war too: the two were one and the same. This was a good indication of what our line of conduct was and would be, and we abided by it at all times.[5]

---

4   We shall quote Carlos Llorens Castillo from his *Historia del Partido Comunista de España*, in which he refers to the attitude existing within the Iron Column in the wake of the events at La Puebla de Valverde: 'That massacre was the cause of the first incident faced by the Iron Column—or 'The Desperado Column,' as one newspaper called it, alluding to its determination to avenge those killed in La Puebla—soon after its formation. Massed in Sagunto in preparation for its trip to Teruel, the Column's men insisted that the Civil Guards from the local barracks enlist and that their weapons be confiscated. When the Civil Guards refused, the militias besieged the barracks. As the Assault Guards and the political parties thought it wiser to not get involved, the governor appealed to the PCE for help. Communist leaders negotiated with the Column's War Committee, and after a round of promises and discussions it was agreed that the weapons would be handed over to the militias and that the Civil Guards would remain under Communist supervision.

5   Roque Santamaría, a member of the CNT and the FAI in Valencia, was secretary of the city's Barbers' Union at the time. As a member of the Iron Column from the very beginning, he was involved in the militarisation process during March 1937, especially with regard to supplies, which subsequently fell under the aegis of the Eighty-third Brigade's quartermaster section. In exile in France, he held the position of secretary of the International Secretariat of the CNT in Exile several times between 1954 and 1965. Approached by us because of his knowledge of the Column, he drafted some notes from which we have quoted as indicated. He died in Toulouse in 1980 at the age of 70.

This witness injects a tone of optimism into the first part of his account, but the truth was that, in view of the conditions in which the militias set off for the front, all they had in their favour was their revolutionary courage and their belief in victory, combined with the psychological element of surprise. But they still lacked elementary things needed to sustain the struggle, such as a proper supply line for transport, arms, ammunition and artillery and—perhaps just as vital—adequate sanitary and hospital services.

Again, according to our eyewitness, the first Iron Column section to leave Valencia was armed with rifles only and had little in the way of ammunition. In such conditions, standing up to the enemy waiting in Sarrión was going to be a crucial test for the militia, which up to that point only had to deal with skirmishing along the route.

Before proceeding, let us return to the point where we left off, with nationalist troops marching from Teruel to Sarrión in order to halt 'that menacing advance.' Martínez Bande narrates the encounter between these troops and the Iron Column:

> Given the danger posed by the enemy concentration (the Iron Column) in Sarrión, Civera resolved to launch an attack: Aguado's column would proceed along the Valencia road, while Pérez del Hoyo's column would make haste for Mora de Rubielos with the aim of closing in on Sarrión from the north. In fact, the operation was unduly ambitious given the strength of the forces allocated to carry it out.
>
> On the morning of 12 August, both columns established contact with the enemy, and Major Aguado's column even made it through to Sarrión. But the reds called in air support, and soon several planes were bombing and strafing the nationalist positions while, after receiving reinforcements, an attempt was launched to outflank the Aguado Column on its right (southern)

The Torres-Benedito Column was so called because its political delegate was Domingo Torres and its military expert was José Benedito, who was an artillery lieutenant and war delegate on the People's Executive Committee in Valencia. The members of the Column were revolutionary workers who, like the members of the Iron Column and all the other anarcho-syndicalist columns on the Teruel front, were at odds with the 'circumstancialist' line of the CNT. The Torres-Benedito Column was complemented by the Mirasol Column of Castellón libertarians and the Gandía Division of the CNT-UGT.

flank. The Aguado Column was thus forced to begin a withdrawal in the face of enemy superiority after its commander lost his life, while the Pérez del Hoyo Column had to do likewise after its namesake was wounded. For the moment, some men remained posted in La Puebla de Valverde, but they would later fall back to Puerto de Escandón.

The loss of morale stemming from the failure of this operation was, of course, considerable. But the high command, having weighed the circumstances, drew up a plan to defend Teruel at all costs and regardless of the risks.

The most advanced positions were Corbalán, Valdecebro, Puerto de Escandón, Aldehuela, Cubla, Villel and Campillo. There were blockhouses at the Muletón and Mansueto peaks, the Santa Barbara convent, the villages of Castralvo and Villaespesa along with the adjacent high ground (the Castelar peak and Hill 992), the Muela de Teruel peak and the hamlet of San Blas.

A last-gasp retreat position was established on the outskirts of San Blas, fortifications were hastily erected and all access routes were blocked.[6]

We now return to our narrative. On 10 August, *Correspondencia de Valencia* wrote that 'the CNT and FAI militias were encountered en route to Teruel following what is now National Highway 234. From the station in Sagunto they were heading for Barracas, with the intention of swooping down upon Teruel from there. These forces are led by a major and four officers.'

Once in control of Sarrión, one of the first steps taken by the Iron Column was to set up a hospital and urgently ask the CNT and FAI Defence Committees in Valencia for medical services. But it is unlikely that this matter was easily resolved when we see that, in a report dated 10 August 1936, the People's Health Committee in Valencia was insisting that 'forty-eight hours prior notification was required if medical services were expected to arrive on time.'[7]

---

6   José Manuel Martínez Bande, *La Invasión de Aragón y el Desembarco en Mallorca*, 94.

7   Archivos de los Servicios Documentales (Salamanca), Sección Político-Social (P.S.), Barcelona, 1420, 'Memorando de la Delegacíon de Guerra del Comité Popular Ejecutivo de Valencia, 30-1-1937,' quoted in Terence M. Smyth, *La CNT al País Valencià, 1936–37*, 42.

Regarding the matter of supplies, clothing, blankets, footwear, etc., the war delegation of the Executive Committee, recalling those first moments, wrote in late 1937: 'The burden of keeping the militias supplied proved to be one of the toughest and most demanding of all, because in those early days the columns of fighters spawned by popular enthusiasm lacked even the most elementary necessities: they had neither clothing nor gear nor boots.'[8]

To all this we have to add the matter of transport and gasoline. It is true that from Sagunto the Central de Aragón rail line could be used, but after the mutineers destroyed the Mora de Rubielos rail bridge on 13 August, half of that line was rendered unusable. Consequently, the most practical form of transport was by truck, but that created a gasoline problem of such seriousness that on 22 August an advance party from the Iron Column was unable to proceed any further because the trucks requested from Valencia were twenty-four hours late in arriving.[9]

Regarding this issue, Terence M. Smyth writes:

The war delegation of the People's Executive Committee in Valencia had to cater to the needs of four independent and poorly-equipped militia columns that were fighting on difficult terrain along a semi-circular 'front' that was between seventy and ninety kilometres long. In addition to the Iron Column, which was predominantly CNT,[10] the others were the Torres-Benedito Column, the Thirteenth Column (also mostly CNT) and the Eixea-Uribes Column, which was made up of UGT members, socialists and Communists.[11] It should be remembered that even

---

8   Ibid.

9   See Valencia's *Fragua Social* (26 August 1936 and onwards) for matters related to the Iron Column.

10   Archivos de los Servicios Documentales (Salamanca), Sección Político-Social (P.S.), Castellón, 329. This is a list, complete with affiliations, of eighty-three names belonging to members of the Iron Column's transport section, three of whom were in the UGT. The ratio is clear.

11   The proportions within the militias on the Levante front were the same as those on the Aragón (Zaragoza-Huesca) front. The numbers overwhelmingly favour the CNT-FAI, clearly indicating its strong influence among the working class while simultaneously highlighting the PSOE's negligible influence (especially in Barcelona), along with the complete insignificance of the PCE prior to 19 July 1936.

though Column Thirteen was not deployed until the month of October, it still must be included as part of the front we have just mentioned.[12]

---

12 Terence M. Smyth, *La CNT al País Valencià, 1936–37*, 41. We complete the scene at the Teruel front with the following:

The Torres-Benedito Column (Column No. 1)—which by early August occupied Corbalan and Valdecebro to the north of Teruel—dislodged the enemy from the road bordering the Alfambra river with an attack from the rear, thereby reaching as far north as Perales de Alfambra and as far south as the Muletón, Santa Bárbara and Mansueto mountains, which were Teruel's natural defences. Colonel Velasco took over from Benedito in September as military advisor. In October the Column was reinforced by Confederal Column Thirteen, organised by S. Tronchoni in Valencia.

The Iron Column (Column No. 2) had been deployed between Aldehuela, which covered access to Castralbo at the foot of the Galiana peak and Castellar mountains, and Trinchera de la Muerte. The Column's territory included Hill 1301 in Puerto de Escandón, which was also called the Posición Pancho Villa in reference to the nickname of the Column's first leader Rafael Martí, who died in an ambush.

The Uribes-Pérez Column (Column No. 3) was mainly comprised of Communists from the JSU, with Juan Antonio Uribes as political delegate and Major Pérez Martínez as military advisor. In September, Pérez Martínez was replaced by Colonel Eixea, which facilitated a name change to the Eixea-Uribes Column. Additions came in the form of the Pablo Iglesias Battalion, which was made up of UGT members from Valencia, and the Iberia Column, which was comprised of *cenetistas* from Alicante who would soon abandon the Uribes-Eixea Column for the Torres-Benedito Column.

The Peire Column (Column No. 4) was a battalion of soldiers under the command of Lieutenant Colonel Peire. It left Castellón for Córdoba on 26 July, turned towards Teruel three weeks later, and on 21 August occupied Villel and Tramcastiel on the Valencia-Teruel road through Ademús. Between the Peire Column and the Uribes-Pérez Column were some POUM and Izquierda Republicana groups operating around Campillo. In mid-October, the Ferrer and Mora Battalions from the confederal militias of the central region arrived in the Montes Universales under the command of Cipriano Mera and Colonel Del Rosal. They liberated a number of villages and fought in Albarracín, which was retained by the nationalists. The Peire Column was then deployed at the other end of the line in Alfambra, where it was joined by the Matteotti Battalion of Castellón socialists. Command passed to Major Serrano, who took over from Peire. The Eixea-Uribes Column moved into the old positions held by the Peire Column and handed some of its own positions over to the Del Rosal Column. To all of these militia columns, bolstered by Valencian troops from Madrid, must be added the Macià-Companys Column, comprising some three thousand men organised by the Catalanists. It was answerable to the Militias Committee in Barcelona and took up a position between Vivel del Rio and Portal-Rubio, which was previously manned by the soldiers of the Martínez Peñalver Column. From there it served as liaison between the Catalan and the Valencian militias.

It must be assumed that the first eight centuries of the Iron Column to leave Valencia on 8 August were followed by others within a few hours, because otherwise it would have been barely eight hundred men who attacked Sarrión, which would have amounted to a real feat given their lack of military experience.

On 13 August 1936 the front page of *Correspondencia de Valencia* carried statements by a war delegate, José Benedito, reporting on the capture of Sarrión: 'The capture of the town of Sarrión prevented the enemy from blowing up the Albentosa railway bridge connecting Barracas and Sarrión.' Looking at the map, it is easy to understand the enemy's intention to slow the progress of the militia columns at all costs, and this was surely dictated by the scarcity of forces at its disposal in Teruel. This explains the counterattack on Sarrión on 13 August, as related by José Benedito in the aforementioned newspaper:

> The Iron Column has today clashed with fascist troops from Teruel, who were brought in by truck. Those forces comprised some four hundred soldiers... But our forces managed to scatter the enemy and capture two trucks, one coach, a car, six machineguns, some fifty rifles and the same number of pistols. The enemy left forty-three dead and several wounded on the field. Our losses amounted to four dead and twenty-seven wounded, four of them seriously... After five hours of fighting, sometimes hand-to-hand, the enemy fled to the safety of Teruel, pursued by our aircraft.

Within days, and despite the lack of transportation, the Iron Column was on the move again. Its objectives this time were La Puebla de Valverde and Puerto de Escandón, which was a fortified pass protecting Teruel.

> At daybreak, the Iron Column—which the previous day had taken La Puebla de Valverde without any resistance—has quickly mobilised. In buses we have begun our advance across the flat ground separating us from Puerto, where we have been told the enemy has dug in. The road snakes through the vast wheatfields—freshly harvested—like a huge reptile with neither

tail nor head. The white trail carries us towards our objective: Puerto de Escandón. The delegates in charge of the Column have a hard time keeping a lid on the men's enthusiasm, especially 'Pancho Villa,' who cautions them against wasting ammunition... The abandoned roadbuilders' huts serve as way-stations along the route, and soon we leave them in our wake. On the one beside which I am writing these notes, we can read this inscription: 'Teruel—18 kilometres. Zaragoza—199 kilometres.' The trucks press on. There is no enemy in sight. Maybe there are none in El Puerto, we reckon, and press on.

Our fighters crown the imperceptible hills surrounding this flattened plateau. Barely visible dots break the line of the horizon. They move. They become more visible. They are comrades who have pressed ahead. A few venture out to greet us. They come for water. August in Aragón, and that spells drought. Thirst. Parched.

We call a halt to our march. Three planes come from the north. Are they friendly? We take precautions, spreading out in order to not make an easy target. We hear a few explosions from a cannon. Rifle and machine-gun fire. But are they enemies? We missed their fly-past and also missed the insignia we were used to seeing on friendly aircraft.

We wait for the rest of the Column. Because of our cars, we've left it behind. The waiting bothers some of us, but good sense prevails. We rest in some shade by the side of the road. Soon the long-awaited orders arrive. We are to deploy on both sides of the road. The enemy is in sight. We scramble up a hill. Look out! A deafening blast rings out. A shell whistles past us. Hit the dirt! We flatten ourselves against the stubble. Another explosion. Another and another. Without a doubt they are aiming at us. Our trucks, sitting beside the station in Puerto, make a fine target.

Our fighters edge forward. But where is our artillery? Where are our planes? As far as we can judge from their projectiles, the enemy is at the top of a mountain, dug into a nearby pine forest. Are they expecting us to walk right into a machine-gun nest in our eagerness to capture their guns?

We take up our positions without giving ground. From behind the station-house we hear new artillery explosions. A ten-calibre shell falls nearby and explodes near a van, which sustains damage. And our artillery? Is it not yet close behind us? We had been told that we would have air cover from a number of planes. Why have they not arrived? We dissolve into speculation. The ghastly pounding ceases. Ah! I set about jotting down this report. Not a shot is heard. Our people occupy the hilltops.

I finish off this report surrounded by the bombast of makeshift strategists and a torrent of commentary.

We are laying siege to Teruel's Puerto Hill. An unexploded shell from the enemy artillery is being passed from hand to hand. It is an iron tube with an elegant bronze decoration.

Two hours of anxiety pass. At last! A friendly aircraft comes into view. It passes overhead and sweeps over Teruel. It drops its payload and flies away. And later on, our artillery arrives!

We take a breath. The fight has evened out. They have planes and we have planes. They have artillery and we have artillery. This means that we will soon be in Teruel.

Night closes in. The fighters, the equipment and the artillery, ensconced in their positions, wait for day to break so that they can give the fascists their just deserts.[13]

Having taken Puerto de Escandón and positioned itself at the gates of Teruel with its very first push, the Iron Column now found itself in the same situation as the Durruti Column, which stood at the gates of Zaragoza. Both were stranded, unable to capture either of these seductive targets which were so crucial to a revolution that politics were transforming into a war.

From that moment on—late August 1936—a period of stability descended upon the front; a breathing space that the nationalist high command exploited in order to reorganise its defences. General Ponte was appointed divisional commander while Colonel Muñoz Castellanos was made military commander of the Teruel front and given the mission of defending it from Monreal del Campo up to the boundary of the Soria Division. The forces at his disposal consisted of some 4,000-odd men, one unit of 75-millimetre guns and a battery of 105-millimetre guns. In addition, there was an auxiliary force

---

13 *Fragua Social* (25 August 1936).

composed of a motorised column under the command of Lieutenant Colonel Galera with 1,835 men, one battery of 75-millimetre guns and another of 105-millimetre guns.

As for the republican forces besieging Teruel, there were four columns:

— The Peire Column, under the command of Lieutenant Colonel Peire, was based in Alfambra with some seven-hundred men, one battery and eight machine-guns.

— The Iron Column, located south-east of Castralvo, was comprised of 600 regulars and 1,600 militias for a total of 2,200 men, with one battery, two machine-guns, five 81-millimetre mortars, two 50-millimetre mortars and two armoured cars.

— The Torres-Benedito Column, commanded by Colonel Velasco Echave, was deployed between Muletón and Valdecebro. It was made up of 800 regulars and 1,800 militias for a total of 2,600 men, with one battery, sixteen machine-guns, two 81-millimetre mortars, two 50-millimetre mortars and three armoured cars.

— The Eixea-Uribes Column, which was deployed along the Cubla-Villel-Bezas front, comprised 850 regulars plus 2,200 militians for a total of 3,050 men, with one battery, two machine-guns, five 81-millimetre mortars, two 50-millimetre mortars and three armoured vehicles.

These were the forces facing each other, and it is no stretch to say that, militarily speaking, by the beginning of September 1936 the defenders had the advantage. Their positions were fortified and naturally suited to defensive purposes, while their supplies and manpower were equal in quantity to those of the columns. However, they had the added advantage of military expertise.

And what about the workers' militias which, right from the start, had relied on the element of surprise and their own revolutionary zeal? By September, both of those factors had begun to decay.

IV
From Theory to Revolutionary Practice

'We anarchists had not marched off to war for the pleasure of defending the bourgeois republic which had murdered us in the streets and deported us to its African possessions in 1932, for having had the effrontery to proclaim libertarian communism in the Catalan mining villages around Sallent. No. We had taken up arms in order to unleash it along the way as we liberated territory wrested from the fascists at gunpoint.'[1]

Forty years later, that statement by an Iron Column member does not merely stand as a testament to the ethos of the Column in 1936. It is also a record of what its members feel to this day, faithful as they are to the pact they signed in blood on the battlefields of Aragón. The *miliciano* in question was one of the those who, after the capture of Sarrión on 13 August 1936, belonged to the tiny group that ventured as far as Mora de Rubielos in order to liberate it and fill its inhabitants with revolutionary zeal. Among his papers he still keeps the report, from the newspaper *Fragua Social*, that chronicles the expedition. We will transcribe a part of that report here, for how could we possibly say no when someone offers us a wrinkled, yellow scrap of paper salvaged from four years of Nazi occupation in France? It is not so much a newspaper clipping as a revolutionary testament:

> After an assembly of peasants, an advance party from the Iron Column along with a delegation of village residents declares libertarian communism in Mora de Rubielos. Nuns marvel at the fine treatment they receive from the anarchists and syndicalists.
>
> The village: We arrived in Mora de Rubielos this morning. On the way here we admired the lush fertility of its meadows and the

---

1   Oral testimony of Patrocinio Martínez Armero, who joined the Iron Column at its inception and later served as company political delegate for the Eighty-third Brigade, as shown by a document dated in Salinas on 26 September 1937 by the Brigade's commissar, Diego Navarro. Martínez Armero gave us this statement in 1974 in Montpellier, where he had been in exile since 1940.

verdant patchwork of its irrigated fields. Our impression prior to entering the village was that poverty couldn't possibly exist in Mora. Its residents, favoured by the generosity and fertility of nature, must surely lead a pleasant and contented existence.

Once in the village, which is overlooked by a feudal castle that dominates one's view, we found streets which could be called broad when compared with those in other villages. Housing of relatively modern construction and neat signs on the village establishments seemed to confirm our first impression.

But the appearance of the residents—weather-beaten and wrinkled like empty old wine-skins; scrawny and desiccated—shatters our optimism and leads us to conclude that Mora may be a rich village, but its inhabitants are poor and wretched.

The proclamation of libertarian communism: As we pass through the streets on our way to the main square, we meet a bailiff who is getting ready to post a notice from the Village Committee proclaiming libertarian communism. That notice, which we now reproduce, reads as follows:

'All villagers, male and female, will make themselves available to the delegated comrades who have taken up arms in service of the community, and will endeavour to bring all usable goods to the castle. All those who need anything will be attended to. Money is hereby abolished and libertarian communism is proclaimed in this village. The Committee. Mora de Rubielos. 18 August 1936.'

The people enthusiastically applaud the proclamation. We note that there are not many around. The left-wingers fled when the fascists swooped and the right-wingers fled when our fighters arrived. The population has been halved.

Consequences of the proclamation of libertarian communism: The homes of wealthy people under suspicion have been requisitioned. We have been in several of them. I marvel at their comfort and splendour. The halls and rooms are luxurious. The cellars are superbly stocked. These are not necessities. This is abundance. It is only here that we see a reflection of the wealth of the sprawling meadows and vast, fertile land of Mora.

In the streets, women and men with sacks on their backs make their way to the castle. We follow them as they zigzag up the slope. Attached to the castle are the Civil Guard barracks and the dungeons where the unfortunate suffered. A rather squat building, the dimensions of which we can only guess at.

The castle has been turned into a warehouse and supply centre. Everyone brings what they can and takes what they need. There is amazement and delight on the faces of women who help themselves to necessary commodities without paying.

The comrades, acting as makeshift administrative personnel, write and explain how the commune operates.

Five nuns with the libertarians: Somebody tells us:

'We have five ex-nuns among us'

'... ?'

'They were in the village. When they heard that we had come, they fled. We went after them and managed to convince them that there was no danger from which to run. Now they help us as much as they can, if they want to. They say that they are very glad to do so, and everyone respects them like sisters. They are amazed that we did not make mince-meat out of them. They have come to understand that we anarchists are quite humane.'

Indeed. At our request the nuns are called. They come quickly, keen to make a good impression on us. All smiles and good manners, they agree to answer our questions, knowing that their words will carry weight in the revolutionary press.

They tell us that they are doing very well. That the comrades—already they have adopted this working class terminology—treat them very well. They perform whatever duties they choose, without anyone asking them to. They have no fear regarding their lot. They will stay with their comrades for as long as seems necessary, unhurried and without fear. When they are no longer needed, they will go back to their home villages. They ask us to let their families know that they are fine, that they need not be alarmed, etc.

We note their impressions, which fill us with satisfaction, and in addition they give us their names so that anyone worrying about them can know that they are with anarchists and syndicalists who show them respect and extraordinary consideration.

Their names are: Trinidad Prats, from Benicolet; Teresa Tortajada, from Villar del Arzobispo; Rosario Llopis, from Beniarrés; Catalina Furió, from Vergel; and María Tormo from Montesa.

These ex-nuns are dedicating themselves to education in Mora de Rubielos. They have no academic degrees. They are living on what the townspeople, in particular, choose to give them. Same old story: When the fascists fled from Mora, reactionary elements advised them to get out of the village because 'those who were coming' would subject them to the worst treatment and outrages. They have now seen what the men who have taken up arms in order to create a new way of life are capable of.[2]

There are various documents of this type from which we could quote, but it would make for monotonous reading. The important point is that the Iron Column—just like the Durruti Column in Monegros—had refused to act as a mere occupying force by putting the villagers under 'martial law,' as was done by other militia columns not informed by anarchist theories, who thought that their fight only consisted of defending the Republic. By contrast, the Iron Column understood that its mission was to make people conscious of the real reasons for fighting: namely, the social and economic transformation of human relationships.

The very fact that property had been abolished and that farming collectives sprang up in the wake of the Iron Column's advance gave rise to a libertarian outlook within the Column. Its men were not soldiers, but workers who had swapped their tools and—painfully for them—had now to lay the foundations of a new world with their lifeblood. Living among the peasantry, as the men of the Iron Column did, made it easier for them to spread anarchist ideas and libertarian practices.

A shortage of weapons on the one hand, and a lack of battlefield activity on the other, ensured that there was always a part of the Column's membership that was not on active duty. From the outset it was understood that, according to our source, 'they could not follow the precedent set by the soldiery—like wasting their time drinking in taverns and upsetting civilian life with their rowdiness—but instead had to cooperate with the peasants working in the fields or on other tasks, according to the needs of the village.'[3]

---

2   *Fragua Social* (20 August 1936).
3   Patrocinio Martínez Armero. See note 1, p. 47.

In reality, their conduct in this sense was not very different from the conduct observed among other CNT and FAI militias operating on the Zaragoza and Huesca fronts.[4]

---

4   We refer the reader to our book, *Durruti, el Proletariado en Armas*, which extensively documents the activities of the confederal (CNT-FAI) columns on the Aragón front. [Available in English as *Durruti in the Spanish Revolution*, AK Press, 2007. KSL]

V

The Achievements of the Iron Column

The situation outside Teruel was identical to the one outside Zaragoza, and for the very same reasons. On the Zaragoza front, both confederal columns (the Durruti Column and the Sur-Ebro Column) were unable to proceed any further due to a lack of adequate weaponry (aircraft and artillery), and shortages of rifle ammunition. Another factor was the low priority given to the capture of Zaragoza by the combined command of the Central Militias Committee of Catalonia. The War Department, quite possibly advised by the 'professional experts' of the Central Militias Committee of Catalonia, made the taking of Huesca its number one priority. But Huesca, while an important objective, would cease to be so if the Zaragoza-Huesca road was cut, and this was a mission that the Del Barrio Column of the Partit Socialista Unificat de Catalunya (Unified Socialist Party of Catalonia—PSUC) was never willing to undertake, in spite of the pressing demands from the War Department in Barcelona.[1]

In Teruel, thanks to other complications more directly related to the central government in Madrid, the outcome matched that in Zaragoza. With their motley assortment of weapons[2] and displays of exceptional daring, the militias had managed to place Teruel almost completely under siege, but they could get no further. Every day that passed represented a squandered opportunity, because the enemy—who was perfectly aware of Teruel's military and psychological value—kept reinforcing its positions until they were impregnable (which would be made plain later, when the 'Republican Army' mounted its massive attack).

Thus, in September 1936 the situation of the militias facing Teruel was as follows: mere kilometres from Teruel, the Iron Column was occupying Puerto de Escandón; on the Iron Column's left

---

1   Paz, Abel *Durruti, el Proletariado en Armas*.

2   At the CNT's Regional Plenum in Levante, the Iron Column's delegation declared that it had received some one thousand rifles and very little ammunition. See *Fragua Social* (12–20 November 1936), which reprints the minutes of this CNT Regional Plenum.

flank, in Villes, was the Eixea-Uribes Column in an advanced position; north of the Iron Column, on its right flank, also just a few kilometres outside of Teruel, was the Torres-Benedito Column in the village of Villalba Baja.

The coordination between these three columns was nearly perfect because they were all answerable to the War Department of the People's Executive Committee in Valencia, which had to keep the troops supplied with both food and weapons. But Valencia was not as well-placed as Catalonia with regard to the development of war industry, and was thus equally dependent on both Barcelona and Madrid. On the other hand, Madrid was not at all pleased by what was going on in the Valencia region (remember the failure of Martínez Barrio's Delegate Council) and was openly hostile in its policies towards the region, decying it and Catalonia 'salt and water.'

The only solution open to the Levante region was to lobby Catalonia for support (which it did during the existence of the Militias Committee in Catalonia)[3] while getting on with the economic reconstruction plan; that planning should be handled by the CNT and UGT union centrals.[4] But that would take time, and in the absence of any guerrilla-style military activity, conventional warfare—with all its drawbacks—was gaining ground with every passing day, while the revolutionary vigour displayed by the working class on 19 July slowly ebbed away.

The Iron Column was aware of this state of affairs, and its members devised a number of schemes designed to apply pressure to the situation. Nevertheless, none of those schemes did anything to change the overall approach, even though some might have made a tiny impact in the rearguard.

Any plan of action designed to alter the course of events had to be very determined if it was to be foisted upon Madrid, which

---

3   See José Peirats, *La CNT en la Revolución Española*, Vol. I and Abel Paz, *Durruti, el Proletariado en Armas*.

4   This refers to the establishment of the Consejo de Levante Unificado para la Exportación de Agrios (Unified Council of Levante for the Export of Produce—CLUEA), which was a central agency created by the CNT and the UGT in order to oversee produce exports and manage profits. The central government would eventually use this body as an excuse for its war on collectivism in Levante. The inspiration behind the government's centralisation policy was Minister of Agriculture Vicente Uribe of the PCE.

represented the main obstacle to revolutionary goals. But how was this to be achieved? Had the men on the front been sensible enough to coordinate with one another independently of their own organisation (in this case, the CNT) and, at Durruti's suggestion, formed a National Defence Council, then it is possible that the pace of the war might have been accelerated.

But the problem stemmed from an earlier time, and could be traced to the lack of initiative at the beginning of the fascist uprising, when General Franco managed to establish a foothold in Andalusia near Gibraltar and began making giant steps towards Madrid. The revolution, as early as September 1936, found itself at a serious impasse.

Be that as it may, one surmounts an impasse not by stalling but by forcing a way through, and the Graphic Arts century of the Iron Column—which included seven young female libertarians[5]—got together and decided to set up a mobile printing press mounted on a truck. They procured the requisite machinery, and the first edition of a four-page bulletin (in 22 x 30 centimetre format) called *Línea de Fuego*[6] [*Firing Line*] appeared in early September.

The bulletin appeared each morning and was distributed among all the Iron Column militians, but its example was soon followed by printers within the confederal Torres-Benedito Column, who also put out a bulletin called *Victoria* [*Victory*].

Victoria and *Línea de Fuego* were the starting points for the launch of a number of propaganda organs that quickly circulated the ideas informing the militias' fight against the fascists.

Meanwhile, one of the many stargazing poets who were born while standing guard on the parapet began to compose a few verses, thanks to which one can feel even closer to the collective spirit of the

---

5   *Fragua Social* (22 August 1936) reports in the article 'Las Mujeres en la Columna de Hierro': 'In the CNT column there are many female comrades who fight alongside us... We, the comrades from Graphic Arts, are pleased to have among our number seven heroines who are a constant encouragement and help to us. Some are like Teresa "La Rubia" ["Blondie"] Piquer, who is like a standard bearer on the front lines; ... others stand guard and work on *Línea de Fuego*, etc. Today we give the names of these female comrades, with more to follow on another day: Carmen and Teresa Piquer, Paquita and Remedios Gómez, Josefina Domínguez, Pepita Castillo and Matilde Prósper.'

6   See the appendices from *Línea de Fuego*.

Iron Column, and from his emotive words grew the song that would soon be adopted by its members:

IRON COLUMN

Iron Column
from iron forged;
Iron Column
of the proletariat.
Rifles that spit scorn
at the reaction;
rifles that roar and sing
of revolution.
Rifles that aim towards infinity
with sights trained on the bourgeoisie;
rifles that write in bullets
the war-song of their rebelliousness.
Iron Column!
In the revolutionary
blast furnaces;
in the forge of slavery,
was forged the iron of the proletariat,
and it became the iron of our youth.
Youth that roars.
Youth that advances.
Youth that fights for freedom!
Peerless youth!
The only hope
for humanity.
Manes in revolt,
eyes flashing brilliantly,
defiant breasts
and raised fists.
The iron and the blood
that flows through the veins
of our workers
and our soldiers!
Soldiers with neither finery

nor mythic history!
Iron Column!
Mettle and heart,
no laurel, no wreath,
no false glory;
Those who only crave
revolution!
And the female comrades
who decisively go
to share the fate
of the fighters,
and bind their wounds,
and place red flowers
on their graves!
Downtrodden women,
sisters and mothers!
Bold female comrades
who have written their motto
of love and labour
in blood
on our banners;
downtrodden women!
Iron Column,
that marches towards destiny
without fear of failure,
because the admirable feat of Francisco Ascaso
marked the road ahead of us
with his blood!
Generous blood of the comrades
who fell dead!
Generous blood of the advance parties
who defended us!
Blood that fertilises
the noble seed
of the sowers.
Blood of a brother!
Of 'Pancho Villa'
who was like a dead bouquet of flowers!

Iron Column!
Copious energy,
engine, brain, arm and heart.
Iron Column!
Column of a world
that shaped revolution
in its forge!
Onwards always,
bold fighters...!
Mane in revolt,
fist of menace.
Onwards always
workers who pioneer fresh trails!
To health! Onwards!
Overwhelming column!
Forged Iron Column!
Brave Iron Column!
The proletariat's Iron Column!

— Muro[7]

As the old Italian anarchist Malatesta used to say: 'One thing leads to another.' In Sarrión, where the Iron Column had set up its headquarters, one thing indeed led to another and countless projects took shape. But before telling that story, we want to leave a record of what Salvador Cano Carrillo wrote about Sarrión:

> The Iron Column established its headquarters detachment in Sarrión, which in those days was in the front line, and the Column's leading members set about organising the village's economic and moral life—which had been completely destroyed in the wake of the fascist uprising—and introducing libertarian communism. Foodstuffs received were made available to all militians and villagers, some of whom had eaten nothing but bread and water for the past month due to a lack of any other food. It had been impossible to even bring in the harvest because of the fear inspired by the fascists, who refused to allow

---

7   Text published by *Fragua Social* (17 September 1936).

the peasants on to the fields so that they might attend to their farming duties.

The Column's economics department promptly got the residents together and explained that basic necessities would be made available to all, but that everyone needed to dedicate themselves to the tasks at hand.

The villagers were intrigued by this news. They later agreed that this was the best policy, because suspension of work would lead to bankruptcy and widespread chaos. All were agreed that the harvests needed to be brought in and placed at the people's disposal.

Once the economy was running normally, the question of public schooling was tackled. The schoolhouse had also been abandoned as a result of the tragic circumstances. Thus, everything was overhauled and the school and public libraries were enriched with new reading materials.

The comrades from the Committee would not embark upon any project unless they themselves had laid the first stone, by way of setting an example.[8]

The Column's War Committee was organised in a manner very similar to those of other confederal columns. The basic unit was the ten-man group. Ten such units comprised a century, which was headed by a general delegate. The novelty of the Iron Column, in comparison with the structure of the Durruti Column, lay in the fact that it had eliminated the *agrupación* (a unit made up of five centuries) for the sake of a more direct internal democracy. Thus, the centuries were in direct contact with the War Committee.

The War Committee members were: José Pellicer, Montoya, Armando, Rodilla, Gómez, Rufino and Rafael Martí ('Pancho Villa'), the last of whom perished during the fighting in Puerto de Escandón.

Ancillary services were split up into sections: Manzanera and Morell looked after general provisions; Diego and Gumbau took care of rations for the front; Serna ran the offices; Doltz was in charge of transport; Cortes and Segarra handled information and liaison services; Canet saw to miscellaneous matters.[9]

---

8   *Fragua Social* (6 September 1936).
9   See the appendices from *Línea de Fuego*.

Roque Santamaría, who handled general provisions for a while, describes the internal operation of the Column thusly:

> With regard to the Iron Column, its internal organisation was collective in nature, which can be seen as symbolising a certain purist interpretation of our libertarian approach. I make no apologies for it. We men are not perfect, and our collectives were not perfect either.[10]

October—autumn of the revolution—had arrived, and a general assembly of the Iron Column concluded that propaganda activity needed to be intensified in order to counteract the defamation campaign that had begun to be directed against the Column. The creation of a radio station was proposed, responsibility for which was entrusted to Cortes and Segarra, given that they were already taking care of information and liaison services.

Just one month after the project was suggested, 'Radio Station EA5—Iron Column—Frequency 42m, 5cm,' began broadcasting the following programs:
— 1200h to 1300h: News in Spanish.
— 1300h to 1400h: News in Italian, French, German and English.
— 1800h to 1900h: News in Italian, French, German, English and Portuguese.
— 1900h to 2030h: News and miscellaneous matters in Spanish.
— 2100h to 2230h: News, music and miscellaneous matters in Spanish.
— 2230h to 0030h: News and propaganda in German.[11]

---

10 Testimony of Roque Santamaría.
11 *Fragua Social* (22 January 1937).

VI
The Bureaucratisation
of the Rearguard

One of the most enigmatic personalities to play a role in the direction of the Spanish war was Largo Caballero, leader of the left wing of the PSOE. Thus, an analysis of his contradictory attitudes becomes crucial to our account of the history of the period.

In his book *Mis Recuerdos*, Francisco Largo Caballero offers little that could give us a sense of the reasons he had for the ideological change he underwent towards the end of August 1936, when by accepting the formation of a government he chose a position that went against everything he had defended until that point, or at least until 22 August 1936, when he declared in the socialist newspaper *Claridad*:

> Some people around here say: 'First let us crush the fascists and bring the war to a successful conclusion, and then there will be plenty of time to talk of revolution and make it if necessary.' Those who talk that way have apparently lost sight of the formidable conflict in which we are all caught up. The war and the revolution are one and the same; aspects of a single phenomenon. They neither exclude nor obstruct each other; rather, they are mutually complementary and supportive. The war needs the revolution if it is to succeed, just as the revolution needed the war to unleash it.
>
> The revolution represents the eradication of fascism. Thus, the first step is to annihilate fascism militarily. Today the people are not fighting for the Spain of 16 July, which was a Spain still socially dominated by the traditional castes, but for a Spain in which these castes will be definitively erased. The mightiest weapon in the arsenal of this war is the total economic destruction of fascism, and that requires revolution. It is the revolution in the rearguard that will lead to and ultimately secure victory on the battlefields.[1]

---

1   Burnett Bolloten, *La Revolución Española*, 109.

When Largo Caballero began to write *Mis Recuerdos* in 1945, he had the chance to retrace his political footsteps and offer first-hand evidence so that historians might better understand his agreeing to become prime minister on 4 September 1936. Not only did he not take this opportunity, but in addition, upon reading *Mis Recuerdos* we are given the impression that he had completely forgotten the political positions that he had espoused up until 22 August 1936.

The main reasons he gives for not refusing to form a government are of a moral character (which suggest to us that he was conscious of just how ominous that government would be for the revolution). He writes: 'It would have been put down to fear and labeled desertion.' This is meaningless.

Largo Caballero opened talks with the CNT, during which that trade union proposed the formation—in concert with the UGT—of a defence organisation that would assume the political, military and economic leadership of the country.[2] This was more in tune with his stance of 22 August. But the socialist declined the responsibility offered to him by the CNT. Nevertheless, he accepted the position offered to him by Manuel Azaña on one condition (which he knew was impossible to fulfil at that time): 'I thus accepted the position with full awareness of the difficulty of the task ahead, but on the condition that the government would not be of any specific political hue and that it would contain representatives of those who were fighting on the fronts in defence of the Republic, without prejudice towards any political or social tendency.'[3]

The facts immediately gave the lie to Largo Caballero's intentions. The government comprised six socialists who took the Ministries of Finance, Labour, the Navy and Air Force, Home Affairs and Foreign Affairs, the Presidency, and War, the latter two of which were held by Largo Caballero himself. Socialist predominance could not have been clearer.

But in addition, there was something even more insidious regarding his selection of personalities. Juan Negrín, who was given the Ministry of Home Affairs, was a novice burdened with real shortcomings

---

2   José Peirats, *La CNT en la Revolución Española*, Vol. I Diego Abad de Santillán's *Por Qué Perdimos la Guerra* is clearly in agreement with Peirats.

3   Francisco Largo Caballero, *Mis Recuerdos*, 181.

that left him unfit for such responsibilities.[4] Indalecio Prieto—Largo Caballero's irreconcilable enemy—had no faith in the revolution and advocated 'a bourgeois republic,' while Julio Álvarez del Vayo was a brazen pro-Stalinist. Yet these were the three men entrusted with three important Ministries, among them Finance (the national treasury), which was crucial to the winning or losing of the war, if it is indeed true that wars can be won with gold.

'To the PCE,' declares Largo Caballero, 'I gave two Ministries: Public Education and Agriculture to Jesús Hernández and Vicente Uribe, respectively.'[5] The remainder of the Ministries were awarded to the scrupulous republicans who looked kindly upon the politics advocated by the PCE, which was the declared enemy of all the revolutionary conquests made by the Spanish proletariat.[6]

Thus, by means of a very much self-interested coalition, the PCE—which had been a minuscule political force prior to 19 July 1936—found itself joining a government containing two ministers from its own ranks, a covert supporter (Álvarez del Vayo) and the seeds of an objective alliance with Indalecio Prieto and the republican ministers. From the outset, Largo Caballero had fallen into a trap of his own making, and as a result he was left genuinely isolated in the incoherent government over which he presided as of 4 September.[7]

But there was still more. With the CNT having no representation in the government, the government could not claim to be representative of the fighting forces. Why had the CNT not been included? Caballero offers this partial explanation: 'Steadfast in my intention to ensure that all sectors involved in the war should be part of the government, I approached the CNT. Those negotiations proved to be the most difficult for me. The CNT said that they had no desire to take part in a government that was bourgeois in character, but after much negotiation I managed to talk them into joining. The thorniest

---

4   Palmiro Togliatti, *Escritos Sobre la Guerra de España*. In a number of places, Togliatti—who, as Stalin's 'advisor' in Spain during the war, was in a position to know—clearly explains these defects.

5   Francisco Largo Caballero, *Mis Recuerdos*, 181.

6   In this regard, a reading of the *Historia de la Revolución y la Guerra en España*, edited by a PCE commission and published in Moscow, is instructive.

7   This was the first time that a Communist party from the 'bourgeois' world joined a bourgeois government.

problem was the size of their representation, for they demanded six posts, and I did not accede to their demand.'[8] This last statement by Largo Caballero perhaps explains his 'evolution'—or regression—as he was still thinking along the same lines as in 1934, when he believed that the PSOE was the only party capable of leading the revolution in Spain. Like many, Largo Caballero thought that anarchists could serve as cannon-fodder: useful when there was fighting to be done, but slated for annihilation once victory had been assured.

As for the CNT, it spelled out its attitude towards the Largo Caballero government in an article carried by *Solidaridad Obrera* in Barcelona, beneath the headline 'La Inutilidad del Gobierno' ('The Uselessness of the Government'). In the article, the CNT analysed the reason why it could not join a bourgeois government and concluded:

> We hope that Spanish and foreign workers will understand the fairness of the decisions taken by the CNT and the FAI regarding this matter. Discrediting the state is socialism's objective. The facts demonstrate that liquidation of the bourgeois state— weakened by asphyxiation—is caused by economic expropriation, and not by a spontaneous shift on the part of the 'socialist' bourgeoisie. Russia and Spain are living examples.[9]

The CNT gave this political statement about the Largo Caballero government the title 'La Inutilidad del Gobierno.' From the anarchist point of view, all governments are useless, but the one in question did have a use: to rebuild the state and to restore its institutions, all of

---

8   Francisco Largo Caballero, *Mis Recuerdos*, 181. In reality, Largo Caballero offers no evidence to back this claim. In fact, the very opposite was the case: the CNT was at that point floating the idea of establishing a National Defence Council together with the UGT. This was proposed to Largo Caballero in mid-August 1936, and at first he took to the idea. But later, after the Russian ambassador Marcel Rosenberg arrived in Spain, he completely changed his opinion and declared the establishment of his government—a government in which the participation of the CNT was resoundingly denied—on 4 September. The issue of the 'six ministers' arose later, in mid-October 1936, at which point the CNT—under siege as it was— had no option but to join the central government.

9   José Peirats, *La CNT en la Revolución Española*, Vol. I., 209.

which had been swept aside by the flood of revolution unleashed in response to the fascist uprising. In order to rebuild the state and form a government that was comprehensively popular and thus recognised by the masses, there was a need for prestigious personalities among the workers: men who were not symbols of 'the dying world', like José Giral and Martínez Barrio for example, but rather strong personalities tied to the world of labour and social struggle. Francisco Largo Caballero fit that bill, at least for those workers who followed the UGT, which was just as important a trade union as the CNT. This much was clear, and José Peirats expressed it perfectly in his analysis of Largo Caballero:

Largo Caballero was the *deus ex machina*. He represented a significant segment of the working class as well as the left wing of his party, which was the only political party spared bankruptcy thanks to the October revolution.[10] Caballero's extremist line within his party, his personal prestige in the eyes of the UGT masses and the regard in which he was held in both confederal and anarchist circles singled him out as the man of the moment.

Caballero would not know how to appreciate future political fluctuations and the ebb and flow of party manoeuvrings, including those of his own party. And the 'Spanish Lenin' would serve as a bridge to the most tragic phase of the Spanish revolution. At the head of a government that was broadly representative of the people, Caballero would lend prestige to damaged republican institutions, rejuvenate the state and realise objectives which had hitherto proved impossible: the militarisation of the army, the reorganisation of the armed forces, the restoration of government control of the military and the disarmament of the rearguard. Afterwards, he would disappear like a shooting star, making way for the counterrevolution and a one-party dictatorship.

As for slogans, there would be no shortage of them: the need for discipline and a single command in response to the

---

10 The reference is to the insurrection that broke out in Asturias on 6 October 1934 in response to the entry of José Maria Gil Robles, leader of the CEDA, a party that was the Republic's sworn enemy, into the government as minister of war. For further information, see the various books dealing with the Second Republic.

misfortunes of the war; the supreme necessity of pursuing and winning the war above all else.

'Would the CNT's entry into the government signify some revolutionary change in the government's economic policy?,' asked a *Daily Express* reporter of Largo Caballero on 30 October 1936. Largo Caballero's answer was clear-cut: 'First the war must be won, and then we can talk about revolution. Of course, civil war has a social character, and during the course of the war problems of an economic and social nature may naturally arise. We will resolve these problems with the help of the CNT, but in any event, the solution will be subordinate to one objective: winning the war. Right now, nothing else requires our attention...'[11]

This was the man who would force a straitjacket on to the revolution, revising his own declarations of 22 August in which he maintained positions totally different from those we have just outlined.

What had happened to him to bring about such a huge leap backwards? Or perhaps he had never even taken a step forward, and his August claims were nothing but a way of making a name for himself: a wink at his rivals to show them that they had to count on him.

On 8 August, Stalin's special envoy M. Koltsov arrived in Barcelona. On 26 August, Koltsov met with Indalecio Prieto in Madrid and they both agreed that Largo Caballero was the only adequate choice to head a new government.

—And you... ?

—I am ready to play my part in that government, to occupy any position within it under Caballero's orders, anything at all. There is no other way out for Spain or for me if I wish to be of service to my country at this time...[12]

The following day, Koltsov spoke with Largo Caballero in the UGT secretary's office, and Stalin's special envoy persuaded 'the doltish Caballero' that he was the best person to form a government capable of defeating the mutinous generals.

---

11   José Peirats, *La CNT en la Revolución Española*, Vol. I., 209.
12   M. Koltsov, *Diario de la Guerra de España*, 55–56.

At the same time that Largo Caballero was putting together his government, inside the Kremlin, Stalin was deciding to directly intervene in the Spanish situation.

Stalin convened an extraordinary session of the Politburo. The Political Bureau is the supreme authority in the Party, and therefore the government. Against the decisions of the Politburo there is no possible appeal. They have the strength of military orders on the battlefield.

At this session of the Politburo, Stalin came out in favour of immediate action in Spain. At that time—early September 1936—the Spanish Popular Front had formed a government in Madrid. With immense help from the Comintern, Largo Caballero had set up a coalition government containing two Communist members, with him taking part as president of the cabinet and minister of war. Like Leon Blum, he was partial to cooperation with the Soviet Union.

Stalin's contention was that the old Spain was a thing of the past and that the new Spain could not survive on its own. It would either have to enter into an alliance with Italy and Germany or with the opponents of those two powers. Stalin said that neither France nor England would allow Spain, which controlled access to the Mediterranean, to fall under the control of Rome and Berlin.

For Paris and London, Spain's friendship was a matter of crucial importance. Stalin was of the opinion that he could create a regime in Spain controlled by Moscow. With Spain in his pocket, he would be able to achieve a permanent alliance with France and England. At the same time, his intervention would revive the faith of the Soviet Union's supporters abroad, which had been badly dented by the purging of the Bolshevik old guard.

With regard to the $700 million worth of gold amassed in Spain, Largo Caballero's government was ready to invest it in war materials. The gold could be transported to Russia as payment for munitions delivered to Spain, and this constituted a problem to be solved without delay, as the Soviet government was officially adhering to a strict non-intervention policy.

The Politburo came out in favour of immediate action. Stalin cautioned his commissars that the Soviet Union's aid to Spain should be undertaken in absolute secrecy in order to avoid all possibility of his government becoming involved in an armed conflict. His final words, which those assembled by the Politburo had to keep in mind and which were passed on as an order to his entire staff, were: 'Poldashe et artilleiskavo ognis' ('Stay out of artillery range').

At the same time in Moscow, Stalin instructed Yagoda—then head of the OGPU—to establish a Soviet secret police network in Spain.

On 14 September, Yagoda convened an urgent meeting at the Lubyanka central offices in Moscow. Present at the meeting were General Uritsky from the Red Army General Staff; the current navy commissar, Frinovsky, who at the time was chief of the OGPU Armed Forces and regarded in Soviet circles as one of Stalin's most promising men; and my comrade, Sloutski, who headed the OGPU's Foreign Department.

From Sloutski, who I often ran into in Paris and elsewhere, I learned that at that meeting a former official from his department had been appointed to establish the OGPU in republican Spain. This was Nikolsky, AKA Schwed, AKA Lyova, AKA Orlov.

The Lubyanka conference also placed Comintern activities in Spain under the supervision of the Soviet secret police. It was decided to coordinate or harmonise the activities of the PCE with OGPU policy.

Another decision reached at the conference was that the OGPU police would take charge of the movement of volunteers from each country to Spain. On the Central Committee of every Communist Party in the world there is a member who carries out secret work for the OGPU.[13]

Francisco Largo Caballero assumed the functions of prime minister under the shadow of Stalin, and it was logical that the Communist leader's decisions regarding the country would follow the line that the Soviet Union had designated for Spain. For the time being,

---

13 W.G. Krivitsky, *La Mano de Stalin sobre España* (Toulouse: Editorial Claridad (Socialista), 1946 [32-page pamphlet]).

Caballero's mission was to apply the brakes to the revolution by any means necessary and to return the country to the position it was in on 18 July 1936.

In the following chapters, the Iron Column's activities should be interpreted as a response to the reactionary policy of the new government as well as to the official CNT and FAI organisations, which were lurching uncontrollably towards the right.

VII
The Iron Column and the Rearguard

We have already stated, although there is no harm in repeating it now, that the Iron Column had been set up by anarchist groups from the Levante region. And in Levante, anarchism enjoyed a strength whose origins went back a long way. In Valencia, as in the rest of the Peninsula, the labour movement began in 1870. Like in the rest of the country, the theoretical conceptions of Mikhail Bakunin were deeply rooted, especially his revolutionary practices. In terms of organisation, these were articulated through the groups comprising the Revolutionary Socialist Alliance, which was a secret organisation founded by Mikhail Bakunin following the infamous Congress in The Hague (1872) at which Karl Marx—resorting to all kinds of trickery—managed to expel his rival from the International as 'a common swindler.' Franz Mehring, a Marxist and biographer of Karl Marx, wrote of this expulsion: 'The unpardonable thing was to sully the name and honour of Bakunin over questions of property, and unfortunately the fault lay with Marx.'[1]

Following the aforementioned Fifth Congress of the First International, the Revolutionary Socialist Alliance was founded in Saint-Imier (Switzerland) in order to provide a rallying point for international anarchist relations. One of its most fervent adherents in Spain was Tomas González Morago, who died in prison in Granada in 1885. But above all, in the person of Severino Albarracin, who worked as a schoolteacher in Alcoy, anarchism found in Valencia a tireless propagandist and agitator for workers' organisations that rallied around the First International in Spain.[2]

Throughout the entire period of proletarian history until 1936, the Alliance and its anarchist groups were a constant fire which flared up during the most severe bourgeois repression of the working class.

---

1   Franz Mehring, *Carlos Marx* (biography), 515.
2   For more about the Alliance, founded by Mikhail Bakunin with the intent of establishing an Anarchist International, see *Miguel Bakunin, la Internacional y la Alianza en España (1868–1873)* (Ediciones de la Piqueta). Also see Anselmo Lorenzo, *El Proletariado Militante*.

Their constant oral and written propaganda kept sowing the libertarian seed and imbuing many of their militants with a character more accented by anarchism than by syndicalism. It was a radicalism that we shall see made concrete in the Iron Column.[3]

After that historical digression, let us now return to what was happening around Teruel, where the militias had not taken kindly to the news of the formation of Largo Caballero's government and the decrees that had been issued announcing the militarisation of the militias.

In the Communist press, which supported Largo Caballero's policy, it was said that if the war wasn't being won then it was the fault of those who clung to militias that were clearly ineffective in the battle being waged.

Another favourite theme of the PCE was to invoke 'the utopian experiments being carried out by the anarchists in the economic sphere.' Such experimentation, they wrote, could do no more than hamper the development of the economy. The time for revolution had not yet come and the important thing was to win the war. Thus, there could be no lack of 'iron discipline.' This underhanded campaign was clearly aimed at destroying the gains of the revolution, thanks to which the economy continued to function, especially in Catalonia, where a war industry had been created through the effort of the CNT unions.[4]

This insidious propaganda fell upon explosive terrain. The fighters massed around Teruel, who were unable to launch a decisive attack due to a lack of weapons and ammunition, were irritated by such chatter. Meanwhile, Valencia's Executive Committee was unable to attend to the needs of the front because it did not have access to war material or ammunition. Such material could only come from Madrid, but the government had decided to boycott the fronts where resistance to militarisation was strong.

In order to illustrate all this to the reader, we will use another's words to describe the Iron Column's actual situation:

The boycott was a serious problem for the Iron Column. Although it had fended for itself during the first months of the

---

3   One clear reflection of this was the Levante Regional Plenum, which we have cited (see note 8, p. 106), and the contributions of the delegations attending.

4   See note 3, p. 54.

war, thanks to its recruitment drives and the requisitions made with the help of anarchist-controlled committees in the villages and cities of the rearguard, its appeals for volunteers were yielding diminishing returns incapable of supplying it with the requisite number of new recruits to relieve the soldiers on the front. This was due to the ebbing of revolutionary fervour and the disrepute into which the Column had fallen in libertarian circles.[5] In addition, the committees were being replaced by regular administrative organs in which the most revolutionary elements were no longer the dominant force.

Still more serious was the fact that the ministry had decided not only to withdraw weapons from all militias refusing to reorganise in accordance with the prescribed regulations, but had also decreed, albeit in carefully chosen language, that the fighters' pay—which in the case of the militias had previously been delivered to each column as a lump sum, without subsequent supervision nor prior consideration with regard to its distribution—would henceforth be issued through regular paymasters and only by battalion. As the decree made no reference to paymasters in units that had not adopted militarisation, it was obvious that if the Iron Column stuck to its militia structure then the time would soon come when its pay would be suspended.[6]

We now look, also using another's words, at the situation regarding weapons and ammunition:

Before the war, Valencia had had no armaments factories. The weapons and ammunition used during the initial outbreak of revolution came from what the militians had obtained for themselves by raiding the armouries, the vessels at anchor in the port, the arsenals in the barracks, etc.

---

5   Because of the Iron Column's intransigent attitude towards militarisation and the CNT's governmental involvement, the 'higher bodies' of the CNT undermined the Column's rank and file support by brandishing arguments concerning the influence on the Column of the 'common prisoners' freed from San Miguel de los Reyes.

6   Burnett Bolloten, *La Revolución Española*, 261.

In November the Iron Column stated that it had only received a thousand rifles from the state. The remaining 80% had been wrested from the enemy in battle.[7] Furthermore, it was common knowledge that the rifles were damaged through use, especially in untrained hands. As a result, ready supplies of replacement parts and ammunition were just as important as the weapons themselves.

The War Department of Valencia's Peoples' Executive Committee had applied itself to the resolution of a great variety of problems, among them the launching of a war industry. But by January 1937, it hadn't managed to produce anything but hand grenades, incendiary bombs for the air force and the some spare parts for use in machine-guns and rifles.[8]

Until January 1937, the Executive Committee hadn't been able to resolve the problem of ammunition, gunpowder and detonator caps. Empty shells were refilled at the risk of making them unusable:

The daily output of ammunition for January 1937 was 62,000 units per day. At the time, there were some twenty thousand fighters on the Teruel front who were dependent upon Valencia, meaning that each one of them had no more than three cartridges...[9]

It was the urgency of all these factors combined that prompted the Iron Column to send some of its men to the rearguard. One of those who participated in this decision explains it to us thusly:

The return to Valencia had been agreed among the Column's leading personnel. Firstly because, even though the regular military had been disbanded, there were still two or three Civil Guard barracks there. And primarily because we did not trust the Civil Guard in light of what had happened in La Puebla de Valverde. Among them there was one person with a degree of

---

7   Statement by the Iron Column delegate to the aforementioned CNT Regional Plenum.

8   Terence M. Smyth, *La CNT al País Valencià, 1936–37*, 49.

9   Ibid.

republican credibility: a captain by the name of Uribarry who had lived up to his oath. But we were still not very pleased.

One of the 'expeditions' in which Column personnel were involved was to disarm the Civil Guard; that is, those who could be disarmed, because most of them had gone over to the enemy and the rest were organised into combat units under Uribarry. The latter brought his men to Extremadura, and there they defected to the enemy. Thus, we had not been mistaken in our intentions.

But in my opinion, the most important 'expedition' was that which set fire to the property register, the archives of the Palace of Justice and the files in the police stations, with the aim of destroying the records on all the people who had passed through there. And to that effect, a great bonfire was set up in the main square in Valencia which burned for 24 hours. This was surely the act that corresponded best to the spirit that motivated the Iron Column.

Did the people approve of what we did? I believe so. At that time a sentiment existed which I wouldn't call fraternal, but which came very close to it.[10]

Terence M. Smyth also relates these events, to which he adds even more details:

It was on 23 September that the men of the Iron Column surrounded the barracks of the Civil Guard, who, after negotiations with the militians, eventually handed over their rifles. Later, the Column raided jewellery shops and even disarmed the Spanish guards on sentry duty at the door of the British Consulate.[11]

On the same day that all this was happening, the CNT's steering committees met with delegates from the Iron Column. Initially, there was no common ground between the two sides. The representative from the Workers' and Soldiers' Council was the first to speak:

'The Organisation must not let itself be overwhelmed by this climate of irresponsibility, allowing a group that will not accept

---

10 Testimony of Roque Santamaría, as previously cited.
11 Terence M. Smyth, *La CNT al País Valencià, 1936–37*, 50.

responsibility for its actions to impose its sovereign will. We have to determine, once and for all, whether it is the Organisation that makes decisions or whether it is a few armed groups.' The Column's delegate stated: 'We gave the Organisation a grace period during which it could have implemented our resolutions, which we think have essentially revolutionary objectives. And since the Organisation has not done so, the Iron Column has done nothing more than put its own resolutions into practice. If the Organisation fails to decisively implement a revolutionary programme, then the Iron Column will return to Valencia and will do what it considers will best serve the revolution.'[12]

The actions carried out by the Iron Column were grist for the PCE propaganda mill, which strove to portray the men of the Column as common criminals, underlining in its reports that their ranks included the convicts freed from San Miguel de los Reyes. To the CNT and even the FAI, the Column's behaviour was an extreme annoyance, particularly because the National Committees of the CNT and the FAI were trying to find a viable formula that would allow them to become part of the institutions of the state. In such conditions, the Iron Column had to defend itself not only from the natural enemies of anarchism but also from those CNT and FAI committees that were already in the throes of bureaucratisation. Thus, on 1 October the Iron Column published the following manifesto:

CONFRONTING LIES

A Manifesto from the Iron Column

To workers,
To revolutionaries,
To anarchists,
The Iron Column, which is comprised of FAI and CNT members along with others who—without belonging to any particular organisation—identify with the ideas and the conduct of anarchists, in light of the consequences of its activities

12 *Fragua Social* (7 October 1936).

in Valencia and the judgements being passed upon it by certain groups, feels the urgent need to fully clarify its conduct so that no one, no matter who they may be, attempts to make partisan propaganda at our expense.

The men who fight against the clerical and military reaction on the Teruel front under the common banner of THE IRON COLUMN are, as anarchists, equally concerned by problems on the front, problems in the rearguard and problems in the city. Thus, when we saw that things in Valencia were not going the way we would have wished; when we realised that the rearguard, far from being a reassurance for us, was a cause for concern and doubt; we decided to intervene, to which end we sent the following demands to the organisations concerned:

1. The total disarmament and dissolution of the Civil Guard.

2. The immediate deployment to the front of all armed bodies in the service of the state (Assault Guards, Carabineers, Security Guards, etc.).

3. The destruction of all archives and files belonging to capitalist and statist institutions.

We based these demands on two points of view: the revolutionary and the ideological. As anarchists and as revolutionaries, we understood that the existence of the Civil Guard—a blatantly reactionary body which, with the passage of time and more particularly during our present activities, has plainly demonstrated its mentality and methods—represented a threat.

To us, the Civil Guard was odious, and we did not want to see it in the city or on the front because we had intense reasons to distrust it. We therefore asked for its disarmament, and disarm it we did.

We asked that all armed bodies be sent to the front because there is a shortage of manpower and weaponry at the front, and given the present state of affairs, the presence of these bodies in the city was not so much a necessity as it was a hindrance. We have partially achieved this aim, and we will not rest until we have completely succeeded in its execution.

Finally, we asked for the destruction of all those documents that represented an entire history of tyranny and oppression against which our free consciences rebelled. We are destroying those papers and we are thinking of seizing those buildings that—like the High Court—once served to bury revolutionaries in dungeons and which today, when we stand on the threshold of a libertarian society, have no reason whatsoever to exist.

These objectives brought us to Valencia, and we realised them through the methods we deemed most apt.

In addition, during our stay in Valencia we observed that, while deals for the purchase of arms failed due to lack of hard currency, many establishments still contained a huge quantity of gold and other precious metals, and this induced us to confiscate gold, silver and platinum from some jewellery shops. However, we must point out that what we recovered is insignificant compared to what was recovered by other organisations who undertook such work before us.

All of the above recounts what we did. Now let us see what we did not do.

We are accused of looting shops, and that is a lie. We defy anyone to produce to us the receipts we issued and show that these were issued on a whim or to whip up trouble rather than to meet the needs of our men.

We are accused of murdering people on a whim. This too is a filthy lie. What have we done to justify this characterisation? What crimes have we committed? An unfortunate accident, which we are the first to regret and condemn, appears to be the damning evidence. The death of the socialist comrade José Pardo Aracil had absolutely nothing to do with us. It was demonstrated on the very same night of the event that no member of our Column had any part in it. WE HAVE NEVER THOUGHT ABOUT ATTACKING SOCIAL-ISTS OR ANY OTHER ANTIFASCIST GROUPING, especially in the underhanded way that Pardo was attacked. Without any suggestion that we have renounced our aims, which are the only reasons for our struggle, we understand that infighting among us would be criminal at this time.

We are facing a formidable enemy; all our efforts must be directed towards its destruction.

We believe that this statement will have clarified our actions. We are revolutionaries and we have behaved as such, with integrity and nobility. No one but a cretin could see evil intent or indiscretion in our conduct.

Our position during this decisive period in Spain's development is clear and definite: with all our manpower, with all our energy, with all our enthusiasm, we shall fight to crush despicable fascism once and for all. But it must be understood that we are not fighting to save a Republic or install a new statist regime. We are fighting in order to realise the SOCIAL REVOLUTION. We march towards ANARCHY. Thus, now and in the future, we will defend all that allows us to live with greater liberty, we will smash the yokes that oppress us, and we will destroy the remnants of the past.

We say to all workers, to all revolutionaries, to all anarchists: At the front or in the rearguard, wherever you may be, fight against the enemies of your liberty and demolish fascism. But also make sure that your exertions do not bring about the installation of a dictatorial regime that would represent the continuation, with all of its vices and defects, of the whole state of affairs that we are trying to obliterate. Now with weapons and later with the tools of labour, learn to live without tyrants and to develop for yourselves the only road to freedom. These are the feelings of the Iron Column, and they have been explained clearly and simply.

Comrades: Death to fascism! Long live the social revolution! Long live anarchy!

Puerto de Escandón, 1 October 1936

VIII
The Revolution Under Siege

When the Iron Column published its manifesto 'to the working class' in order to let the workers know that the people's rifle still had a few bullets left in the breech for fighting the counterrevolution, it was correct; as were Durruti's words in his final address to the working class, which cautioned them against the new bureaucracy that was beginning to ensconce itself in the rearguard. But by then the capacity for fighting back was minimal, because the initiative—which thus far had been in the hands of those at the bottom—had passed to those at the top due to the political manipulation of both the revolution and the war by the PCE and the PSOE.

The Popular Front thesis peddled by the PCE and the PSOE had already triumphed as the political stratagem through which the revolution of 19 July could be reduced to a straightforward war of 'national independence.' This was not an inevitable occurrence, but it was genuinely desired by Joseph Stalin and León Blum: the former aimed to secure an alliance with France and England against the threat of Nazi Germany and the latter wished to placate the Anglo-Saxon capitalist bourgeoisie, which was exactly what the Conservative politician Churchill had in mind when he advised Blum to 'let the Spaniards cut one another's throats.'[1]

The PSOE and the PCE had submitted to their masters, and in order to keep those masters content, the two parties were unashamedly sacrificing the Spanish working class. On the other hand, the CNT—through its committees, which were later invited to that same sacrifice—clung to the idea that the only way to move forward was to subscribe to the Popular Front thesis, and this attitude gave birth to the policy of compromise that ultimately led to their absorption into the government. It was a policy that was not only futile, but would

---

1   We have not found a source for this quote. In 'Can the powers bring peace to Spain?' (dated 2 April 1937 and published in *Step by Step* (Thornton Butterworth, 1939) Churchill says 'There must be perseverance to reduce this Spanish tragedy to its true proportions, and to make sure as far as possible that only Spanish blood flows in it.' (p.119.) [KSL]

also bring about terrible consequences for the CNT's traditional revolutionary practices.

And so, that September the liberation of the people was sacrificed to the appetite of international politics by the PCE and the PSOE. Worse still, as the old saying goes: 'When the fool becomes useless, send him to prison.' The workers were fooled and imprisoned, who through their own initiative had revived industry. The peasants were fooled and imprisoned, who in twenty-four hours had transformed the structure of agrarian property and resolved at one stroke what the Republic had proved itself incapable of resolving over a five-year period. Those very people were fooled and imprisoned who ventured into the countryside in order to contest territory with the mutinous military, stopping the mutineers in their tracks in a number of places and routing them in many others.

Now that the militias had salvaged territory, thanks to which the Republic still existed; now that the industrial workers had created an economic organisation and a war industry from nothing, without any technical expertise other than their own instinctive knowledge accumulated from their revolutionary tradition; now that the peasants had not just saved the harvests but also prepared for the next ones; now it transpired that those who had had nothing to offer but 'grand theories' were sentencing and condemning the militias and the working class for having cut the apron strings and ruptured the fabric of bourgeois society.

In the name of the revolution and in order to save it, those who had not lifted a finger were now asking the militians to become soldiers and the workers to turn the factories and fields over to their former owners. If there was to be a reversion to the society that existed on 18 July, then why carry on with the struggle? This was what the worker and the peasant was asking Largo Caballero, the likes of La Pasionaria, and even the CNT and its leaders. And since there was no response, the authentic revolutionaries and the working people had suddenly been transformed by the language of politics into 'uncontrollables,' 'bandits' and 'provocateurs.'

And the people accepted all this in the face of the crude reality of the war and the massacres brought on by fascism wherever it trod, all the while thinking that the last word was still theirs. But there would be no last word, because that September the working class was stripped of its best weapons for defeating fascism. The revolution was under siege, and as a result the war was being lost. Those who were losing the war were the same ones who had no will to win it; those who, drunk on the prestige derived from authority, had seized the rudder of the state and were steering the boat towards certain shipwreck.

Why had Largo Caballero, as head of the government, clung to the bourgeois defence of international compromises that the revolution and the people had rejected? Hadn't there been revolutionary strikes protesting the policies of Alfonso XIII towards Morocco? Hadn't Abd el-Krim been hailed as a brother when his warriors, having defeated the Spanish army, proclaimed the Republic of the Rif in 1921? Hadn't the people refused, as far back as 1909, to go to their deaths in Morocco? Hadn't the PSOE and PCE alike condemned the colonial policy of the Spanish monarchy? Now, facing a military revolt, when general Franco was making Moroccan territory his main springboard for attacking the Republic, why wasn't the republican government publicly declaring that Morocco belonged to the Moroccans? Even if only for reasons of military strategy, that was a card that should have been played for the sake of a republican victory.

Nevertheless, Largo Caballero said no to three representatives of the Comité de Acción Marroqui (CAM—Moroccan Action Committee) when, that September, their delegation offered to start an uprising among the Kabyles in exchange for the granting of autonomy by the republican government. Was Largo Caballero serving the interests of the Republic and the Spanish people by declining to accept the offer made by the Moroccan delegation? No! He was in fact serving Anglo-French colonial policy, because that is what León Blum—socialist leader and president of the French government—was asking him to do. Was Largo Caballero alone responsible for all this? No! The responsibility was shared by the PCE, which had two ministers in the Caballero government. The PCE was also responsible for this policy because it was serving Stalin, and at that very moment Stalin was negotiating—through Stashevsky, his business agent in Spain—the transfer of 700 million gold dollars (part of the Spanish treasury) to Russia; to the 'homeland of the proletariat,' as the Soviet Union was called back then. The transfer was completed in October 1936 with the consent, naturally, of the PSOE and its leadership.[2]

---

2   Abel Paz, *Durruti, el Proletariado en Armas.*

And the application of this policy of handing over—of embezzlement—was what permitted its supporters to call the peasant collectivists, the fighting militias and the genuine revolutionaries 'uncontrollables.' Thus, the war, which the militias and the people had been winning, was being lost by the politicians.

IX
The Prelude to May 1937

Events in republican Spain were moving along at a dizzying pace. On 28 August the Republic opened diplomatic relations with the USSR. Marcelino Pascua was sent to Moscow while the USSR sent Marcel Rosenberg to Madrid, with Antonov-Ovseenko following behind as consul to Barcelona.

Marcel Rosenberg was a diplomatic service bureaucrat in the same way that Largo Caballero was a UGT trade union bureaucrat. These two bureaucrats eventually bumped into each other, and as Largo Caballero relates in his memoirs: 'He was wrapped around my legs like a serpent.' But by then it was too late to react, for Spain's gold was already in Russia and Largo Caballero was dependent upon Stalin.

Largo Caballero had two ways to get out of the pit he had dug for himself: resign or wait until he was driven out. He didn't choose the first option, which would have been the wiser course, but instead waited for the second to occur, absurdly playing along with his beloved enemy by doing his best to sink the worker collectives and revolutionary militias: denying the former every assistance while compelling the latter to submit to a militarisation program that handed supreme command of the new army over to Russian advisors operating under cover of their PCE patsies.[1]

Antonov-Ovseenko was an old revolutionary still capable of mustering enthusiasm for a revolution like the one happening in Spain, so Stalin sent him to Spain to die. Nevertheless, like Largo Caballero, he faithfully carried out the order he had received from Stalin: put an end to anarcho-syndicalist power in Catalonia. But before achieving that objective, he had to infect certain CNT and FAI leaders with his poison: 'Russia will help you so that your economy can move forward and your militias can finally get on with the war in Aragón, but you must change the image the outside world has of your role in the life of your country. The same things can be accomplished through lawful, democratic means: militarise your militias, join the Generalitat as councillors and dissolve this Central Militias Committee of Catalonia, which reminds

---

1 Indalecio Prieto, *Convulsiones de España*, Vol. II, 121–151.

the international bourgeoisie of the Committee of Public Safety during the French Revolution.' And he managed to win them over.

On 24 September 1936 a Regional Plenum of Unions, attended by 505 delegates representing 327 labour unions, took place in Barcelona. The Plenum was to debate economic matters arising from the economic arrangements that had been set in place on 20 July. The Plenum concluded on 26 September, and on 27 September the Barcelona press startled the public with the sensational news that the CNT was joining the Generalitat government.

The news came as a bombshell to the CNT rank-and-file, so much so that the Catalonian Regional Committee of the CNT had to publish a notice in order to sweeten the pill: 'What has been set up is not a government but a new entity, in keeping with the circumstances we are in, which is called the Generalitat Council.'[2] Much later, Santillán was more explicit: 'We knew that success in the revolution was not possible without success in the war, and we were sacrificing everything for the war. We were sacrificing the very revolution, without realising that such a sacrifice also implied the sacrifice of the aims of the war.' And he continues:

> The Militias Committee guaranteed the supremacy of the people in arms; it guaranteed Catalonia's autonomy; it guaranteed the purity and legitimacy of the war; it guaranteed the resurrection of the Spanish heartbeat and the Spanish soul. But we were told time and time again that, as long as we remained faithful to popular power, no weapons would reach Catalonia, nor would currency be made available to purchase them abroad, nor would we be allocated raw materials for industry. And since losing the war was equivalent to losing everything and returning to the conditions that prevailed in Spain under Ferdinand VII, in our conviction that the impulse given by us and our people would not disappear from either the militarised armed forces or the new economic life planned by the central government, we left the Central Militias Committee behind in order to join the Generalitat government's Defence Department and other essential departments of the home rule government.[3]

---

2   José Peirats, *La CNT en la Revolución Española*, Vol. I, 217.
3   Diego Abad de Santillán, *Por Qué Perdimos la Guerra.*

That step was a crucial one in the commitment to an irreversible process of concession-making that strayed ever further from its starting point, because the appetites of the Stalinists were insatiable. Two months after the formation of this Catalan government, one of its members was condemned to death by Stalin. Antonov-Ovseenko told Generalitat president Lluís Companys: 'Bring me the head of Andreu Nin.' Companys complied, thus triggering the government crisis that heralded the events of May 1937. In this way, Companys and the CNT remained prisoners of the diabolical Antonov-Ovseenko. And he was an irrepressible demon, because after Nin's head he became even more demanding: now he wanted the heads of the entire Barcelona proletariat. This made Lluís Companys's hair stand on end. It was too many heads!

Among the various arguments used by Antonov-Ovseenko to consolidate an alliance between the ERC and the PSUC, it is likely that one concerning the 'Reverter' case—a madcap conspiracy hatched by the notorious Dencas—was the one that managed to seduce some leading Catalanist figures in November 1936. The affair had been previously hushed up by ensuring that Reverter, who was then general commissioner of public order in Barcelona, disappeared from the scene.[4] But if the matter was to be reopened, where would that leave Companys and the ERC? Thus, to preserve a state secret, Companys gave in to Antonov-Ovseenko and sealed an alliance between his own party and the PSUC that would eventually put paid to Catalan autonomy thanks to the scheming of 3 May 1937.

This plan proceeded little by little, but not so secretly that the CNT's intelligence services didn't know about it, for they monitored the conversations between Antonov-Ovseenko and Rosenberg[5] from

---

4   'The Reverter case' is an obscure page from the history of the era. Certain opinions are expressed in the following works: Jacinto Toryho, *No Éramos Tan Malos*; Manuel Cruells, *El Separatismo Catalán Durante la Guerra Civil*; Montserrat Roig, *Rafael Vidiella, la Aventura de la Revolución*; and Juan García Oliver, *El Eco de los Pasos*. [Playboy Andreu Reverter i Llopart was Companys's surprise choice for Generalitat Commissar-General of Public Order until he was arrested by anarchists in connection with gold and platinum ingots being smuggled out of the country into France. He allegedly threatened to implicate Companys unless his release and escape from Spain were expedited and was discovered, shot, in a ditch shortly after he was released from custody in Montjuich. KSL]

5   Jacinto Toryho, *No Éramos Tan Malos*.

the Telephone Exchange while keeping an eye on the comings and goings of various Catalan political personalities from Barcelona to Paris and Brussels.[6] Krivitsky describes all of the foregoing with the detail and aplomb of a specialist in such matters:

> Sloutski (the OGPU chief in Spain) had done sterling work. By December 1936, the terror was raging in Madrid, Barcelona and Valencia. The OGPU had set up its own private prisons. They had their own courts and their own control patrols, members of which carried out killings and arrests. They filled their hidden dungeons and mounted lightning raids.
>
> Naturally, they operated independently of the Loyalist government. The minister of justice (at the time, García Oliver) had no authority over the OGPU, which constituted an empire within an empire, a force before which some of the highest-ranking members of the Largo Caballero government trembled. The Soviet Union seemed to have Loyalist Spain all fenced in as if it were already a Soviet possession.

On 16 December 1936, Largo Caballero delivered a thrilling speech in defiance of Franco: 'Madrid will not fall. Now that we have the necessary weapons, the war is just beginning.'

The following day, the newspaper *Pravda*—Stalin's mouthpiece in Moscow—explicitly declared that the purge that had already begun in Catalonia (the Nin affair) would be expedited with the same vigour as the Soviet Union's infamous purges.

Stalin's goal seemed to be within his grasp, but the main obstacle in his path was Catalonia. The Catalans were anti-Stalinists, and furthermore they represented one of the main sectors of Largo Caballero's support. In order to secure absolute control, Stalin still had to bring Catalonia to heel and oust Largo Caballero.

---

6   Juan García Oliver, *El Eco de los Pasos*. García Oliver describes in great detail how he 'handed Largo Caballero a file of some hundred pages, complete with photographs and documentation revealing the conspiracy being hatched against the Republic by certain Catalan and Basque politicians.' But Caballero 'spilled the beans at a press conference, although by doing so he did not prevent the bombshell of the tragic week in Barcelona in May 1937.'

Stalin had assigned the task of making him master of Spain to the OGPU. This was disclosed to me in a report from one of the leaders of the Russian anarchist groups in Paris, who was a secret OGPU agent. He had been sent to Barcelona, where as a prominent anarchist he enjoyed the confidence of the autonomous government's anarcho-syndicalist wing. His mission was to operate as an agent provocateur in order to incite the Catalans to engage in acts that would justify the army's intervention to put down a revolt in the rearguard.

When the events of May 1937 came about, Krivitsky wrote:

I was reading reports of 'Catalan revolutionaries taking to the streets in an attempt to seize power by treachery...'
The absurdity of such reports was striking. The Catalan revolutionaries already controlled the government, so why would they have been trying to seize control?
The fact was that the Barcelona revolt was a plot hatched successfully by the OGPU.[7]

In Valencia the OGPU was also operating behind the scenes, and the socio-political conditions there were almost identical to those in Barcelona. The CNT was a powerful force, forming part of the People's Executive Committee and—together with the UGT—serving as the driving force behind the CLUEA, which basically put control of the region's agricultural production in the CNT's hands. Since September, when Vicente Uribe (PCE) had become minister of agriculture, there had been ongoing warfare between that ministry and the CNT.

Uribe intended to destroy the CNT-supported agricultural collectives and, naturally, put an end to the CLUEA. It was not easy to find grassroots backing for this initiative, because the UGT in Valencia—which was quite radicalised from a revolutionary point of view—maintained a close alliance with the CNT.

Nevertheless, the PCE went ahead with its policy of provocation, the aim of which was to irritate the most radical elements in the CNT and thereby lure them into violence which could then be used as the pretext for widespread repression. The most radical elements were in

7   W.G. Krivitsky, *La Mano de Stalin sobre España*.

the Iron Column, and they were targeted for what could be called the general onslaught that preceded the 'May events' in Catalonia.

In late October, one Tiburcio Ariza González was shot dead in a street in Valencia.[8] It turned out that he was a delegate from an Iron Column century who was serving in the city. The news reached the front quickly, and the confederal columns—the Iron Column, the Torres-Benedito Column and the Thirteenth Column—agreed to send a sizeable delegation to the funeral, which was scheduled for Friday 30 October.

Terence M. Smyth relates what happened on that day:

Along the way, the delegation got itself into a few scuffles with the Guardia Popular Antifascista (People's Antifascist Guard—GPA), but when it arrived at the Plaza de Tetuán it fell into a trap. On that central square, near the river, sat the headquarters of the PCE and the former residence of the Captain-General, which had been converted into the militias office. It is unclear whether or not the Iron Column was planning to attack those buildings, but it was nevertheless caught in a hail of machine-gun crossfire originating from both structures, and it was forced to scatter with heavy losses, which amounted to between 150 and 160 dead.[9]

---

8   Quoting 'Ana' a female militian who served with the Iron Column's 10th centuria, Group 9, left forward position, Romero names the murder victim as Alfredo 'el Barbas'; from the column's 4th Centuria. She admits that 'he may have been drunk but he was unarmed. So how come the GPA (People's Antifascist Guard) shot him?'

Of the massacre, Ana says that the Iron Column sustained 30 dead and 80+ wounded, but says that the Torres-Benedito Column sustained 38 casualties, dead or wounded. She says the Iron Column held an impromptu meeting to decide not to retaliate before taking up their positions at 3.00 am., after they were informed of the risk of an enemy breakthrough.

'Next there was intervention by the regional committee, about which much might be said in fact. Above all, comrade Rodilla spent part of a night perched atop a crate of vegetables, explaining to us how we had to remain calm, that we had to be sensible, that the Regional Committee in conjunction with the National Committee was going to do this and do that, that Bakunin this and Kropotkin that; to no avail, we all wanted to get away. We wanted to take to the streets immediately and put paid to the 'Guapa' (GPA) and the rest. We could have, we were strong enough to do so. But in the end, we were 'sensible" (Romero, *'Los Incontrolados': chronique de la 'columna de hierro' (Espagne 1936–1937)* p. 108). [KSL]

9   Terence M. Smyth, *La CNT al País Valencià, 1936–37*, 57.

After that provocation by the PCE, unmasked in the eyes of the working class after advancing a policy of 'weapons to the front' yet now showing that it had at its disposal not just rifles but also machine-guns, the Iron Column printed a manifesto that was published as an editorial in issue 37 of its bulletin, *Línea de Fuego*. As what was written faithfully reflects the Column's position, we reprint it in its entirety:

IRON COLUMN

Once again, the Iron Column has to confront a defamation campaign waged against it whose sole aim is to discredit the Column in the court of public opinion. Once again, we have to explain our actions to the people and refute the lies propagated by the usual backstabbers, who, incapable of understanding or accomplishing anything which has a renewing and progressive spirit, are therefore enemies of the anarchist movement and of revolutionary action.

Without getting involved in more arguments or ideological assumptions, we are simply going to state the facts, because they and they alone are clear enough to demonstrate beyond all doubt where each one of us stands.

The Guardia Popular Antifascista [GPA—People's Antifascist Guard]—a police organisation with a short history, yet already very much hated for their activities—murdered an unarmed comrade from our Column in the most vile and cowardly way possible.

This crime, justified only by the GPA's rancour towards us, caused unanimous outrage within all the confederal and anarchist columns on the Teruel front. After liaising with one another, we resolved to travel down to Valencia the next day in order to attend the funeral of our fallen comrade and to exact justice upon those responsible for his death. This is what the Iron Column, the Torres-Benedito Column and the CNT's Thirteenth Column set out to do on Friday, 30 October.

The funeral procession, which was a magnificent expression of protest, left the Salesian convent without any trouble. But upon arriving at the civil government building, we were surprised by the formidable precautions in evidence: doors closed, a tank positioned to defend the balconies, windows barricaded with pillows and sand-bags, rifles trained on the street, strategically occupied rooftops... We continued forward, and upon reaching the Plaza de Tetuán we found that in both the PCE headquarters and the militias office there were people prepared to either repel or mount an attack.

Nevertheless, the front of the cortege continued on its way and had already left the square when the first shot rang out from the PCE headquarters, followed by several heavy volleys and abundant machine-gun fire, all of it aimed at the group of people who were peacefully and quietly following the coffin.

Although we returned fire, given the surprise nature of the attack and the position we were all in, we were totally ineffective. Whereas their shots, fired cold-bloodedly into a mass of people caused mayhem. It was not a case of some unavoidable clash but of a deliberately prepared attack. It did not stem from the natural defence instinct, but from the cruellest and most cowardly viciousness.

As evidence, we note that their machine-gun expertly followed—to the point of stalking—those unarmed or injured comrades who, with their hands raised in the air, wanted to get out of the square. Nor was any mercy shown to female comrades or those who, guided by their humanitarian spirit, went to recover the bodies of the fallen. In short, the 'brave' combatants of the COMMUNIST PARTY achieved a resounding VICTORY, scattering 30 DEAD AND MORE THAN 80 WOUNDED among us. The casualties did not just include personnel from our Column, for the Torres-Benedito Column alone sustained 38 losses, some dead and some wounded.

To sum up, the treachery of one party—utterly heedless of the situation in which we all find ourselves, and forgetting that its efforts should be deployed at the front against the fascists and not in the rearguard against the anarchists—spilled enormous quantities of proletarian blood; the blood of revolutionaries who, from day one of the uprising, have been fighting with all their energy against the reaction...

But we, who have more understanding and more sense of responsibility than our attackers, immediately analysed the potential implications of internecine strife in the rearguard. And we swallowed our bitterness, contained our feelings and—though perfectly placed so to do—refused to take reprisals or continue the fight initiated by them. With a menacing and emboldened foe called fascism confronting us, we decided that this was not the time to respond to the PCE's aggression and engage in a suicidal brawl.

But understand this: our attitude does not in any way signify fear or forgetfulness. We are too well-known to be accused of the former, and we are far too wise for the latter.

Even though we are now returning to the front in order to finish off the fascists, the day will come when we reexamine and remember these events and give the responsible parties what they deserve.

Finally, we say without any hidden meaning that on the very night of these events, after our men had agreed not to take to the streets, upon being alerted to the danger of a possible fascist attack at 3:00 a.m. they got up and unanimously went to occupy their designated positions without incident. It was a superb display that many others should learn from.

Comrades, we have nothing more to say. The IRON COLUMN, in spite of adversity and come hell or high water, holds fast to its revolutionary stance. Without any of the old womanish shrieking and hullabaloo that is unfortunately so prevalent, we will continue to fight everywhere for the triumph of the revolution and of liberty.

Puerto de Escandón, 3 November 1936.[10]

Santamaría writes:

One of those who had opened fire on the crowd was a bullfighter who was by no means a revolutionary and who had wormed his way into the PCE. His name was Enrique Torres. Let the historical record show that.

---

10 *Línea de Fuego* 37 (5 November 1936).

Upon returning to the Column, the problem was discussed and the idea arose to seek vengeance; in other words, an emphatic response. And it was on this occasion that a confrontation broke out between the columnarios—which we jokingly called ourselves—and the people from the committees. Those very committees—in the name of antifascist unity—defended the idea of compromise, while we felt that the time for compromise had passed... But we were won over by the 'pacifying spirit of the committees' combined with the aggravating circumstance of 'militant responsibility,' and so the massacre went unavenged.[11]

---

11 Testimony of Roque Santamaría, as previously cited.

X
The CNT Enters the Government

The delicate situation in the Levante region was not unconnected with what was going on in the remainder of the country: clashes between CNT and PCE militants were also everyday occurrences in Barcelona, Madrid, Murcia and Jaen, which were focal points of the CNT's militant activity and its Regional Committees.

In Barcelona the situation was particularly red hot due to comments made by the USSR's consul in reference to the POUM. These comments followed the POUM's demands that the Generalitat grant political asylum to Leon Trotsky, who had just been expelled from Norway. The consul's direct interference in the internal affairs of a foreign country clearly demonstrated the extent to which Stalin already considered Spain to be yet another region of the Soviet Union.[1] With regard to this matter, it is helpful to quote the writing of Jesús Hernández:

> The decision to eliminate the POUM was made in November 1936 at the Soviet embassy in Valencia, during a meeting between Soviet ambassador Marcel Rosenberg and the Chekists 'Marco,' 'Orlov' and 'Vielayev.' [Belayev][2]

In his memoirs, Largo Caballero also complains about the Russian ambassador's meddling in Spanish domestic affairs to the point that the he had to eject the Russian from his office. But unfortunately, all of this was going on amidst extremely serious circumstances that threatened to bring about the complete collapse of the republican zone: General Franco's troops were advancing towards Madrid from the south and a column led by General Mola was descending upon the capital from the north. Madrid was therefore under severe threat and, worse still, the weaponry needed for her defence was unavailable.

---

1   Julián Gorkin, *Caníbales Politicos*, 68.
2   Jesús Hernández, *Yo Fui Ministro de Stalin*. Also see José Díaz, *Tres Años de Lucha*, especially the section regarding the Plenum of the PCE Central Committee on 5 March 1937.

As a result of the government shipping off Spain's gold reserves to Russia, republican Spain found itself at the mercy of Stalin, who was the exclusive supplier of its arms. It was Stalin's decision whether Spain would or would not receive weapons, and that being the case, Spain had no other recourse but to submit to his impositions. This explains all the concessions made to Russia at the time; concessions that unfortunately had positive repercussions for the PCE, which was hoarding the new military commands of the nascent Republican Army.

This is the political context in which we have to place the CNT's incorporation into the Largo Caballero government on 4 November 1936 and its acceptance of four ministerial positions.

The CNT had avoided, as much as was possible, joining government bodies. But after becoming part of the Generalitat government at the end of September, the inevitable next step had to be incorporation into the central government. The CNT had tried to come to an intermediate solution through the creation of the National Defence Council, which was composed primarily of CNT and UGT members, but Largo Caballero could in no way accept that. He was Stalin's prisoner, and he was also unwittingly under a political death sentence.

So the CNT had only two options left: either take a place in the government or bring about a revolutionary situation that would destroy the entire governmental apparatus that Largo Caballero had been rebuilding. After the CNT joined the Generalitat the latter option no longer existed, thereby leaving only the former, which in practice was the most feasible thanks to the minimal protest occurring within the CNT ranks. Thus, the Generalitat episode had been a kind of trial run with which to silence voices of protest and, in time, get the membership used to an extraordinary situation.

One of the first reactions of protest came from the Iron Column, and *Línea de Fuego* published the following communique on Wednesday, 4 November:

THE GOVERNMENTAL CNT

Over the wire comes news, which we have reproduced elsewhere, that the CNT is going to join the government.

Thus, it is embracing what it has always attacked, thereby destroying the basis of our ideas.

From now on there will be no more talk of liberty, but rather submission to 'our government,' the only agency capable of directing the war and economic life.

The confederal organisation has secured four ministries for itself, yet none of them correspond to the arguments raised in support of the creation of a National Defence Council.

Four second-rate ministries will be filled by four individuals who have never shown any interest in the matters that they must now concern themselves with. We will see a member of the Weaving and Textile Union, surely with much expertise in matters of war, in the Ministry of Justice; a public speaker and writer on matters of the heart and social issues in the Ministry of Health; and a professional propagandist in the Ministry of Trade.

In summary: instead of departments there are ministries, and instead of experts in their fields with their own initiatives there are incompetent, inept politicians.

History moves on, the state survives, and all in the name of an organisation that professes to be libertarian.

For how much longer, comrades?[3]

It is clear that the Iron Column was not alone in protesting against the CNT's decision to enter the government. There was widespread unease among the grassroots membership of the CNT, mostly because the process by which in which the CNT made the decision to join the government was unclear. The precedent of the resolutions passed at recent CNT National Plenums could not be considered as a justification for entering the government.

In mid-September 1936 at a National Plenum of Regionals, the decision was taken to invite the UGT to form a National Defence Council together with the CNT so that a programme designed to solve the problems pertaining to the war and the economy could be developed for immediate implementation. It was proposed that the political issue be resolved through the adoption of political federalism, and to that end 'the Regionals shall be empowered to establish

---

3 . *Línea de Fuego* (4 December 1936), 3.

proportional representation of antifascist forces within the Regional Defence Councils so as to introduce whatever local modifications are required by surrounding circumstances and opportunities.'[4]

The UGT was given a grace period of ten days during which to make its response, and if the UGT failed to give its assent during this period then it was agreed that another National Plenum would be held. That Plenum took place on 30 September, and it was made clear that neither the UGT nor its general secretary Largo Caballero had paid any attention to the CNT proposal for the establishment of a National Defence Council.

But since—as we have seen—the CNT had already gone on to form part of the Generalitat government in Catalonia in the interim, it is our understanding that resolutions should have been passed at the CNT National Plenum on 30 September regarding entry into the Largo Caballero government. In any case, these resolutions could not have been very clear, since we also understand that at the beginning of October it was agreed at an Aragón Regional Plenum in Bujaraloz to undertake the formation (in compliance with CNT accords) of the Regional Defence Council of Aragón, which was comprised entirely of CNT members. Thus, just when the National Committee of the CNT was showing signs of compromise, in Aragón there was an ultra-radicalisation occurring upon which the National Committee did not look kindly. José Peirats writes:

This Council, formed in accordance with the CNT's most recent Regional Plenums, did not obtain recognition from the central government.[5] The PCE described it as cantonalist and factionalist. The Marxist columns sabotaged it by spreading confusion in those parts of the rearguard under their control. Nevertheless, the Aragonese peasants conducted the boldest revolutionary experiment throughout the liberated territory, supported by the confederal Durruti, Ascaso, Ortiz, Hilario-Zamora, Aguiluchos, Solidaridad Obrera and Roja y Negra Columns. All these forces would later be amalgamated into three famous Divisions: the Twenty-fifth, the Twenty-sixth and the Twenty-eighth. The Twenty-seventh and Twenty-ninth

---

4   José Peirats, *La CNT en la Revolución Española*, Vol. I, 225.
5   It was recognised by the government in December 1936.

Divisions would fall under the influence, respectively, of two irreconcilable Marxist groups: the PSUC and the POUM.[6]

Immediately after its formation, the Council of Aragón announced its existence and—as a warning to the militia columns—its position of intolerance towards militia columns behaving like an occupying army in Aragón. A harmonious coexistence between militians and peasants was advocated, but their respective spheres were well-defined: 'The antifascist columns should not and will not meddle in the socio-political life of a village whose essence and personality are liberated.'[7]

Nevertheless, none of this prevented the National Committee of the CNT from joining the government, and news of this event was released to the press by the head of the government at 10:30 p.m. on 4 November 1936.

The CNT was awarded four Ministries, the most important of which—Justice—was assumed by Juan García Oliver. Health went to Federica Montseny, while two conflict-laden Ministries—Trade and Industry—were filled by Juan López and Juan Peiró, respectively. In fact, the CNT had not been invited aboard merely to strengthen the government, but also to regulate the collectivised economy through these two economic ministries; to the detriment of the working class, of course.

Even as the CNT was joining the government, shells from Franco's guns were falling on Madrid. The republican government, fearing that the capital might fall into the enemy's hands, suggested at a cabinet meeting that the government leave Madrid and move to Valencia. The CNT ministers were initially opposed, but ultimately agreed to accept the move in order to avoid a government crisis. On 6 November 1936, with everyone awaiting Madrid's imminent fall into the hands of the mutinous generals, the government settled in Valencia while the people of Madrid—in an act of desperation—rose up en masse and proceeded to paralyse the fascist advance and save Madrid.

Inevitably, the arrival of the government in Valencia affected the city, undermining the authority of the People's Executive Committee of Valencia while threatening the columns fighting on the Teruel front. On 15 November, by order of the Ministry of War, Colonel Jesús Velasco Echave was appointed commander of the Teruel front.

---

6   José Peirats, *La CNT en la Revolución Española*, Vol. I, 225.
7   Ibid., 227.

XI
The Government Settles in Valencia

According to General Vicente Rojo, the central government's transfer—or flight—to Valencia was of crucial assistance to a besieged
Madrid, as it fired the city's determination to resist because,

> along with the government went the pessimism, the apprehen-
> sion, the discord and the defeatist outlook of certain selfish elites
> ... as well as—why not also say it?—the panic that hundreds of
> people could not overcome, even though they held positions of
> great responsibility. In Madrid, along with the expected victims
> there emerged the beginnings of a genuine unity of belief rooted
> in the people; that feared and insulted people. And this belief
> yielded an absolute, epic and anonymous selflessness, as well as
> truth... The long, anguished night of defeat seemed to vanish
> with those who fled, and the light of a new dawn began to shine
> for those who deserved to triumph.[1]

Vicente Rojo hit the nail on the head, and—especially coming
from a military figure like him—his focus upon and praise for the psychological forces that defended Madrid in the absence of war material
warrants the highest form of respect.

The mobilisation of the populace began immediately. As far as
the CNT was concerned, it spelled out its attitude on the very same
night that the government fled the city:

> Madrid, free of ministers, commissars and 'tourists,' feels more
> confident in its struggle... The people—the Madrid work-
> ing class—have no need for all these tourists who have left for
> Valencia and Catalonia. Madrid, free of ministers, will be fas-
> cism's tomb. Forward, militians! Long live Madrid without
> government! Long live the social revolution![2]

---

1   Vicente Rojo, *Así Fue la Defensa de Madrid*, 73.
2   Abel Paz, *Durruti, el Proletariado en Armas*, 481.

But in Valencia the CNT and the FAI were much more aggressive in their response to the government's flight, notwithstanding the fact that the government included four ministers from their own ranks. The Local Federation of CNT unions issued a statement which read: 'For the women, for the children, for the aged and the wounded of Madrid: our homes and our bread are there for the asking. But for the cowards and deserters who drive around and show off their weapons: our disdain. Comrades, we must shun them and make their lives impossible!'[3]

At 10:45 a.m. on 15 November 1936, the concluding session of the CNT's Levante Regional Plenum began in Valencia's bullring. It was addressed by Pablo Monllor, Tomás Cano Ruiz (on behalf of the Plenum), Serafín Aliaga (on behalf of the National Committee) and Minister of Industry Juan Peiró.

Tomás Cano Ruiz's speech was an uncompromising condemnation aimed squarely at the 'confederal' ministers and all those who fled Madrid. His words mirrored the tone of the debates and the resolutions of the Plenum:

> The Plenum has called upon me to simultaneously deliver a complaint and a protest: the arrival in Valencia of the government of the Republic has brought hundreds, if not thousands, of bureaucrats who have completely infested the city and who are using up all of its economic and housing reserves. Comrades of the Levante region, we are faced with the contrast of these thousands of bureaucrats invading our hotels, guest-houses and restaurants and eating up the reserves we have here while a column like Durruti's (applause) passes through Valencia with a heroic and humane purpose: the sublime purpose of going to the Madrid front and driving the enemy from that very Madrid front which those same bureaucrats have abandoned in a most cowardly way. But the comrades from the Durruti Column have to stand around, squat in the gutters or sleep on the pavement, without anywhere to sit down for a meal or find a bed to lie in for the night, while these bureaucrats—I will say it again—use up all the available resources in the city.
>
> The Plenum, which is aware of these matters and is outraged by this plague that has descended upon Valencia, hereby

---

3   Ibid.

registers its most strenuous protest before the people of Valencia and affirms that its first and only responsibility is to the militians fighting on the fronts: that they should never go without a bed, that they should never lack any food, that if anyone in Valencia should have to go without a bed or food then it should be those bureaucrats, those statists, those petty celebrities and characters who—having abandoned the capital of the Republic at the first sight of danger—have come to Valencia to consume our reserves and keep themselves well out of danger (thunderous applause).[4]

After Cano Ruiz spoke, there was a moment of great discomfort among those on the rostrum who were presiding over the meeting. Serafín Aliaga, the representative from the National Committee, became quite displeased now that he could no longer ignore the position that the Plenum had taken with regard to the CNT's participation in the government and the transfer of the National Committee to Valencia.

However, the one who came under the most criticism was without a doubt Juan Peiró. But Peiró was an old CNT militant, and therefore quite experienced in such matters. He perfectly understood the reaction of the CNT rank and file and he also knew that the best way to win them over was with sincerity; a well-timed *mea culpa* with which he could round the Cape of Storms without any undue trouble. He had the patience to sit through Serafín Aliaga's long-winded speech, and when his moment to speak arrived, the effects of Cano Ruiz's address had already diminished. Naturally, Peiró raised the issue of trust:

Anyone who knows me—any of my acquaintances—knows that I am a man who likes to always stand on solid ground, and therefore I must know if I am standing on solid ground on this rostrum. If I am not, then I would have to abandon this rostrum and yield to someone else who could stand here with more dignity.

It pains me greatly, but I have to recall an allusion that perhaps was not directed towards me personally. It is also possible that it was not directed at those who represent the CNT in the Spanish government.

---

4   *Fragua Social* (17 February 1937), 5.

It has been said in broad terms that those who fled Madrid came to Valencia in order to escape danger and gobble up your stores. Before I proceed any further, I want to tell you that the four ministers who represent the CNT in the government are continuing to do our duty. What I have to tell you is that we four confederal ministers—listen carefully—are the first victims of what one comrade has condemned.

I repeat that we have done our duty. And if you hold the opposite opinion then say so with the same candour as he who speaks to you right now, because if that is indeed your opinion then there is no place for me on this rostrum, no place for me in Valencia and no place for me in the government. All that is for you to say.

(Comrade Cano Ruiz makes some explanatory remarks to the speaker and the audience asks that the speaker continue.)

Comrades: each has his own sensibility, and I have mine. I am very sensitive, and thus—although I have profound feelings about addressing this issue—I realised that I could not continue without clarifying things. It seems that all has been cleared up, and I shall now continue.[5]

The Levante Regional Plenum concluded by this rally—although, according to the minutes, the Plenum was still not over—was an important plenum for the CNT in Levante. It was important for various reasons: it tried to determine an economic course of action for the CNT in Levante in both an industrial and an agricultural context, and it tried to find a way of addressing the unavoidable political question surrounding the CNT's entry into the government.

From the rank and file's point of view, the latter signified a jarring about-face for the CNT and the FAI. Nevertheless, one by one the Regional Committees—more informed than the rank-and-file militants due to their attendance at National Plenaries—were to smooth the National Committee's path in slipping certain irregularities such as the CNT's entry into the government past the rank and file membership.

At the Regional Plenum we are currently examining, all these objections emerged through various delegations, particularly the

---

5   *Fragua Social* (17 February 1937).

delegation representing the Liberal Professions of Alicante and Gandía, which actually presented the central question in the context of its real implications by asking the National Committee exactly how the CNT's entry into the government was agreed to and why the decision to proceed with the formation of the National Defence Council was not respected.

The National Committee responded like this to the incisive questions posed by the Gandía Local Federation:

> When the National Committee was faced with the choice of abandoning the idea of the National Defence Council idea or initiating a course of action likely to save it, we were reluctant to proceed on our own, so we entered into communications with all the Regional Committees. The Levante Regional Committee received a telephone call during which it was told that all the means for forming the National Defence Council had been exhausted... A National Plenum of Regionals was convened; I don't know if the comrade from Gandía was aware of that. At that Plenum, after the National Committee had detailed the reasons why it could not form the National Defence Council, it was agreed that we accept participation in the government on the basis of all the points in the programme accepted by the Plenum, which stipulated the formation of the National Defence Council. Thus, we told the government: we won't make an issue out of what the cabinet is called, we accept our participation in the cabinet in order to avoid international complications, but we bring these accords and this programme. That was the agreement.[6]

Based on their explanation, the National Committee must have known that they were not standing on the 'solid ground' referred to by Peiró. How could the militants of an organisation not know about a plenum tasked with determining the theoretical future of that very organisation? How could the Gandía delegation not know about this 'Plenum?' Peiró was correct when he said: 'We have been pushed into joining the government.'

But at the Levante Plenum, the National Committee gave a wide berth to that slippery slope, choosing instead to show that the issue of

---

6   Minutes of the Plenum in *Fragua Social* (17 February 1936).

the ministers was of little importance and that what truly mattered was that the CNT had brought about the creation of the Supreme War Council, on which it was represented by Juan García Oliver.

And with regard to this point and its effect on the Iron Column, the National Committee declared: 'There will no longer be anarchist columns, CNT columns, or UGT columns. There will only be revolutionary antifascist militias controlled by the Supreme War Council.'[7] Or, to put it another way: the militias would be reorganised in order to constitute the basis of the mixed brigades of the People's Army, which was an idea defended by Largo Caballero since 4 September 1936. Thus, what had not been possible in the past now became a reality—thanks to the CNT's participation in executive bodies—that would ultimately lead to serious problems within the CNT, like those created by the Iron Column, which we will discuss later.

At this Levante Regional Plenum, the delegation representing the Liberal Professions of Alicante took on the difficult task of saying no to the National Committee, albeit in vague terms: 'The National Committee presents us with a *fait accompli*.' This statement seems to indicate that the resolution to participate in the government was not really debated thoroughly within the bosom of the CNT, but was rather an executive agreement supported by the National Committee relying upon certain 'recommendations' from previous Plenums. Nevertheless, it was clear that the majority of the delegations attending the Levante Plenum rejected taking ministerial posts as well as the transfer of the National Committee to Valencia.[8]

At the Plenum's ninth session, the Iron Column intervened through its delegation, which included José Segarra:

> Ideologically, we remain enemies of all governments. Facts are what interest us. There is much talk of fascism and the threat it poses, and we agree. But we see everyone saying that they are compromising in order to help those on the front lines, that

---

7   Ibid.

8   In fact, the National Plenum of Regionals was held in Valencia immediately after the National Committee's arrival in the city, at which point it was agreed to reprimand General Secretary Horacio Prieto. The punishment was his dismissal, and his replacement was Mariano R. Vázquez, who had until then been general secretary of the Catalonia Regional Committee.

everything being accepted is being accepted in order to render our struggle more effective, yet we have not seen any effect of all this compromise and all this acceptance of things that have always been repugnant to us.

Let us pose a clear and concrete question. On the Teruel front everyone knows that [two lines censored] and everyone knows that the remedy for it is in the hands of the government. It was not remedied before, when we were not in the government, and it is not being remedied now, when we are. It was refused before and it is also being refused now.

At a meeting of all the comrades from the Iron Column, we said: 'Can we continue like this?' [two lines censored] and that the delegate from the Regional Committee should say it to the representatives in the government. And we want an answer. We demand that they tell us; we can help you or not. If they can help then show us the results, and if not then let us know.[9]

At the tenth session of the Plenum, there was a reading of a proposal that set forth a position regarding the third point on the day's agenda, which related to the militias:

Those presenting this second proposal,[10] who have been tasked with setting forth a position regarding the third point on the day's agenda—the structuring, organisation and control of the CNT militias—after noting the climate reflected in the sessions of the Plenum and the resolution jointly approved by the CNT and FAI columns operating on the Teruel front, have taken the line that

9   *Fragua Social* (18 February 1937).

10   The first proposal was presented to the sixth session (*Fragua Social* (14 February 1937), 6), and it was limited to two points: 1. The creation—under a single command—of a National Council of Antifascist Militias, comprised of the various organisations and political parties fighting fascism; 2. That those fighting on the front and those who join them should depend economically on the state. This proposal was rejected by a huge majority of the delegations on the basis that it failed to abide by the deliberations of the Plenum, and it was agreed to draft another proposal for which the Iron Column delegate would act as advisor. During the course of the debate, this delegate made an interesting contribution in which he defended the initial spirit of the militias and rejected the idea of the state paying the militians, as it was the responsibility of the trade unions to continue looking after the well-being of the needy families of the militians.

this resolution be inspired by the federalist principles that guide the CNT and the FAI, which are the organisations responsible for their militias. Therefore, this proposal sets forth the following:

1. That the structuring of our militias is adapted to the following stipulations:

a. That, starting with the individual as an autonomous cell in relation to the group, century and column, ten individuals shall comprise a group that elects one delegate; ten groups together make one century, which elects its own delegate; and several centuries together form a column, which elects a War Committee that is divided into a number of sections according to the needs of the column.

b. The century delegate will be directly responsible for all the actions—military, social and moral alike—taken by the century. He will be the liaison between the century and the War Committee, and he should communicate all the wishes and desires of the column—in every sense—to the War Committee.

c. In turn, he should brief the members of his century on all matters relating to the state of the war, so that the militian may precisely monitor its progress. In this way we will ensure that our militias, upon mounting any specific military operation, will completely understand the objective to be achieved.

d. The militian should abide by the instructions issued by his century delegate, provided of course that the latter adheres to the agreements reached by the century or, failing that, the War Committee.

e. In no way does the status of group, century or War Committee delegate imply any rank or privilege, because at the very moment the delegate fails to respond to the needs of the group, century or column, he will immediately be stripped of his duties and replaced by another.

2. Regarding the organisation of our militias, our view is that the Levante Plenum of Unions should speak out against the planned militarisation and offer the following organisational model for our militias:

a. All members should consider themselves mobilised and should stand by to receive instructions from their respective Committees.

b. Upon entering a CNT barracks, a comrade should keep in mind that the word 'barracks' does not signify an obedience to odious military orders such as saluting, parading and other such trifles which are completely theatrical and negations of all forms of revolutionary spirit.

c. The comrade entering the barracks should be inspected, a dossier containing all his information should be compiled, and he should undergo a health examination as well as provide references from his trade union in order to guard against suspicious infiltrations.

d. We define the term 'military instruction' in the sense of preparing the comrade for the tasks of war (handling a rifle, guerrilla deployment, withdrawal, etc.), all of which contribute to a warfare education that makes the comrade an expert at combat.

e. In the disciplinary sense, we understand that moral self-discipline should be applied by the militian, that he should maintain an interest in the struggle, and that he should listen to any opinions about the progress of the war from those who may wish to express them at meetings.

f. In specific instances of drunkenness, desertion, fraud, suspicious and inexcusable misconduct, etc., the individual should be sanctioned by the century to which he belongs.

g. Comrades enlisted with militias organised at the behest of the War Committee will not quit their jobs until they are ordered to depart to the front. Military preparation should be undertaken during their two or three daily leisure hours.

h. For rearguard militias, whose mission is relatively secondary (guarding bridges, controlling the roads, etc.), use should be made of those comrades who are ineligible for service on the front owing to a duly verified lack of aptitude.

3. The view of this proposal with regard to the control of our militias is that once the internal organisation of a column is in place, then the next step is for it to liaise with columns belonging to other political or ideological formations. To which end, it is our opinion:

a. That operations Committees be formed, one per column, on the basis of two civilian delegates and one expert military delegate in an advisory capacity. It would be for these Operations Committees to steer and direct the struggle on the front concerned.

b. At a national level, we suggest that a National Militias Council be set up which is comprised of all the representatives of all the columns fighting on the various fronts. Therefore, no direction in the struggle would be acknowledged unless it emanated from the combatants themselves.

c. The better to ensure harmony between all the forces fighting on the front and in the rearguard, we are advising our delegate to the next Plenum of Regionals to lobby for the dissolution of all government forces which do not inspire the confidence of our organisation, owing to the fact that they are not under the supervision of the antifascist organisations.

d. Said suggestion, which is applicable to the Assault Guards, National Republican Guards, Carabineers, Volunteer Army, etc., is to be implemented in such a way that the individuals making up those forces can transfer to the militias of whatever political or ideological grouping is most consistent with their particular outlook.

Broadly speaking, this proposal takes the view that the utmost possible expediency must be shown in converting those industries in the metalworking and textile sectors—as well as ancillary sectors such as transport, construction, farming, foodstuffs, etc.—into war industries.

Lastly, we believe that all CNT-affiliated health personnel, civilian and military alike, should be under the exclusive supervision of the CNT and should be placed at the service of our columns. Trade union control of militia health personnel will shift exclusively to the CNT Health Unions.

And now to conclude. If we publicise this proposal properly, if it is approved, if our representatives in the government enthusiastically champion this structure, if we can interest the Spanish people—who have always been essentially antimilitarist—then we have every confidence that our reasoning will be acceptable to all antifascists who are honourably fighting against fascism. *Salud*.

Proposal Delegations: General Trades, Segorbe; Metalworkers, Alcoy; Construction, Alicante; Street-traders, Alcoy; Health, Valencia; General Trades, Gandía; General Trades, Moncada;

General Trades, Orihuela; Labourers, Biar; Iron Column and CNT Column 13 delegation.

Valencia, 13 November 1936

The Orihuela delegation indicates to the Plenum that a few comments are required before the proposal is discussed. It says:

'The proposal is consistent with the climate of the Plenum on the morning when the proposal was first discussed. Some suggestions from the Iron Column and other delegations have been accepted on account of the federalist spirit of their organisations.

'With regard to the aspect of structuring, the federalist ideas of the CNT unions and the federalist concept of libertarian communism stemming from the Zaragoza Congress were taken as models. Our view is that the individual or militian is a thinking entity with every right to an opinion about all aspects of the war that we are waging.

'Regarding the other bodies, there is a dualism that needs clarification inside our organisations. In requesting that the Carabineers, Assault Guards, etc., be disbanded, we are not trying to start a conflict with the comrades who are part of the government. What we want is for the voice of the CNT to speak very clearly about this matter. We have frequently found that individuals belonging to the Carabineers, Assault Guards, etc.—perhaps acting on orders from their superiors—have disarmed comrades from the CNT columns, along with individuals belonging to corps under CNT control who carry cards signed by Durruti which vouch for the fact that they had served with him on the Aragón front. We therefore ask for the dissolution of these bodies.

'As for a single command, this cannot be accepted in any form. One must bear in mind the ideological tendency of the militias, who wish to be guided by their comrades on the battlefront. And at the national level we recommend that a National Militias Council be created in order to ensure the coordination of each front separately and all fronts together. Clearly, this approach is not quite the single command that the Marxist and political organisations want to impose on us.'

The Torrente delegation says that the proposal and the explanations pertaining to it precisely reflect the rationale of the Iron Column and the essential features of its organisation. In addition, it believes that it is important to fix guidelines for the conduct of the CNT-FAI in the rearguard, for if the comrades who stayed there had done their duty, then Teruel and Zaragoza would be ours by now.

The Alcoy Paperworkers delegation says that the government is conditionally imposing the adoption of chains of command on the columns, with all the ranks of captains, lieutenants, etc. Thus, one can give the example of a column organised in Alcoy with more than one thousand militians enlisted in it that, because it has not adopted ranks, has not been armed by the government. Meanwhile, the numerically inferior socialists, by conforming with the ranks requirement, have been able to raise a column and secure the requisite arms. Many CNT comrades have enlisted in these Marxist columns because of the delays their own columns are suffering due to a lack of weaponry. Thus, the delegation feels that it would be advisable to adopt ranks within the CNT columns for legal purposes only, while ignoring those ranks in the context of internal matters.

The Valencia Foodstuff Workers delegation says that the matter has been adequately debated this afternoon and evening in advance of its submission to the Plenum, and that there has also been plagiarism from the explanation given by comrade Segarra, who is the Iron Column's representative. Although the proposal seems admirable in that it encapsulates the principles of the CNT, the delegation does not believe that this is enough, because it remains to be seen whether the CNT is in the position to address all the needs of the CNT-controlled columns. Since it is almost certain that the CNT cannot meet all the needs of these columns, especially with regard to the acquisition of modern weaponry, the Valencia Foodstuff Workers delegation believes that there is no other remedy besides trusting the comrades who have joined the national government.

The Valencia Buses and Trams delegation highlights the importance of the matter under discussion, not just in terms of what is happening right now, but in terms of what can happen once the common enemy has been defeated. It adds that the vanguard and the rearguard have to trust each other, otherwise, with arms at hand, there could be regrettable conflicts.

A proposal delegate replies to the Valencia Foodstuff Workers and to Torrente, and says that the proposal has not addressed the concerns of the Iron Column alone. He says that, since Catalonia and Valencia are the CNT's two strongest regions and account for more than 70% of the combatants, the CNT's character should be respected.

The Alicante Liberal Professions delegation asks whether service with the CNT militias should be voluntary or compulsory. It wants the proposal to clarify this point.

A proposal delegate replies that the militias are volunteer militias, and that if they were made compulsory then there would be individuals who would not be serving of their own volition, which would be a breach of CNT principles.

The Alicante Liberal Professions delegation agrees that the militias should be voluntary, but believes that the CNT militias in isolation are superfluous, just as the isolated militias of other trade unions or political groupings are also superfluous. It believes that united and indivisible People's Militias or Revolutionary Militias should be formed. For example, the CNT is unable to organise its columns because it does not have the means to do so, while under this other arrangement the public treasury would meet the needs of the new militias.

The Burriana Retail Trades delegation cannot accept the proposal because in practice it would run into obstacles. Mainly, because as the comrade from Alicante has said, war materials will be in short supply. Just as the Marxist columns have adapted to the circumstances, so should the CNT columns, now that the organisation has responsibilities in the government.

A member of the working party replies to all the comrades who have spoken and declares that the working party took counsel from no one. Torrente referred to the working party's having been briefed by the Iron Column. The Alcoy Paperworkers' Union does not see eye to eye with a National Militias Council. Valencia Foodstuffs says that the motion borrows heavily from the report submitted by comrade Segarra, the Iron Column representative.

'The motion takes cognisance of the atmosphere evident in the initial debate at the Plenum. With an eye to efficient operations, we came up with a Council offering representation to the various front-line columns.

'Mention has been made of organising columns with technicians, captains, sergeants, etc. And we said that, since the CNT does not concern itself with asking the UGT how its columns are organised, it should not be anybody else's business how we organise ours. We want absolute freedom to do this, and if we have a personality of our own, we should insist that we are respected. We say that what the government should be concerned about is our readiness to face the music when the time comes.

'It can be no one else's business that the CNT organises its columns however it wants. We are antifascists, and we are not going to halt our advance or deny our entire history by going against our principles. Nor is any harm done to the battlefront if the CNT organises its columns as it wishes. If the CNT were to accept the mobilisation envisaged by the government then it would be accepting a fascistic mobilisation that is not consistent with the spirit of our organisation. People's Militias have been mentioned by the comrade from Alicante, but it should not be forgotten that the CNT-FAI columns are militias of the people. And with regard to the National Militias Council, it will be comprised of delegations from each and every front, because on a National Council it is logical that all fronts should be represented.'

The proposal delegate concludes by saying that had the Iron Column mentored the proposal, the collaboration would have been welcomed with pleasure due to the fact that the column from the Teruel front is the very model that the CNT should be presenting to its other columns.

The Iron Column delegate makes a few clarifications in order to advise the comrades. The delegate believes that, since the government's entire focus was on the Madrid front, it was unable to send sorely needed material to the Teruel front. The delegate cites the case of the Uribes-Eixea Column, which despite having a complete chain of command, still does not have what it needs.

The chair asks if the proposal has been sufficiently discussed, and upon receiving an affirmative answer, asks if the proposal is accepted. It is approved.

The Plenum closes at 2:00 a.m.[11]

At the end of the final (thirteenth) session of the Regional Plenum, the Iron Column reported on its activities: 'The Iron Column delegate took the floor to read out a lengthy report on the work realised by the Column in the rearguard on the various occasions it had spent time there.' At the end of this briefing, the Alicante Liberal Professions delegation asked that 'just as we have had a run-down of what has been going on in the rearguard, so we shall have an account of what has been achieved in the forward positions.'

The Iron Column delegate duly obliges, and having finished, the Alicante Liberal Professions delegation still asks some further questions. Once these are answered, the Plenum accepts the report and endorses all of the work accomplished to date by the Iron Column.

A delegate from the Valencia Workers' and Soldiers' Council says that he finds the report hurtful. He regards the Iron Column delegate as controversial but not deceitful.

He adds: 'I am going to refute the information pertaining to the disarming of the Civil Guard. A committee was created within the Civil Guard, on which there was a delegate from the CNT Guards. When the attempt was made to disarm the Civil Guard, this committee intervened, and were it not for the committee—believe me—the disarmament would not have happened.'

The delegation from Alcácer asks the Regional Committee to ensure that that the Iron Column is shown the utmost respect, like the other CNT columns, because in Alcácer—for instance—there are several comrades who belong to the Column but are unable to serve at the front because they have no rifles.

The delegation from Albalat dels Sorells proposes that not only should the CNT fully support the Iron Column, it should also hold the government and the military responsible for sabotaging the war effort.

---

11 *Fragua Social* (19 February 1937), 9; *Fragua Social* (18 February 1937), 10.

This motion is endorsed by the Plenum.

The Regional Committee explains that it has always shown the utmost respect to the CNT columns because they have clean and unblemished records.

Thereafter, discussion turns to the issue of provisions for the Durruti Column (bear in mind that this is on the morning of Sunday 15 November), newly arrived in the city and en route to Madrid from the Aragón front. The Regional Committee gives a report, as does a militant from the Column who just happens to be at the Plenum.

The delegation from the Alicante Fishing Industries says that the comrade from the Durruti Column has given the Plenum a real education: 'When the Iron Column comrade finished delivering his report, the delegate from the Valencia Workers' and Soldiers' Council stood up to refute it, as did the Valencia Local Federation. But now it turns out that the matter of the Durruti Column is not the responsibility of the Valencia War Council, but rather the Barcelona War Council, and this is unconscionable. It is unconscionable that these comrades were sleeping in the Plaza de Castelar, like many of the delegates attending this Plenum (remember what Cano Ruiz had told the rally), and at the last minute had to go sleep in the streets... This is the result of a lack of organisation, competence and shame on the part of the Local Committee.'

Various contributions follow along similar lines: 'The defence delegate from the Valencia Local Federation says that the Durruti Column was expected two days earlier yet had arrived that very day, which was unforeseeable. In addition, the Local believed that the Column would march directly to Madrid, [but] it has only just discovered that the militias intend to spend the night here.'[12]

But allow us to recount two paradoxical items from the last page of a concurrent issue of *Fragua Social*. One refers to a rally held on 22 November at which 'comrade Tello, in deeply pained language, gave the public the sad news of the death of that heroic fighter for the libertarian cause, Buenaventura Durruti.'[13]

---

12 *Fragua Social* (25 February 1937).
13 The Durruti Column went into battle on the night of 15–16 November 1936

The other item is an appeal to the residents of certain Valencia neighbourhoods to assist in the accommodation of militians passing through Valencia. The note is signed by delegate José A. Uribes, from the Valencia Antifascist Militias.

One of the main problems that this Plenum had to resolve was the question of the financing of the militians. Initially, the factories or workplaces that provided the columns with volunteer fighters assumed responsibility for the upkeep of the families of the militians. Afterwards, as the war dragged on, the Central Militias Committee in Catalonia took over this duty. But in Valencia, the War Department only took care of the militias that had begun to militarise (such were the instructions issued by the Largo Caballero government in order to pressure the confederal columns to militarise),[14] while the CNT unions tended to their own militias.

As was evident at the Plenum, this situation proved very onerous, and it was suggested that the matter be resolved through the imposition of a mail tax, but this would have been a very uncertain solution as long as the postal service was controlled by the state. In the meantime, the problem remained unresolved and was tabled for discussion at a National Plenum of Regionals.

---

in order to close the gap at the Manzanares River left open by the flight of the PSUC's Libertad-López Tienda Column. This fact has always been covered up by the PCE, who in all their literature have accused the Durruti Column of the error committed by the Libertad Column. Curiously, forty-four years after the event, and despite the fact that I cleared the matter up completely in my book *Durruti, el Pueblo en Armas*, memoirs are still being written without the slightest corrections being made. The memoirs of Gustavo Durán, titled *Una Enseñanza de la Guerra Española*, are a case in point. On page 68 he writes: '17 (November). The Catalan forces from the Durruti Column have shamefully chickened out. So much for the great general of the FAI!' Duran, with these words, continues to cover for the PSUC forces that really fled, and at the same time slanders 'the great general of the FAI.'

14 Burnett Bolloten, *La Revolución Española*, 261, note 2.

XII
Militias or Army?

The Levante Regional Plenum that we have just discussed represents a clear example of the ambiguous situation in which Spain found itself during those first months of the fight against fascism. Revolution and counterrevolution were two different concepts, yet so united and interwoven that they could not be separated.

The mortar holding together the different groups fighting in the republican zone was the Popular Front pact against fascism. But this mortar did not unite. Rather, it opened up cracks in what claimed to be a granite block. Everything was clear as day, but all that clarity was blinding. The harsh reality of the war was the factor that truly obscured the daylight.

The political panorama was clear. Who would carry the revolution forward? Only the working class. But the working class had failed to take the necessary measures to ensure the consolidation of its initial gains, and as a result its gains were in jeopardy because—one by one—they were being whittled away, eroded and nullified by the counterrevolutionary forces growing in the republican zone.

Having right on one's side was not enough to stop the advance of the counterrevolution. One needed the determination to tear it up from the roots once and for all, and this was precisely what was not done. There was a desire for discussion, as if chatting with a friend who was defending the same interests. But this was not the case, because the component parts of the counterrevolutionary onslaught were cut from the same cloth as those beyond the front lines whose ideology was plainly fascist. This remained unclear for the simple reason that the first instinct of the people was to defend the bourgeois republic represented by Manuel Azaña, which resulted in the imposition of the antifascist front and the alliance with the bourgeois and social democratic parties: in other words, the counterrevolution.

The revolution lacked the strength needed in order to arrive at its ultimate conclusion. And because of this deficiency, everything that happened during the month of November had a fatal logic, although it would take a lot of intense pain before the serious error that had been committed was finally understood. An attempt was made to remedy this error with preventive measures, which merely postponed any waking up to this shortfall.

The reactionary bloc that planned the military coup d'etat was not revolting against the Republic of Azaña and Casares Quiroga, but rather against the revolutionary forces that were revealing themselves—each time more boldly—in the bosom of the Spanish working class and peasantry. To this reactionary bloc, the revolution in Asturias had represented a warning that they could not ignore. Thus, seeing that the Republic was incapable of stopping the revolutionary development of the working class, the reactionary bloc planned its military uprising in order to establish its dictatorship and eradicate the 'bad seed' forever. The battle lines were clear: on one side, the reaction; on the other, the necessary revolution demanded by the working class and peasantry.

But the wretched antifascist pact, entered into by the enemies of the real revolution, attempted to erase this battle line. Ideologically, republicanism and social democracy were on the side of the state, religion, nation, private property, etc. Objectively, they agreed with those on the other side who had taken up arms against the working class. They were thus counterrevolutionaries who happened to be active in the republican zone and who, for that very reason, were eager to reconstruct the state and its authority under any pretext.

This reorganisation was not designed to destroy the fascist forces, but rather to eradicate the revolution that the people had instinctively set in motion. This was the hard fact that the harsh reality of the war had obscured to the point of blinding everyone. The addition of Stalinism to this equation, this labyrinth, was a circumstantial element that only reinforced the counterrevolution, because the counterrevolution also turned out to be an ally of the foreign policy that Stalin was pursuing at that time.

The revolution, the authentic revolution, had lasted but one short summer. Durruti had fought against the tide without giving in, until at the very end he was liberated from his internal turmoil. To die as he did, without compromise, was his greatest triumph over himself. Now it was time for others to act, and among these others were the desperadoes of the Iron Column.

The Iron Column had demonstrated that its methods could bring about a revolutionary victory over the enemy, and that is exactly why it saw and feared the counterrevolution hiding behind the ministries in Madrid. What kept the counterrevolutionary bureaucrats awake was the knowledge that the counterrevolution would not be safe while forces that were capable of advancing down the path of revolution still existed. Therefore, these forces had to be crushed somehow, and one of the best ways of domesticating them was to absorb them into the counterrevolution.

The CNT's integration into the government was the counterrevolution's most resounding success, but it would be the CNT itself that would take charge of drawing the teeth of its intransigents. And one of the most overwhelming proofs of this was the outcome of the Levante Regional Plenum of Unions, which was unanimously opposed to the National Committee's political line yet deferred to the *fait accompli*, as the Alicante Liberal Professions delegation conceded.

The Iron Column, faced with the practices of militarism, demonstrated that an effective coordination of forces can exist without having to fall into the militaristic trap. As its delegate told the Plenum:

> At a meeting held in Valencia and involving the CNT, the FAI, the Iron Column, the Torres-Benedito Column and CNT Column 13, it was deemed necessary to create an organisation to liaise between all the forces fighting on the Teruel front.
>
> This organisation, called the Operations Committee, should be made up of two direct delegates from each column, an expert military consultant and a representative from the Valencia Popular Executive Committee. And it would be this organisation that acts as liaison to the War Committees of the respective columns on the Teruel front.[1]

This organisation was sufficient for coordinating action, overseeing the fighting and maintaining the continuity of operations, thereby ensuring efficiency. But the government could not accept it because it did not fit the militaristic plan to destroy the spirit of the militias and build a conventional army. The Iron Column had reason on its side, but the scales had already tipped in favour of the counterrevolution, which planned a superb trap—as we shall later see—by creating the

---

1   See the notes pertaining to the CNT's Levante Regional Plenum held in November 1936 (see note 8, p. 106).

Supreme War Council 'in order to harmonise and unify everything having to do with the war and its direction.'[2] This Supreme War Council was to be made up of Largo Caballero himself, as minister of war; the very moderate Indalecio Prieto, a socialist and minister of the navy and air force; Vicente Uribe, the Communist minister of agriculture; Julio Just, the Esquerra Republicana's minister of public works; García Oliver, the CNT-FAI's minister of justice; and Álvarez del Vayo, the pro-Communist minister of foreign affairs and commissar-general of war.

The Supreme War Council came into existence on 10 November, and having commissioned García Oliver—the CNT-FAI minister—with the task of organising War Colleges, the government sprung into action on the closest front: Teruel. On 15 November, Minister of War Largo Caballero issued an order appointing Colonel Jesús Velasco Echave commander of the Teruel front. Up until that point, Velasco Echave had been in charge of Column 1 [The Torres-Benedito Column] on the same front. That Column was now entrusted to Major Ramírez Jiménez.

There was nothing ambiguous about the mission that the government had given to Jesús Velasco. He was to convert all the militias and troops operating in that sector into the Levante Field Army, with headquarters in Barracas. In order to facilitate this mission, a General Staff was organised with Colonel Pérez Serrano and the Russian advisors 'Ivan' and 'Petrov' taking charge.

The first columns to agree to submit to the authority of Jesús Velasco Echave were the Eixea-Uribe and Del Rosal Columns, both of which were commanded by regular soldiers. These Columns became part of the Fifty-seventh and Fifty-eighth, and the Fifty-ninth, Sixtieth and Sixty-first Brigades, respectively, although some military and political commands were given to CNT and FAI personnel. But the militians from the Peire Column refused to become the Twenty-second Brigade, and those from the Torres-Benedito Column declined to join the planned Eighty-first and Eighty-second Brigades. As for the Iron Column, it adopted an attitude of steadfast opposition to the militarisation.[3]

---

2   As recorded in *Gaceta de la República* (10 February 1937).
3   José Manuel Martínez Bande, *La Invasión de Aragón y el Desembarco en Mallorca*, 202.

However, the Iron Column's attitude was not shared by the so-called 'higher committees' of the CNT and the FAI. Nor was it shared by militants from the two organisations who believed that—now that the move towards militarisation was irreversible—it was crucial to quickly get the jump on the Communists, who had been busy monopolising commissar appointments and military commands from the very beginning.

Another argument set forth by the Committees and other like-minded parties concerned the issue of armaments. From the outset, Largo Caballero, as minister of war, had made a point of arming only those militias that complied with the militarisation order. And the minister honoured his word to the letter, for—as the Iron Column delegate told the Levante Regional Plenum (9–15 November)—the confederal columns on the Levante front were without arms, as were those operating along the Belchite-Zaragoza-Huesca front.

This stance by the Ministry of War (with the solid backing of the PCE) made one thing very clear: winning the war was of little importance because the real point was to kill off the revolution, which was the driving force behind the militias. The first of these charges is serious but true, because by not arming the militias, the militias were not in a position to withstand an enemy offensive—as was indeed the case in several places—and doesn't that surely mean that winning the war was of little importance?

The only people with a real interest in winning the war were the workers, because they knew that wherever fascism went, a proletarian massacre was ensured. This overwhelming argument was the factor that made them accept militarisation, albeit grudgingly, and determined that that they would not be made into soldiers but would retain the same spirit as before. The concessions began with ranks, a half-hearted concession to begin with, as Burnett Bolloten explains:

> As a result of all this, the libertarian movement—far from being able to utilise its participation in the government to increase its presence in the military arena or slow the progress of the Communists—was eventually obliged to confine its efforts to maintaining control of its own militias and securing arms from the Ministry of War. This was no easy undertaking, for the

minister had decided not to issue weapons to those militias that were against conversion into regular units with the required officers… In order to circumvent this requirement the anarcho-syndicalists decided that their units would feign compliance by adopting military names, which strategy was adopted by most of the CNT-FAI units including the ones on the central front, where, to quote the director of the anarchist *Castilla Libre* newspaper, 'everything, except the name, was the same as before.'[4] But this strategy was of no assistance to the libertarian units in securing the weapons they needed, and in the long run they found themselves obliged to submit to militarisation.[5]

Meanwhile, despite sabotage by the Supreme War Council, García Oliver—who had been designated by Largo Caballero to oversee the organisation of the War Colleges—devoted himself to the task with such passion that he earned the admiration of the so-called military advisors. Martin Blasquez, an official with the Ministry of War, later wrote:

In all fairness, it must be conceded that Largo Caballero afforded Oliver his unconditional support. Cordón and I established contact with him, but all that remained for us to do was to put his orders into effect. Barracks, instructors, equipment and every requirement were immediately forthcoming. Oliver was indefatigable. He arranged and supervised everything himself. He immersed himself in the tiniest details and personally checked if they had been adequately addressed. He even took an interest in the students' schedules and the cooking. But above all, he insisted that the new officers should be trained in the strictest discipline.

No believer in improvisation, I was startled by the organisational talent displayed by this Catalan anarchist. Observing the skill and confidence of his every action, I realised that this was an extraordinary man.[6]

---

4   Eduardo de Guzmán, *Madrid Rojo y Negro*, 200.
5   Burnett Bolloten, *La Revolución Española* , 253, note 25.
6   Ibid.

The extraordinariness to which Martin Blasquez refers was nothing more than the organisational capacity displayed by the Spanish proletariat in all the activities that it undertook from the very beginning of the revolution. García Oliver was not an exception. He was the rule. The proletariat was prepared to see the revolution through to a successful conclusion. Its excess of enthusiasm and its confidence in its own strength were its only faults, which defects should be remembered so that the proletariat, in future battles, does not rely solely on its own organisational capacity but also on its firmness in defending its work.

The CNT National Committee organised a Defence Secretariat with all the features of a general staff, complete with military advisors, thinking that this Secretariat would really coordinate all the confederal columns while they were being converted into military units. Despite militarisation, it intended—and it should be said that it generally succeeded—to keep the confederal units homogeneous in terms of their commands and their membership, and not to accept dispersal into mixed brigades as the Ministry of War intended. To better achieve this objective, militarisation had to proceed rapidly, and the future commanders of the confederal units would have to be sent to the War Colleges. Bolloten writes:

> It is worth pointing out that although Largo Caballero had, on political and technical grounds, approved the militarisation of the militias as the basis of the mixed brigades, his desire to maintain good relations with the CNT—a desire fuelled by his increasing antipathy for the Communists—discouraged him from making any serious attempt to enforce the provision. The result was that the anarchosyndicalist units, while submitting to the general staff for the purpose of military operations, remained under the exclusive control of the CNT and were composed of men and officers belonging to that organisation. That Largo Caballero had assented to rather than merely tolerated this evasion of the strict militarisation agreed to with the Russians is demonstrated by the fact that, in February 1937, General Martínez Cabrera—who was Chief of the Central General Staff and who enjoyed Largo Caballero's implicit confidence—authorised the War Committee of the anarchist

Maroto Column to organise a brigade comprised of members of that same Column.[7]

The change experienced by Largo Caballero was that of the 'repentant sinner.' He had clung to the notion of rebuilding the state, perhaps thinking that it would be a socialist state. But since the state does not tolerate qualifying adjectives and expresses only what it is— the source of authority—the authority of the state wound up crushing Largo Caballero, who walked into his own trap when he agreed to collaborate with the USSR and thus with the PCE.

Stalin knew exactly what he wanted, and when Largo Caballero finally understood this, he resisted to the point of raging against the pressure being applied to him by the 'Russian advisors' and the ambassador, Rosenberg. Thus, as Indalecio Prieto explains, some incredible situations came about:

> A situation of unbelievable tension arose between the two (Communist) ministers and Largo Caballero. Scenes of extreme violence occurred during plenums of the cabinet, while Largo Caballero was at the same time having tempestuous meetings with the ambassador of the USSR, Mr. Rosenberg. I am not in a position to say whether Mr. Rosenberg's attitude reflected the anger of the Communist ministers or if their anger was a reflection of the attitude of the Russian ambassador. What I do know … is that Russia's diplomatic action concerning the president of the cabinet—or, to be more accurate, against the president of the cabinet—and the Communists' pressuring of the head of the government were simultaneous and equal.[8]

When he had to confront the PCE and the Russian agents, Largo Caballero found himself betrayed and abandoned by his supporters. He could not find any allies besides his rabid enemies, the anarchists. And this fact explains Largo Caballero's change of position with regard to the CNT's new militarisation strategy. He knew that the CNT rank and file had only involuntarily accepted their organisation's joining the government, and he also had proof aplenty—the Iron Column was

---

7   Ibid., 256, Note 36.
8   Ibid., 245, Note 70.

supplying a constant stream of it—that the CNT would never accept military organisation in the form of mixed brigades, because that would imply collective suicide. Thus, the best way to resolve the matter was for the CNT to militarise its men yet still maintain control. And Largo Caballero also knew that, in the end, this would be no easy task.

XIII
The Iron Column and Militarisation

It would be utterly irrational to consider the militia system perfect. The militias were born out of an overriding necessity to confront the army that had mutinied against the Republic. They were hastily organised by the trade unions and the political parties. Thus, in essence, each one constituted a political organisation loyal to its parent organisation or party.

The essential point of the system was social equality between officers and men. Everyone from general to private drew the same pay, ate the same food, wore the same clothes, and mingled on terms of complete equality. If you wanted to slap the general commanding the division on the back and ask him for a cigarette, you could do so, and no one thought it curious. In theory at any rate each militia was a democracy and not a hierarchy. It was understood that orders had to be obeyed, but it was also understood that when you gave an order you gave it as comrade to comrade and not as superior to inferior. There were officers and N.C.O.s but there was no military rank in the ordinary sense; no titles, no badges, no heel-clicking and saluting. They had attempted to produce within the militias a sort of temporary working model of the classless society. Of course there was not perfect equality, but there was a nearer approach to it than I had ever seen or than I would have thought conceivable in time of war.

But I admit that at first sight the state of affairs at the front horrified me. How on earth could the war be won by an army of this type? It was what everyone was saying at the time, and though it was true it was also unreasonable. For in the circumstances the militias could not have been much better than they were. A modern mechanized army does not spring up out of the ground, and *if the Government had waited until it had trained troops at its disposal, Franco would never have been resisted.* [emphasis added] Later it became the fashion to decry the militias, and therefore to pretend that the faults which were due to lack of training and weapons were the result of the equalitarian system. Actually, a newly raised draft of militia was an undisciplined mob not because the officers called the privates 'Comrade' but because raw troops are *always* an undisciplined mob. In practice the democratic 'revolutionary' type of discipline is more reliable than might be expected. In a workers' army discipline is theoretically voluntary. It is based on class-loyalty, whereas the discipline of a bourgeois conscript army is based ultimately on fear. (The Popular Army that replaced the militias was midway between the two types.) In the militias the bullying and abuse that go on in an ordinary army would never have been tolerated for a moment. The normal military punishments existed, but they were only invoked for very serious offences. When a man refused to obey an order you did not immediately get him punished; you first appealed to him in the name of comradeship. Cynical people with no experience of handling men will say instantly that this would never 'work', but as a matter of fact it does 'work' in the long run. The discipline of even the worst drafts of militia visibly improved as time went on. In January the job of keeping a dozen raw recruits up to the mark almost turned my hair grey. In May for a short while I was acting-lieutenant in command of about thirty men, English and Spanish. We had all been under fire for months, and I never had the slightest difficulty in getting an order obeyed or in getting men to volunteer for a dangerous job. 'Revolutionary' discipline depends on political consciousness—on an understanding of *why* orders must be obeyed; it takes time to diffuse this, but it also takes time to drill a man into an automaton on the barrack-square. The journalists who sneered at the militia-system seldom remembered that the militias had to hold the line while the Popular Army was training in the rear. And it is a tribute to the strength of 'revolutionary' discipline that the militias stayed in the field at all. For until about June 1937 there was nothing to keep them there, except class loyalty. Individual deserters could be shot—were shot, occasionally—but if a thousand men had decided to walk out of the line together there was no force to stop them. A conscript army in the same circumstances—with its battle-police removed—would have melted away. Yet the militias held the line...[1]

---

1   George Orwell, *Cataluña 1937*, 35 ff. [*Homage to Catalonia* 26 ff.]

The quotation is long, but in assessing the militias and the cause they defended with weapons in hand, what better testimony could there be than that of someone like Orwell, who came to Spain without any preconceived ideas and only because he sympathised with the republican cause?

All the drama, the intense drama experienced at that time by the men who had left for the front during the early days, consisted of their being convinced that their system could keep alive the reasoning behind the struggle. But if the militarisation sought by the government and the political parties was accepted, then that struggle would be devoid of meaning because the class society against which they were fighting would have been restored. For what, then, would they be fighting?

To accept militarisation was to deprive the cause of its best weapon: enthusiasm. And enthusiasm, as General Rojo recalled, was the greatest weapon in the defence of Madrid. With enthusiasm, up until that time, the enemy had been fought and important positions had been conquered. And if there could be no further continuation of this, it was clear that it was because of the government's and the political parties' fear of revolution. For that very reason, they did not arm the most extremist militias, like the Iron Column.

Thus, the militia system was not at fault, but rather the idea that drove it. And all the forces opposed to the revolution had conspired against this idea.

Nevertheless, it was hard to give up if one still had the wherewithal to take hold of the situation and defeat the counterrevolutionary forces: not just the ones up ahead, but also the ones operating treacherously in the rearguard. It was for this reason that the Iron Column learned certain lessons which it then applied in practice as time passed. The experience of these lessons was translated into the Column's structural changes in order to achieve greater effectiveness in action.

The Iron Column, along with the other confederal columns operating on the Teruel front, had quickly realised that the coordination of forces was crucial. This coordination had been practised from the beginning among the confederal forces, but they encountered other forces that did not share the anarchist ideal. These forces continued to lament the lack of a single institutionalised military command, as if such a thing could miraculously alter the outcome of the war.

This was the real obstacle to the implementation of the plan devised by the confederal columns, which consisted of a Central War Committee with direct delegation from all the columns and a delegate from the War Department within the Popular Executive Committee advised by military experts. What better general staff could there be? But no, this general staff could not be effective because it preserved what others wanted to destroy: the militia ethos.

Nevertheless, the Iron Column continued to maintain and improve its structure in the belief that by doing so it could, if necessary, continue fighting on the front as a force autonomous from but in solidarity with the rest of the forces battling against fascism.

In mid-December the Column was completely reorganised. There were already three hospitals that catered to minor injuries, with the two most important ones located in Sarrión and in La Puebla de Valverde. Consequently, wounded members of the Column no longer needed to leave the area controlled by the Column.

The decisions regarding the Column's structure were not dictated from the top down, but rather emanated from the rank and file. In other words, the Column did not want to lose its greatest strength: its internal solidarity.

Luckily, we possess various documents that illuminate the manner in which these changes were brought about:

> Extract from the minutes of the meeting between the century delegates and the War Committee, held on 23 November 1936:
>
> It is agreed that tank and armoured train personnel should form a century and lend their services to the rearguard.
>
> In view of the fact that the weather (in other words, the cold) is making the normal provisioning of our right flank difficult, it is agreed that said sector should be provided with a kitchen for its exclusive use.
>
> Century delegates are hereby empowered to order the final discharge from the Column of those whose physical constitution cannot withstand campaign life. Guards are to be posted at the hospitals. The chronically ill will be definitively discharged, without entitlement to war benefits.
>
> The Clothing Union will only be able to repair clothing, as it is not equipped to manufacture garments.

The quality of female comrades doing essential work within the Column will have to be looked into.

Monitoring of this will have to be endorsed by a meeting of delegates and the War Committee.

No militian will be able to send packages outside the war zone.

Comrades travelling to Valencia will have to carry a warrant before they can draw upon the stores at Las Salesas (general headquarters of the Column in Valencia).[2]

Another document:

To all comrades:

By unanimous agreement of the century delegates in conjunction with this Committee on 4 December, and also taking into account that the requirements of the war in which we are engaged demand certain formalities if maximum yield is to be obtained from minimal effort, the centuries will be reorganised and restructured in the following manner as the result of an investigation into the problem. But it must be understood that this is not about militarising anyone; rather, it is about learning useful lessons for the war.

The centuries are to be organised as follows: the century will be comprised of eighty-one men; nine delegates, each representing one ten-man unit; three delegates, each representing one thirty-man unit; and one century delegate.

The century is also to include a group that, while not a combat unit, is headed by a delegate and is responsible for provisions, water, munitions, war booty, first-aid and liaison services.

To sum up: Eighty-one fighters, nine delegates from the ten-man units, three from the thirty-man units, one century delegate, six stretcher-bearers, six in charge of munitions and water and four for liaison. Total complement: one-hundred-ten men.

All fighters will be armed, along with those responsible for liaison, munitions and water. Lest it impedes their noble duty to carry the wounded, stretcher-bearers are to hand their weapons over to other comrades engaged in actual combat missions. Thus, all comrades are reminded that, since the war demands certain

---

2   *Línea de Fuego* (27 February 1937).

sacrifices that ultimately benefit the cause of liberty, they should set aside any attitudes at odds with these guidelines, as all of these organisational methods are likely to help hasten our victory.[3]

And another:

PROPOSAL ON THE RESTRUCTURING OF THE COLUMN AND THE WAR COMMITTEE

Submitted to the meeting of century delegates and published for their scrutiny.

Comrades:

We need not delve into history to appreciate that our Column today is not, in any way, what it once was. That 'little column' formed by spontaneous enthusiasm, shunned by some and very often deceived, has—within the space of a few months and thanks to its consistent revolutionary anarchist conduct—become a seasoned, hardened and vigorous Column with a defined personality. This personality—despite a complete absence of propaganda on our part—has become known in the capital, racing across the countryside and achieved national stature, while also winning the sympathies of the producing masses, who see us as something more than just a makeshift Column.

Why mince words? This is the reality. Nothing remains of the 'gang of bandits and ex-convicts' that, thanks to a defamation campaign waged by politicians and gossips, was the 'bane' of gentle workers and rearguard committees. Today we are respected for what we are; not for having compromised and behaved like 'good little boys,' but precisely because of the constancy of our ideas and our vision for these times.

We have paid with our blood. Dozens of comrades are gone forever and others have been left crippled, but in the end we were recognised for what we were.

But not everything was a success. There is one detail, one little

---

3   *Línea de Fuego* (13 December 1936).

matter today, that can be corrected with time. But if left uncorrected, it would cause us serious problems. Due to inactivity, our organisation has become a bit rusty. Matters of no importance arise; minor details originating mostly from annoyance and which in the long run create real conflict with those who, in their thirst for action, would espouse completely anti-anarchist positions. And things cannot continue this way, comrades. Ideologically speaking, it would be the death of our Column.

Are we going to permit that? Never. The death of our Column? Because, let us be clear about this, this is our Column: born out of ourselves, sustained by our blood and by the very lives of those we hold dear, formed by our bodies and defended by our rifles against Hell and high water. Today this Column is our great accomplishment, forged day by day, hour by hour, from hope and zealous faith.

No, comrades. That shall not happen. We have too many things to do ahead of us. And that shall certainly not happen, because the blame lies with us. Yes, literally with us: with the Committee for succumbing to tedium and deviating from its strict obligation, and with you century delegates for failing to articulate and champion the agreements of your respective centuries.

We are not going to argue. The facts are beyond contesting. What is required are solutions, and we will try to give them.

You all know the approximate number in the Column. That number, added to the thousands of workers involved in our offices and in the plan to create recruiting centres in all the districts in the region—as requested by our peasant comrades—leads us to assume that before long we will comprise a very sizeable column. This would cause a series of difficulties for us if we did not first adopt an organisational framework that constituted the firm foundation on which the future can rest.

That framework could—as it has been thus far—be based on centuries, with the provision that every ten centuries would constitute a body of one thousand men which could be called, for example, a division. This would greatly facilitate the grouping and mobilisation of the centuries.

Should this be approved, we would form a fixed number of divisions with the comrades from the front and from Puebla.

The five hundred comrades we have assigned to the Torres-Benedito Column, along with others, would form another division. Apparently, we would have at our disposal in Mora and in Sarrión one or two more divisions to act as reserves for use in relieving the front-line forces.

The remainder of the recruited comrades could form sub-divisions by district, doing their normal work until called upon.

The Structure of the Divisions

On active service, there is no change: there are group delegates and century delegates, and the latter are to meet with the Committee periodically.

The divisions on the front, in Mora and in Sarrión are to be considered on active duty.

In reserve: The units active in the districts are to be considered reserve units. These units shall be comprised of a foundation of exactly ten centuries, with the same features as the units on the front.

Thus, each division will have ten century delegates plus one divisional delegate, whose roles will be 'purely administrative' until such time as the division is brought to the front. These comrades will never be able to make changes, requisitions, etc., by themselves without previously consulting the liaison comrade delegated by the Committee, and they will have to subordinate themselves to the general interest.

Otherwise, they will be expelled.

The Role of the Century Delegate

He will not confine himself to acting as his century's spokesman, but will also make use of every opportunity to explain all agreements reached and the importance of their fulfilment to the comrades for whom he acts as delegate.

He is to be responsible for all equipment issued to his century, whether war materials or provisions, and the group delegates are to be answerable to him for the same.

As for the rest, there is no change.

The Committee

In progressing from a relatively small column to what could be called a small army, necessity dictates—in view of the burden of work and responsibility and, let us be clear about it, the lack of intelligent, trustworthy comrades to take part in those committees that should be formed—that a Committee be created, composed of six comrades who will assume full responsibility for the Column and collate and coordinate the wishes of the delegates and the rest of the comrades.

In order to be able to perfectly oversee the entire Column, this Committee can be sub-divided into:

1. Four delegates from each war zone.
2. One delegate to liaise with the reserve units, district units, etc.
3. One delegate from the offices in Valencia.

The Role of the Committee Delegates

1. War Delegates:

Complete oversight of, and responsibility for, everything pertaining to the front.

These comrades, in concert with the century delegates, will elect those who are to take charge of the various sections that, until now, comprised the War Committee. This will yield a comprehensive improvement in this area, because when a comrade is assigned to a section that is completely unrelated to the work of the Committee, it will be his only occupation and he will thus feel a greater identification with his position. At the same time, the Committee, being thus restricted, will more carefully oversee the various sections, which can continue without change.

2. Liaison Delegate:

This delegate will have no other duties besides periodically visiting the district recruitment centres and the various sectors in which our Column's forces are operating and communicating any reports and petitions received to the rest of the Committee, which in turn will forward such information to the century delegates.

3. Office Delegate:

This comrade will take charge of everything pertaining to recruitment, propaganda, press, attendance at CNT and FAI committee meetings, the War Delegation, etc.

To that end, he will endeavour to set up an office capable of correcting any deficiencies that have arisen thus far.

This, in broad outline, is the proposed reorganisation of our Column. Now, you shall have your say.

We only wish to remind you of one thing: now that we are a force to be respected and feared by some, yet loved infinitely by the finest, let us not disappoint the latter. Remember that they, the revolutionary workers and peasants, see in ours their own strength and in our ideas the true revolution.

There you have it.

On behalf of the proposal group,

Pellicer

The century delegates, having approved in principle and expanded this proposal, proceeded to name those comrades who were to constitute the new Committee and its different sections, the posts being allocated as follows:

War Committee: Pellicer, Segarra, Cortés, Espí, González and Montoya.

General Provisioning: Morell.

Health: Quiles.

Transport: Serna.

Equipment: Gumbau.

Divisional Delegates: Rufino, Villarroya, Navarro,. Sanchís, Rafael Alonso and Mármol.

It is understood that these appointments will not come into effect until the centuries give their approval today, after which the matter will be considered definitively settled at this meeting.[4]

---

4   *Línea de Fuego* (4 December 1936). Also see *Fragua Social* (19 December 1936), which contains the complete text of the proposal for the restructuring of the Iron Column and the War Committee.

This restructuring of the Column introduced a new feature: the division, comprised of ten centuries, at the head of which is a divisional delegate who liaises with the Column's War Committee. The Divisional Committee would be composed of the ten delegates from the centuries.

The innovation of the division was designed to avoid the multitudinous meetings between century delegates and the Column's Central War Committee. At any rate, the assemblies of century delegates still applied in relation to matters of importance affecting the Column as a whole.

As a result, the component parts of the Column were as follows: group (ten men), section (three groups), and century (one hundred and ten men). The largest units remained the division (ten centuries) and the flank sector, which was a strategic war formation that could be commanded by a delegate who was assisted by other delegates from the combat forces or from the Sector Committee.

The War Committee also underwent a modification, and on 4 December 1936 it consisted of: Montoya, Rufino, Serna, Espí, Rodilla, José Pellicer and Peñarrocha. This Committee subdivided into sections as follows: equipment, Canet; offices, Gómez; transport, Dolz; supplies, Morell, Manzanera and Diego; information, Cortés; war commissar and delegate to the confederal organisation, José Segarra; health, Quiles; delegate to the general headquarters and offices in Valencia, Pedro Pellicer.

In keeping with this restructuring:

> All comrades are hereby cautioned that they may not abandon their parapet or the revolutionary task they have been assigned without express authorisation from the century delegate or from the comrade in charge of the department.
>
> Any comrade in breach of this decision by the century delegates and War Committee will be expelled from the Column and named in the antifascist press as an undesirable.[5]

If we analyse the texts that we have transcribed, we see in them a desire not to impose but to persuade. These were not military orders, but rather decisions made more or less democratically and

---

5   *Línea de Fuego* (19 December 1936).

with reasonable explanation, in an effort to persuade and to instruct in reference to the relevant idea.

The last order mentioned turned out to be the very model of moral obligation. Going on the assumption that the people who filled the ranks of the Column were all members of trade union organisations (mainly the CNT-FAI), the term 'expulsion' signified, in this case, the strongest sanction that a militant worker could expect from his organisation or political party. Why resort to the firing squad? Moral sanction was stronger and had the advantage of appealing to everyone's revolutionary honour.

Elsewhere we stated that the Iron Column suffered from a comprehensive boycott by the government. But even more serious was that it also began to receive the same treatment from the 'higher committees' of the CNT and the FAI. In any case, the Column could count on the support of the region's trade unions and collectives, as is apparent from following communique:

DONATIONS TO THE COLUMN

The following goods have been donated to our Iron Column by the Cieza Local Committee:

CLOTHING: Fifteen tee-shirts, fifteen pairs of socks, seven towels, forty-five ponchos, thirty-six bedsheets, three greatcoats and two jackets.

FOODSTUFFS: Sixteen baskets of grapes, one sack of beans, two sacks of oranges, two sacks of lemons, five cases of tomatoes, ten sacks of oranges, eighteen hens, fifty pigeons, eighty arrobas of olive oil and one sack of rice.

The Magadoras comrades from Cieza, who are members of the CNT, have made a donation of 657.35 pesetas for all the comrades at the front, regardless of gender. The money in question has been spent on clothing.

. On behalf of the Magadoras section and on behalf of the Committee: Mariana López, José Morcillo and Dolores Azala.[6]

---

6   *Línea de Fuego* (3 December 1936). [1 Arroba = 11.5 kg. KSL]

At roughly the same time, there was an item published in *Línea de Fuego*, entitled 'We Are':

> This Column of ours was created out of nothing. Dynamism and faith in victory against the nationalist worms were the only things that we had in abundance.
>
> But we were all young, and the raging storm—against which we went into battle with nothing but our minds and our muscles—mattered little to us.
>
> And so we came to Barracas, after which we travelled kilometre after kilometre through the silent land of the Aragonese.
>
> We fought and we won; we spread our ideas and we were heard.
>
> We watched the golden wheat grow and our band of fighters grew alongside it.
>
> They flocked to our Iron Column because they were iron-willed, and our struggle was and will be as hard as iron.
>
> We are rebels and we keep the banner of rebellion flying high.
>
> We fight in the war and in the revolution: on the front, in the vanguard, our weapon is muscle; in the rearguard of the city, our weapon is the mind.
>
> Some hate us, while others love us.
>
> But the 'others' are the workers, who see us as the faithful guardians of revolutionary principles.
>
> The bureaucracy that sprouted out of the revolution hates us, because we unmasked it and held the real pariahs up to the light of day.
>
> But we do not care about their hate.
>
> What matters to us is that the factory and the field are on our side, and on the side of the revolution.
>
> We are vilified and denounced as heretics.
>
> But our heresy honours us, dignifies us, and raises us up to the very summit of truth.
>
> We are the true light of the new life, because we were born for liberation.
>
> We are the immense legion looking for completeness, so that all may love one another.
>
> We have no pay to offer other than the path of light and brotherhood.

Let us discard the current set-up lest it plunge us back into extreme corruption and filth.

We offer solid ground upon which the city of true men can be built, with mortar seasoned by free minds.

Youth and iron: because of that, because of what we are, we will win.[7]

7　*Línea de Fuego* (14 December 1936), article by Jaime Serna, a member of the War Committee.

XIV
The Counterrevolution on the Move

The Iron Column was a grain of sand in the desert of the republican zone. The CNT and the FAI—on political grounds—were made to accept a part in a government that, given its characteristics, could not have been revolutionary in the sense in which the proletariat understood revolution. No government can be revolutionary in that respect, least of all one headed by Largo Caballero, whose mission was precisely that of derailing the revolution by invoking reasons of efficiency in order to win the war.

Because of all this, the CNT inevitably had to pressure its militant rank and file to conform to its political strategy, because otherwise its participation in the government would prove pointless. And here was where the first difficulties arose: the rank and file rebelled against the leadership because the former understood the trap into which the latter had walked.

Miguel González Inestal, a distinguished FAI militant, wrote: 'In the libertarian camp, everyone, absolutely every single militant, had his share of scruples to overcome, beliefs to readjust and—why not admit it?—dreams to bury. And this was not just due to a practised position derived from experience, but also because we justly feared the resurrection—in whole or in part—of the old army: the caste privileges, the poisoning of young minds, the reversion to the past, the trampling underfoot of all social rights and, above all, that there was a danger of its turning into the devourer of the revolution, into a partisan instrument.'[1]

All that the CNT and the FAI could gain from this course of action was certainly not the triumph of the revolution, but rather to prevent the Communist Party from making a massacre of the libertarian movement, as it did with Nestor Makhno's Ukrainian anarchists in Russia during the years 1919–1921. Perhaps if all this was said clearly to the anarchist rank and file, things might have gone another way. But this was not the case. Instead, an attempt was made to maintain a triumphalist front, and it was this that surprised the members of

---

1 Burnett Bolloten, *La Revolución Española*, 255.

the Iron Column as well as those of the Durruti Column, the Ascaso Column and the rest of the libertarian columns. It must be admitted that, following the CNT's entry into the government, many influential CNT militants became dizzy with power and passively reverted to the militarisation argument, as if it could offer some magical solution to every problem. What we are essentially saying is that confusion had taken root inside the CNT and the FAI, and that this confusion had naturally begun with those militants whose ideological grounding was the least sound, as was the case with Cipriano Mera: a man of indubitable moral integrity but who went to the extreme of expressing a determination 'to bandy words only with generals, officers and sergeants.'[2] Mera offers us this account of his own evolution:

'It was at that moment—after the loss of Aravaca and Pozuelo, on the outskirts of Madrid—that all my ideas about discipline and militarisation turned upside down,' confessed Cipriano Mera, leader of the anarchist militias on the Central front, some months later. 'The spilling of my brothers' blood in battle made me change my opinion. I understood that in order to avoid a comprehensive defeat we had to build an army of our own; an army every bit as potent as the enemy's; a disciplined, capable army organised to defend the workers. From then on I never ceased to advise every combatant about the necessity of submitting to the new military regulations.[3]

Cipriano Mera's arguments were untenable from all angles. An army like the enemy's could not possibly be conjured up. The enemy would only be destroyed by a distinct strategy: guerrilla operations, serious infiltration in the rearguard, the sowing of revolt in that same rearguard, and the destruction of bridges. In other words, a 'scorched earth' policy. For this type of war and this type of warfare we had fighters who were superior to the enemy.

But the same could not be said about conventional warfare. The 'spilled blood of comrades' that Mera regretted seeing ran in rivers later on, because that was the inevitable result of the military tactics

---

2   Cipriano Mera, quoted in *CNT* (23 February 1937).
3   Cipriano Mera, quoted in *Solidaridad Obrera* (1 December 1937).

used by the Russian experts, the clearest examples of which were the battles of Teruel and the Ebro.

But the inferiority complex surrounding the war infected the bosom of even the healthiest revolutionary organisations like a virus. The accidental death of Durruti, not so much because he was a gift from God but rather due to an array of circumstances, was an awful loss for all those who championed the more radical position within the anarchist camp, even, as we shall see, within the Iron Column itself.

Before the question of militarisation was seriously posed to the Iron Column, the matter was logically discussed at all levels within the Column, from those with the greatest responsibilities to the modest militians on the parapet. The tone of those discussions is related to us by Roque Santamaría:

> We talked amongst ourselves about militarisation, and I wish to place on record the arguments that I heard during those con-versations. One of them was: 'If we continue fighting as we have been doing and we win the war, those counterrevolutionaries ensconced in the rearguard will surely ambush the victory. Thus, our efforts are going to be futile, in that we will lose the best of our militants on the battlefields and the victory will be co-opted by people who will not make any revolution. Isn't it better to accept the principle of militarisation, which will impose the same obligations on everyone?' The discussion always remained unfinished, because later on came those 'principles,' about which we were intransigent. Nevertheless, the problem was there and there was no way to avoid it.[4]

The noose was tightening around those groups that were tena-ciously resisting the idea of militarisation. Structural reforms were made which included the acceptance of military titles, but certainly no one wanted to talk about changing their way of life! Nevertheless, the government controlled the supply of weapons and money.

For quite some time, the Iron Column had more or less been sorting out its own problems by raiding enemy territory with the aim of capturing weapons and ammunition, and it had also received assis-tance from Catalonia in the form of war material. The problem of

---

4 Roque Santamaría, testimony cited above.

provisions was resolved by the peasant collectives, which supported all the confederal columns in Levante.

But it was obvious that this situation could not continue. Militarisation was being imposed all around, even taking root in the area in which the Column operated, where there were already other militarised units. It was as if a dream was coming to an end, and the reaction of the people was brutally honest: if militarisation—even in its most moderate form—was imposed on them, then the most rebellious section of the Iron Column would threaten to quit the front.

It was in these circumstances, with the Column facing danger from all sides, that the War Committee drew up a report for circulation among its members at the end of 1936. It stated:

> When all this began, the state was a phantom, to which no one paid attention. The workers' organisations—the CNT and the UGT—represented the only security for the Spanish people. Politics then came into play ... and, almost unnoticed, so did that lifeless, powerless phantom. As a result, our beloved CNT, using its strength and its prestige to reinforce the state, has become nothing more than an appendage of that very state and yet another hose dousing the fires of revolution that the labouring masses of the UGT and CNT trade unions so brilliantly began.
>
> With the government thus reinforced, the task of purely governmental organisation begins. And now we find ourselves with an army identical to those armies that serve the state, complete with the customary old coercive forces. Just like before, the police go against the workers who are attempting to realise something socially useful. The people's militias have disappeared and, in short, the social revolution has been strangled.
>
> Had we been able to rely on the support of the government and our own organisation—we are speaking of the responsible committees—we might have had more equipment and more man-power, with provisions for relief and leave. But since it did not happen that way, since we have had to put up with comrades serving month after month behind the parapets, the end result is that such a spirit of sacrifice can no longer be demanded or expected, and each day brings tremendous problems... We acknowledge that the Column's internal problems are difficult to

resolve. And before something serious happens, before the combination of fatigue and a loss of morale spreads and delivers a tremendous blow to what has already been conquered and sustained with the strength of peerless sacrifice; before that, we say again: we need to look for a formula that leaves all of us well placed...

We alone remain unmilitarised, opposed to the agreements of the CNT and the FAI, and we continue to be denied assistance from the government as well as from our own organisation. This Column of ours, which might, with proper assistance, have preserved undiluted the revolutionary principles that suit our character, must, because of this deficiency, this absence of such aid, acknowledge that our system for making war has failed.

We are well aware that the immense majority of comrades will be furious with those who are at fault for this, but we also want to alert these comrades that their protest would be violently suffocated by the agencies of the state, for it is no longer possible to organise anything against it or its partners. It is sufficiently strong to crush anything that gets in its way. Additionally, in these extremely serious times it is advisable that we swallow our outrage. Once again we must don the mantle of Christ...

We know the disadvantages of militarisation. The system is inconsistent with our temperament and the temperament of all who have always had a clear conception of liberty. But we are also aware of the drawbacks that accompany our operating outside the orbit of the Ministry of War. It is sad to say, but only two paths remain: dissolution of the Column, or militarisation. Anything else would be pointless.[5]

At the end of the report, the War Committee left the decision regarding this delicate issue to an assembly of the Column. The assembly was unable to come up with a definitive solution, but the campaign in favour of militarisation intensified, especially among Communist Party spokesmen. The campaign was orchestrated with attacks on 'the uncontrollables' and 'the tribes,' names the Communists used to describe the confederal forces on the Aragón and Levante fronts.

---

5   *Nosotros* (16 February 1937). This newspaper was launched by the group of the same name in November 1936. At the time, almost all of the group's members were in the Iron Column along with José Segarra and the brothers José and Pedro Pellicer.

At the beginning of February 1937 the city of Málaga inexplicably fell into the hands of the fascists. The general in charge of the city was General Villalba, who had a very bad reputation stemming from the days when he was in charge of the Huesca front, which he was accused of paralysing in order to impede the taking of Huesca. Now it was widely believed that Villalba had handed Málaga to the fascists, which signified more than just the fall of that city, for during the first three months of fascist rule there some ten thousand workers were shot.[6] The loss of Málaga profoundly affected the republican zone. The Communist Party, aiming to attack Caballero, highlighted the fact that he was being weakened by his clashes with the 'Russian advisors.'[7] In order to deliver the death blow they went after General Asensio, the undersecretary of war, holding him responsible for the fall of Málaga. The objective of this Communist Party policy was to cover for Villalba, who had become a 'fellow traveller,' and to bring the president of the Republic into disrepute. Naturally, the PCE demanded 'an end to the uncontrollables' and the 'utopian projects of libertarian communism.'

In the midst of this serious crisis, Largo Caballero and the CNT reached a tacit agreement that gave the anarchist trade union carte blanche to control its combat units through its own organisations, provided that the militarisation of its columns proceeded immediately.

On 2 February, *Nosotros*, which was both the organ of the FAI in Levante and the mouthpiece of the Iron Column, published the following article on page four:

MILITARISATION?

The CNT, by way of *Nosotros*, calmly has its say regarding this delicate problem:

---

6   Antonio Bahamonde y Sánchez de Castro, *Un Año de Queipo*, 132. The author, a nationalist who served on the staff of Queipo de Llano, writes: 'During the first week, when no one could enter Málaga, FOUR THOUSAND people were shot. They were shot down in groups by machine-guns on the Playa del Palo. Later on, court martials were set up. At dizzying speed, the people were tried—if that is the right word—in groups of fifty to seventy. In this fashion, by the third month of Málaga's liberation TEN THOUSAND people had perished.'

7   Francisco Largo Caballero, *Mis Recuerdos*; Burnett Bolloten, *La Revolución Española*; W.G. Krivitsky, *La Mano de Stalin sobre España*.

Let us be blunt. Whenever the word 'militarisation' is spoken, we worry, we become uneasy and we tremble, because it brings to mind countless crimes against dignity and the human personality.

Until not too long ago—and there are many today still seeking the same thing—to militarise was to dragoon men in such a way that their wills were annihilated as their personalities were broken on the wheel of barracks life. The commander, in the name of a discipline that had all of the features of despotism, issued the orders. And the soldiers—our brothers—obeyed them not because they freely chose to do so, but through imposition, which as a result kept us and our people inferior in status to the bourgeoisie, who were always represented by the officer corps.

Through militarism, which was a kind of Caesarism adopted by the ruling caste, we were persecuted, insulted, vilified and decimated. And today, our wounds still fresh, we cannot just forget militarism as if the very word did not disturb and frighten us.

Our preaching and our practice were always opposed to regimentation, which means degradation. And we should proceed with the utmost good judgement and caution, lest we be caught in the snares that the militarists of every school—both white and red—have placed in our path.

Those comrades who are fighting—the spirited youth in the trenches, the warriors of the revolution, our brothers who risk their lives on the battlefields—have spoken to us, somewhat shaken up and surprised, because they have seen in all this a danger to individual liberties.

And wishing to give them an explanation—not just to calm them down but to reassure them that the militarisation of which we are all so fearful is not going to happen—we have interviewed comrade Marianet, secretary of the CNT, so that he might give us his word, which is the very word of the CNT, on this matter.

—What can you tell us, comrade Marianet, regarding this problem of militarisation?

—Firstly, the comrades should not worry just because the word sounds bad to them. Whether we like it or not, we are already militarised in that, voluntarily and from the very beginning of the war operations that fascism has brought upon us, we agreed to the command and discipline that every collective undertaking requires. Secondly, this militarisation—even if it is true that other sectors might be against it—will be nothing more than the necessary cohesion, harmony and mutual understanding between the military expert planning a defence or an attack and the expert on the parapet who, with peerless courage, defends his territory. And let no one see in this a castrating subordination of some men by others, as we will not allow any renaissance of militaristic privileges. Rather, we will only concede the necessity—the indispensable necessity—that while some defend our territory with rifle or machine-gun in hand, others work out the best way to defend a position or capture a city in the solitude of the office: consulting maps and observing the terrain, taking into account the human factor and the importance of ammunition, examining the enemy front, and preparing a surprise attack.

—Will our columns disappear?

—Yes, they are to go. They have to go. By the time we joined the National Committee, the agreement had already been reached that our columns would, like all the rest, become brigades—not that the name matters—and be given everything that they need in order to operate effectively. Now this conversion does not, if examined carefully, imply a fundamental change, because upon conversion the brigades will keep the same commanders who served with the columns. This means that comrades who have formed an attachment to those who are responsible for operational decisions can be assured that they will not be obliged by capricious changes to accept people whose ideology, and therefore personal bearing, are not to their liking. In addition, the political commissars, who are the real commanders—don't let the word scare you—of the brigades, will be appointed by the confederal organisation, to which they will be answerable at all times, although they may first be required to undergo training at the military academy established for this very purpose.

—I have heard it said—and this is another point that worries our fighters—that these brigades will be mixed; or in other words, that they will be composed of regular battalions, Marxist battalions and confederal battalions. Is this the case?

—There is a grain of truth to that, as it is one of the existing proposals regarding the formation of the brigades. But we also have our own proposal, which states that the brigades we will logically need to form in the future should be comprised of comrades from the CNT and the FAI and controlled by those two organisations, while at the same time subject to the orders—another word that jars our hearing—that issue from the sole command, which all the forces voluntarily accept.

The secretary of the National Committee continued: 'I would ask that you comrades from *Nosotros* do what you can to dispel this despotic view of militarisation which some, we don't know with what intention, are propagating. From day one of the revolution, without any orders, we all voluntarily accepted a measure of discipline in matters of defence and attack. And this, which was a spontaneous thing, is what we are trying to channel, order and regulate in order to better achieve our common aspirations. That is all.'

We concluded the interview, and just as comrade Marianet said, we are communicating it to our comrades.

The matter is thought-provoking and of immediate relevance. We shall be returning to it in these pages.

Burnett Bolloten says that this interview about militarisation and the mixed brigades—given by Mariano R. Vázquez, secretary of the National Committee of the CNT, in *Nosotros*, which was the mouthpiece of the Iron Column—proved 'very significant,' and 'was published without comment by the Ministry of War.'

But, for all these declarations from the CNT, the Column's misgivings were not assuaged. It was plain for all to see that acceptance of militarisation, even under CNT supervision, would be a terrible backwards step and would represent a slide down a slippery slope that would lead inevitably to the foot of the cliffs of self-contradiction.

XV
Teruel Torn Between Franco and Largo Caballero

In the zone dominated by the mutinous generals, the question of power remained unclear. Ever since General Sanjurjo's death in a mysterious accident, the fascist generals were without an overall leader. Each one considered himself lord and master of his zone: Queipo de Llano in Seville did not feel that he had to submit to anyone, and the same was true of General Franco in Morocco, Mola in Navarra, and Cabanellas in Zaragoza. Each mutinous general was at loggerheads with the rest, and regarded himself fit to exercise supreme command exclusively.

Then again, the Requeté was against the Falange and the Falange was against Franco. The Falange had waited patiently for its leader, a prisoner of the republicans in Alicante, to be released. But José Antonio Primo de Rivera, the Falange's founder, was stupidly shot by the Republic (it would have been more politically astute to release him into the mutineers' territory in order to better stir up the political contradictions among them), and from that moment on the Falange had lost its bearings. Its leadership accidentally fell to Manuel Hedilla, who did not have the character for such a position.

During these power struggles General Franco was patiently manoeuvring to ensure that he would be named head of the 'Nationalist Movement,' which position he attained on October 1936 and took advantage of in order to amalgamate the Falange and the Requeté, thereby converting two enemies into a single organisation. And from this moment onwards the reconstruction of the state began.

Even in the fascist zone, the state had been broken into pieces. The reconstruction process in both the fascist and republican zones took on a curious parallelism owing to a coincidence of factors and circumstances. In the republican zone, the reconstruction of the state had begun through the efforts of Largo Caballero, with Stalin in the background. In Burgos, the fascists' capital, General Franco, with help from the German ambassador, was doing the same work.

But the state would not come to consolidate itself in the republican zone until, after the 'May events' of 1937, Juan Negrín took power as an authentic dictator and continued the statist work initiated by Largo Caballero. In the fascist zone, the same consolidation took place in the wake of the 'Salamanca incidents' of April 1937, when the Falange was virtually decapitated with the imprisonment of Manuel Hedilla and then 'put in its place' by Raimundo Fernández Cuesta and Serrano Suñer. Thus, Franco and Negrin were mirror images of each other in their statist endeavours. But Franco combined the upper hand in the war with incessant help from Hitler and Mussolini, as well as the conscious support of those republican politicians who, as declared enemies of the popular revolution, were helping to lose the war through their counterrevolutionary efforts.

More or less, this was the politico-military panorama at the beginning of 1937, when a republican attack was launched in the Teruel sector, whose front—as we know—had been undergoing militarisation by the Republic since 15 November 1936. Franco was restructuring his side of the front with the intention of initiating a general offensive in Aragón, which began in October 1937 as a response to the offensive launched by the Republican Army between June and September 1937.

Teruel, semi-besieged, had not been taken by republican troops due to their lack of weaponry, and for this reason—after the Iron Column militias had advanced as far as Puerto de Escandón and Aldehuela between August and November—the front had stabilised and work had begun on fortifying the lines. But in late December, the republican General Staff mounted an offensive on that front.

At the moment the offensive began, the republican forces deployed around Teruel consisted of, from right to left: Column No. 4 (Peire), which was to operate around the village of Celadas, the Santa Bárbara peak and Cerro Gordo; Column No. 1 (Torres-Benedito), operating around Concud; the Thirteenth International Brigade (recently transferred to this sector), whose immediate objectives were the cemetery, the monastery of Santa Bárbara and the Mansueto peak; the Iron Column (Column No. 2, according to the republican command), which would advance down the Sagunto road towards Teruel; and the Del Rosal Column, which would take Albarracín and Gea de Albarracín. Preferably, Teruel would be occupied by the Thirteenth International Brigade.[1]

---

1 It is advisable to keep in mind that during any military operation involving a Communist unit, that unit was assigned the task of occupying the city centre if things went well, thereby allowing it to claim all the 'honours.' But if things did not

In charge of all these forces was Colonel Velasco Echave, whose chief of staff was Captain Arderius and whose 'special' advisor was Colonel Petrov, a Russian. The command post was located in Cedrillas.

The republican attack was scheduled for the night of 25–26 December, but just a few hours before it began the commander of the 'Henry Vuillemin' battalion defected to the enemy and, from enemy lines, exhorted his friends to do the same.

On the 26th, following an artillery barrage, the attack on Teruel began in the Celadas-Mansueto sector. That night, republican forces managed to cut Teruel's telegraph communications and close the main highway. And on the 27th, 'heavy pressure was applied in all sectors, but especially in the Alfambra valley and against the capital. Fifteen armoured cars and eighteen aircraft intervened. Column No. 4 was unable to get past the Santa Bárbara peak, Celadas village and Cero Gordo, while the same fate befell Column No. 1 at Concud. The 'assault force' (Thirteenth International Brigade) captured some positions opposite the cemetery but later lost them in the face of tenacious resistance by the defending forces. Column No. 2 (Iron Column) advanced slowly, without substantial results, and dug in on its left in Las Alvarizas, which was unoccupied. Column No. 3 established itself in Los Altos de Marimezquita, La Muela de Villastar, Las Carboneras, El Cerro de Perdigón and to the west of La Hoz, but it was unable to enter Villastar. No news was received from the Del Rosal Column.'[2]

The offensive continued on the 28th, especially in the Mansueto-Santa Bárbara sector manned by the Thirteenth International Brigade, which suffered heavy losses and was unable to achieve its objective. Column No. 3, in conjunction with the Del Rosal Column, managed to cut the Bezas road between Campillo and San Blas, which left Albarracín in a difficult position.

The enemy also took heavy losses, and their commander Muñoz Castellanos asked for reinforcements from Zaragoza, which arrived immediately with a *bandera* from the *Tercio* and a *tabor* from La Mehal-la in addition to a motorised column. The mutinous Colonel Castellanos estimated that he was being attacked by a force of 20,000 men.

---

go well, the blame was shifted to other units because they 'had chickened out.' This was the PCE's usual technique.

2　José Manuel Martínez Bande, *La Invasión de Aragón y el Desembarco en Mallorca*, 202.

On the 29th and the 30th there was fierce fighting throughout the sector, but on 1 January 1937 the fighting was concentrated around the Concud-Teruel line, where the Torres-Benedito Column managed to occupy the Chantre hills and cut the railroad tracks. The fighting continued in varying degrees of intensity until the 13th, on which date the Iron Column improved its positions in Puerto de Escandón overlooking Teruel. A republican dispatch from this day reads as follows:

> Today, the Iron Column bypassed Puerto de Escandón on the right flank, thereby severing the highway between kilometres six and eight and amid heavy combat. Ten trenches have been taken from the enemy—including two heavy machine-guns and one light machine-gun—while a great number of losses have been inflicted, causing sixty soldiers to defect to our ranks with weapons and ammunition, along with several families. One second lieutenant and two Moors have been taken prisoner. Our guns pounded the enemy positions to great effect, thereby maintaining an effective counter-bombardment. The Galán Brigade assisted in this operation.[3]

After accepting that the nationalists suffered six hundred losses, the military specialist José Manuel Martínez Bande summarised the battle with the following commentary:

> From a technical point of view, Colonel Velasco (republican sector) managed to occupy Gea and Castralvo temporarily and to surround Albarracin, the results of which we can only describe as fleeting and incidental, with no real significance.
> Once again, the lack of overall operational coordination along the entire Aragón front was less than impressive, which was the reason why an operation that attempted to be decisive—or at least of real significance—was not accompanied by other simultaneous diversionary operations along the length of that front.[4]

---

3 Dispatch from the War Delegation of the Popular Executive Committee in Valencia, reproduced in the press.
4 José Manuel Martínez Bande, *La Invasión de Aragón y el Desembarco en Mallorca*, 214.

XVI
The Prologue to Militarisation

After the aforementioned military operation, the Iron Column had to confront the problem of militarisation once again:

> In a ministerial order, particularly directed at accelerating the militarisation of the Iron Column and which had undoubtedly been issued following consultation with his CNT and FAI colleagues in the cabinet, Largo Caballero announced that the forces on the Teruel front would come under the control of the Ministry of War in every respect—including administrative matters—as of 1 April. In addition, he named José Benedito, commander of the anarcho-syndicalist Torres-Benedito Column, to the organisation section of the General Staff with the aim of implementing the requisite reorganisation. At the same time, the Iron Column received notice that the Decree of 30 December 1936, which provides for the distribution of salary through battalion paymasters who are subordinate to the paymaster-general, would be imposed.
>
> Whatever the War Committee's particular opinion may have been regarding these matters, it was washed away by the wave of indignation that swept through the Column. At a general assembly of Column personnel, the men refused to submit to the military reorganisation and the new financial regulations, and a large number of them decided to abandon the front as a gesture of protest.
>
> Fearful that this defiance might give the Ministry of War a pretext on which to conscript members of the Column into service with the regular army, or that the CNT in Valencia might attempt to incorporate them into other libertarian units, the War Committee drafted the following cautionary note:[1]

IRON COLUMN

To the comrades belonging to the Column:

---

1   Burnett Bolloten, *La Revolución Española*.

As a response to the many comrades who have asked us about the situation of our Column and what should be done about it, we write the following note.

The Iron Column has not disbanded, nor is it thinking of doing such a thing, nor has it been militarised. The Iron Column, in compliance with the agreements reached by all of its members, asked to be relieved for the purposes of rest[2] and reorganisation, and this is all that it has been doing. At present there are only some three centuries waiting to be relieved, after which, according to agreement, an assembly of the entire Column will be held at which we will determine our position and course of action with the seriousness and responsibility that we have always displayed.

Thus, until that assembly occurs, no comrade should enlist with any other organised forces—whether brigades or army—because as members of a Column that is on leave, no one can force you to do so. At the same time we warn all that this WAR COMMITTEE has not authorised anyone to go around organising battalions or brigades—with which we have nothing in common—using the name and the prestige of the Iron Column.

We believe that these declarations clarify the situation sufficiently for no one to be mistaken.

THE WAR COMMITTEE.[3]

The period between 6 and 21 March, when the Column's general assembly took place, was a time of great tragedy and debate within the Column as well as within the various bodies of the CNT. Curiously, it was also during this period, on 9 March, that a large assembly of militias from the Zaragoza and Huesca sectors of the Aragón front took place in Barcelona (mainly involving international units of an anarchist persuasion). The French-language supplement to the *Boletín CNT-FAI* of 19 March 1936 carried a report on the results of that latter

---

2   According to Roque Santamaría, only part of the Column was withdrawn for rest, while the remainder stayed behind in order to protect the positions for which it was responsible.

3   The text quoted here was published in *Nosotros* (6 March 1937). Bolloten summarises it, but we have opted to reproduce it in its entirety.

assembly. Due to its illustrative character and its accurate reflection of the situation at the time, we shall quote from it at length:

EXTRAORDINARY ASSEMBLY OF MILITIANS

At 1800 hours on 9 March, the assembly of militians—particularly those who recently arrived from the Zaragoza and Huesca fronts—began in the meeting hall of the Casa CNT-FAI in Barcelona.

The following were designated to chair the gathering: Alfred Lobel (French section), chairman; Fernand Fortin (propaganda delegate from the French section), vice-chairman; C. Styr-Nair (French section) and Flodig (militian on leave from the front), advisors; and Félix Danon (French section), minute-keeper.

The proceedings began once the aims of this assembly of militians—who had come to Spain as volunteers—were defined, with a succession of speakers taking the floor.

Georges Bougard (miliciano): I am not speaking as a delegate, but rather as an individual. I agree that a degree of discipline is essential, because the army against which we are fighting is formidably well-organised. Obviously, there is no question of militarising in the manner in which many expect. It must be understood that we have come here in order to see things through to the end. Militarisation as I see it is nothing more than a properly understood and applied self-discipline. In addition, we need more expert military training, which can be secured because we have in our midst, among others, a number of French 'officers.' We find ourselves faced with the dilemma of militarisation or the complete disbanding of the militias. The disbanding or dissolving of the militias cannot be allowed to happen. I thus ask that the militias remain under the control of the CNT, which is the strongest organisation in Spain.

Julien Cadot (miliciano): I am against militarisation. Not everyone in the CNT is an anarchist and therefore the FAI should control the militias.

Lovi (militian): We cannot isolate ourselves by dealing only with the war. We must also spare a thought for the revolution. They want to blind us with cries of: 'Everything for Madrid! Everything for the children!' There are two capitalisms that intend to crush the revolutionary movement: a domestic capitalism represented by the power of the Generalitat, and a foreign capitalism represented by England, America, in France by Leon Blum, etc. To us, the CNT is more than just its 'leaders.' We have confidence in the opinions of the entire CNT membership. The post of army officer is and always has been a dishonourable calling for us. If we do need military experts, these should be supervised by trade union and political delegates ... but it already seems that the intention is to leave the trade unions out of the matter, like in Russia. They want to crush the revolution, but since they cannot do that, they intend to strangle it.

Raoul Tarrou (miliciano): I will not speak as an antifascist but as an anarchist. I oppose all authority, especially military authority. Two months ago in Gelsa we were presented with the ultimatum to militarise. But all we want are technical delegates with no power to command us or make us march in lock-step... If our proposal to form an autonomous body is not accepted, then there will be no way for us to get along, in which case I would be disposed to return to France.

Moneck Krsech (militian): Right now it is no longer a question of a 'barricades revolution.' The Spanish people cannot and should not continue to play around with heroism. This is a real war and it must be won at all costs. The intention was to toy with the theory and the spirit of the anarchists in order to thereby disarm us. Our militarisation has nothing to do with parades or military salutes. What we need are good commanders on the front so that we are not required to watch absurd scenes like our artillery firing on our infantry. We acknowledge that we in the Durruti Column have officers who conduct themselves like true comrades... There should be no playing around with the word militarisation.

Fortin (chairman): I remind the assembly that what we are interested in finding out is why comrades have abandoned the front and what those comrades want to do.

Joaquin Cortés (CNT Regional Committee): I was asked to attend this assembly so that I might expound upon militarisation. Obviously, I am a member of the CNT Regional Committee, but I do not feel qualified to speak of matters with which I am not familiar. For this reason, I defer to our comrade Ascaso.

Domingo Ascaso (Ascaso Division): We Spanish anarchists are no less sensitive than our French comrades, but we find ourselves facing a militarised enemy. The militias are not schooled in the art of war, if indeed war can be called an art. All of this is very hard for an anarchist, but we have even had to organise military academies in order to maintain military control over the militias. Spanish anarchists have had to accept the necessity of discipline and responsibility.

With regard to the experts, 75% of them will be chosen by us and 25% by the Valencia government, and they will be genuine military technicians. We have reached a truly critical moment. At certain times the enemy was advancing at will. We have accepted ministerial appointments, but we will not accept militarisation unless it is under the condition that we ourselves select 75% of the technical commanders. It is necessary to accept this if we are to go into battle. Also, we will have our own army. We must not forget that 'lieutenants' will be replaceable when necessary or when their conduct is not to our liking due to the way they command our militians. The moment is truly critical. The Spanish comrades have accepted this and there can be no going back. Understand that we are also anarchists like you.

Sacha Pietro: I am not a *miliciano*, but I have been to Russia, where I experienced the revolution and was able to observe the way in which the anarchists were liquidated (at this point the comrade summarised the Makhnovist movement). I have been in Spain for the past eight months, and I know that as long as we have weapons in our hands, everything is possible. Here we are still living the revolution, the true path, and I am always interested in the spirit that motivates events. We do not yet have to acknowledge defeat, we have not yet lost, and the worldwide revolution is at stake right here. I believe that certain comrades criticise too easily. What counts is to maintain the spirit of anarchism and, equally, to try to find the resources that will give us strength.

Souchy: Some comrades have accepted militarisation and discipline without discussion. Our militarism has nothing to do with the militarism that prevails in the fascist countries. Here we have endured an attempted fascist putsch, and the following revolution has turned into a war. Thus, if we really want that revolution, and if we accept it, we must accept it with all its consequences. A revolutionary force opposed fascism. A military force rose up against us and against that military force we must oppose another military force. What we need is a little more discipline and a little more order. Germany and Italy are doing everything in their power to crush the Spanish revolution, because the worldwide revolution depends on it. Our CNT comrades have accepted militarisation. Militarisation, properly construed, can save us.

Blumenthal (militian): 19 July represented a backlash from the common folk, not a backlash from the multitudes. An attempt is being made to divide us with the principle: 'First win the war.' In Barcelona I saw some truly repulsive things, including stripes and stars! I do not think that is how we can win. I am an anarchist and I stand with other anarchists. I refuse to be a soldier and a servant of capitalism.

Máximo (militian): (Comrade Félix Danon translates what Máximo says in French into Spanish) I am also antimilitarist, but let the comrades reflect for a moment, as I have done. Our struggle is not just a fight among Spaniards, but an international fight. If we remain vigilant then nothing bad will happen. The day we lose confidence in our captains and lieutenants, we will ask them to step down. Our militarism has nothing in common with bourgeois militarism.

Blondino (militian from Gelsa): I am emphatically against militarisation. I understand and accept discipline, but only in combat, where it is necessary. As a result, unless we negate the anarchist ideal or adopt a kind of revisionist anarchism, it is not possible to understand and accept this hierarchical ladder and its outward manifestations: salutes, uniforms, decorations, etc.

Styr-Nhair: Fundamentally, I believe that what is happening stems from a lack of information among militians, which is perhaps excusable among isolated combatants. The CNT has lacked a scrupulously informative French-language newspaper. It seems that the militians do not want to take a beating for the sake of the bourgeois Republic. That is their right, although right now no one is in a position to say what kind of social system they are taking a beating for. The CNT certainly has not said that we are fighting in order to institute libertarian communism or anarchy. Since 19 July, the French-language CNT-FAI Information Bulletins have been content with examining the limits and possibilities of revolution while making antifascist declarations without any precise content. One always struggles for the maximum in order to obtain the minimum. That is the law of all social struggles. There is always some middle ground between the ideal and reality.

The antifascist front, composed of different elements, was not and is not fighting for anarchism, and obliging it to do so would amount to doing violence to other political persuasions that do not share our ideas. This cannot be. And why? For precisely the reason that we do not agree to struggle and fight for ideas that are alien to us. That would yield the dissolution of the antifascist front and the triumph of Franco. Thus, it has been necessary to renounce such a strategy.

In order to impose our watchwords—the possibility of which still has not been demonstrated, given that our comrades, for all their heroism, would never have been able to win had they not been armed from the beginning by some police who were loyal to the Republic; of this much we are certain, because in the regions where such assistance was unavailable our comrades were defeated—without breaking up the antifascist front, we would have had to resort to dictatorship: the very thing to which the CNT is opposed. And these prigs who today take the CNT to task for its concessions, which according to them represent a pure reformism turning away from the revolution, would have been the first to reproach it even more vehemently had it resorted to authoritarian methods!

Nevertheless, Catalonia is not the whole of Spain, and if we would have taken advantage of our strength here in order to crush our political enemies then they would have adopted the same principle wherever they were stronger and duly routed our comrades, and the responsibility for such a massacre would have been ours for having started the whole thing.

The Spanish anarchist organisations have preferred to come to an accommodation with the moderates instead of fighting against them, because that was the only feasible solution. Concessions are merely the consequence of this alliance, and every bit as indispensable and inevitable as the alliance itself. To reproach the anarchist organisations for the concessions they have made is tantamount to reproaching them for having taken part in the revolution and its defence.

To renounce armed struggle in order to avoid a militarisation that the CNT accepted a long time ago is akin to desertion. In the name of principles, the CNT could have abandoned the revolution from the very beginning!

Furthermore, there are real concessions and there are formal concessions. Militarisation is primarily a formal concession, since the spirit of the militian has not changed. Acceptance of a certain code, like the one that guided the Durruti Column, was a real concession because the sanctions dictated by that code had nothing to do with the classical military code. True, it was never applied. But during a campaign, the formal barrack-style provisions of the classical military code are also never applied. All depends on the intelligence of the officers. In the Catalan People's Army, the CNT says that it has the highest percentage of military posts. The bulk of the officers there will be comrades. What is it, then?

I feel that the rejection of militarisation is a pretext to retire from combat. These militians feel fatigued, and fatigue is only too human… But I take a critical view of the invocation of this pretext, as it could be harmful to our anarchist organisations and our revolution, as they are perceived abroad.

Blanchard (militian): In Sariñena, the Russians are giving the orders.

Domingo Ascaso: That is not true.

Lobel: We must get back onto solid ground so that the comrades can determine their own positions.

Fortin: We are wandering off the topic somewhat. This is not a matter for discussion, because a discussion about whether militarisation is good or bad would lead us very far from the point. Militarisation exists and that is an incontrovertible fact. This meeting has been organised in order to determine the situation of the comrades who have left the front and who, as a result, have become confused. To me, these comrades fall into three categories:

Firstly, there are those who categorically reject all forms of militarisation. At present, in Barcelona we are very acutely suffering from the repercussions of the war. There are people going without, and every person not making himself useful in accordance with his abilities represents another needless mouth to feed. The best thing for these comrades to do would be to return to France or to some other democratic country. We will not judge their decisions. They came here voluntarily, and they can leave here voluntarily.

Secondly, there are a certain number of comrades who are either deserters or draft-dodgers, or who have been sentenced to terms of imprisonment in their absence. Obviously, these men cannot be handed over to the authorities, which would likely be the case if they went to France. We can look for work for them with the assistance of the Grupo Francés de la CNT and of the Casa Internacional de Voluntarios.

Finally, that leaves those who wish to continue fighting. They have a choice: either they return to the front and accept militarisation and its consequences, or if possible, they can attempt to create a free corps, as some comrades have already suggested. It is up to the Spanish comrades to let these militians know whether the possibility of establishing a free corps still exists.

Domingo Ascaso: That is asking the impossible. Strictly speaking, the Spanish anarchists did not make the revolution on 19 July. For the first time, what we did was raise a counter-revolution in response to the fascist uprising. The CNT and the FAI have begun to accept positions of responsibility and have agreed to militarisation. But this does not mean that we feel any less anarchist than you (very emotionally, Domingo Ascaso acknowledges the efforts made by the international anarchist comrades and all that they have done on behalf of the cause of liberty). Those unwilling to fight can stand down, but the others who want to continue fighting have to accept militarisation. As a result, we cannot allow the creation of a free corps.

The session concluded after many militians had had their say in Spanish, French, German and English. They all indicated that they had come to Spain to fight for the freedom of the entire world, and not just for the freedom of one country. Most of them called for greater discipline and for a new technical reorganisation of the militias.[4]

---

4   Text published in the French-language supplement to the *Boletín de Información CNT-FAI* (19 June 1937), a–d. There is a note that explains the delay in publication. Possibly, 'the circumstances beyond our control' were the 'May events' of 1937 in Barcelona. Cipriano Mera, in his memoirs (*Guerra, Exilio y Cárcel* [Ed. Ruedo Ibérico, Paris, 1976], 112), alludes to a meeting called by the Iron Column at the beginning of February 1937, to which the confederal (CNT-FAI) columns were invited in order to discuss the problem of militarisation. At the time, Cipriano Mera was already a major in the army, and he commanded the Fourteenth Division (comprising the Tenth, Seventy-seventh and Seventieth Brigades). He writes:

Some days later, the Iron Column, which was made up of comrades from Levante, called a meeting of the confederal militias in Valencia. The Regional Committee of the Centre and its Defence Committee selected me and Feliciano Benito to attend the meeting as representatives of our militias serving on the Madrid fronts, and to argue for the necessity of militarisation. At the beginning of the meeting the Iron Column explained its position: that the decision to militarise or not should be left to the militias' own representatives. We delegates from the centre objected that, for our part, we were answerable to a Regional that had already adopted concrete accords, and that in addition there had been irregularities in the organisation of the meeting, for which reason there should be no deliberations until the CNT National Committee was present. This proposal was endorsed and a commission was designated to communicate to the National Committee the necessity of its presence at the meeting. Initially, it refused on the grounds that it had not been previously consulted, but it eventually accepted the invitation due to the importance of the matter at issue and it appointed two comrades to attend, one of whom was Manuel Amil.

The first representative to speak was the National Committee's. He pointed out the irregularities in the organisation of the meeting and further indicated that, having not been consulted beforehand, his presence would be limited to listening and transmitting what was said to the National Committee so that it could make an informed decision. The delegation from the centre spoke next, acknowledging that the irregularities pointed out by the National Committee were by now largely moot due to the presence of its representatives. It then argued the reasons for its support of the militarisation of the militias, which was regarded as an indispensable measure towards winning the war. To this effect, it revealed that the Centre Regional was converting its militias into regular military units. The ensuing debate resulted in all the delegations save two—the Iron Column and the Tierra y Libertad Column—accepting militarisation. In this way, the true feelings of the vast majority of the CNT's fighters were made clear, and the National Committee kept that in mind when making its final decision.

XVII
The Iron Column Against Itself

By March 1937 the militarisation of the militias was an irreversible fact. All the confederal units had submitted to it. The speed at which this militarisation advanced depended on the intensity of the fighting on the front lines and the presence of Russian advisors. As for the militias operating in Aragón, the militarisation to which the confederal columns were subject—which created the Twenty-sixth Division (Durruti Column), the Twenty-fourth Division (Antonio Ortiz Column), the Twenty-fifth Division (Vivancos Column) and the Twenty-eighth Division (Ascaso-Jover Column)—did not change anything about their internal life.

One transformation had been made: those who were group, century, and association delegates became sergeants, lieutenants, captains and majors, with the innovation that—starting from the company level—military commands were duplicated by commissarships, which posts were held by those comrades deemed most deserving by the militians. The units were thus the same, the only change being the simple appearance of military stripes ('bars' or 'little sardines,' as the militians jokingly called them).

But everything began to change as far as Aragón was concerned—we are referring to the internal social life of the militias—at the beginning of June 1937, albeit slowly. There were two reasons for this: the first was a consequence of the 'May events' in Barcelona,[1] and the second stemmed from the republican offensive against Zaragoza and Belchite, which began that June.

The defeat of the workers in Barcelona had profound repercussions on the militias, which felt it as a sudden slowing of the revolution. This became palpable by August (in the middle of the republican offensive against Belchite), and was exploited by the Eleventh Division under the command of the Communist Enrique Líster, who launched a generalised attack against the Aragón collectives.

---

1   The events in Barcelona during May 1937 were the culmination of the Stalinist conspiracy of which we have previously spoken.

These three factors that we have mentioned—taken together—conspired to slightly change the internal relations between commanders and soldiers in the confederal units, but not to the extent that the spirit which had previously animated the militias was lost, for the soldiers' constant vigilance towards the commanders impeded the degeneration into an abuse of power. In spite of this, there were many symptomatic cases which demonstrated that the exercise of authority and power tended to corrupt even the most wholesome, and the anarchists were no exception.

We have mixed up the chronology a bit, but not unduly so, for in March on the Central front, militarisation was already a perfectly managed reality.

The Iron Column—which, as we have already said before, was organising in the rearguard—had taken some time to reflect. But serene reflection came with great difficulty now that events, provoked by the Communists, were rushing along.

That March, the Levante region had a foretaste of what was to come in the 'May events' in Barcelona, or the Communist drive to encompass the entire republican zone in order to make an end of what they described as 'uncontrollables', who were virtually the only resistance to their monopolisation of power.

At the centre of the provocation in Levante was Minister of Agriculture Vicente Uribe, who had declared war on the agricultural collectives. The agricultural collectives were doing well, so much so that the CLUEA agency created by the CNT and the UGT was managing the economic life of the region independently of the government. As a revolutionary project it was already a success, and it was precisely this that the Communists could not tolerate, because it showed all their bourgeois democratic policies to be devoid of content. In this sense, it is useful to refer to what García Oliver wrote regarding the matter:

> Ángel Galarza was the minister of home affairs. He was a socialist of the Caballero school, a fair player, capable and intelligent. But he never attained control of the Assault Guards, with their quasi-fascist or emphatically pro-Communist commanders. In the orchards of Valencia, the Assault Guards undertook an operation to invade and raze the local unions and collectives.

Anarcho-syndicalist comrades and Caballero socialist comrades from the UGT who had allowed themselves to be provoked by card-carrying Communist smallholders were arrested by the hundreds. The prisoners, due to a lack of prisons or police stations in which to hold them, were packed wherever they would fit.

For my part, I spent the night moving from one place to another (with Galarza), and made a concerted effort to extinguish the various fires, which yielded excellent results. The anarcho-syndicalists and the Caballero socialists were freed, some of the weapons seized from them were returned, and—while not completely put at ease—we had the satisfaction of having thwarted many agents provocateurs who had skilfully manipulated the Communists and Prieto socialists... It seems that the Levante firewood was not adequate for making large bonfires. Or else things are still not quite ready...[2]

In fact, the time was ripe for a generalised eruption, since one of the prime objectives of the Communists was to seize control of a foundry operating in Burriana. A small munitions plant was in operation there under the supervision of the CNT's Defence Secretariat, the output from which was used to meet the needs of the forces in the Levante confederal columns, which were still being boycotted by the government.

The Assault Guards showed up to seize the plant, but there was a vigorous backlash. The entire district was mobilised but the Assault Guards received reinforcements, and just when it appeared that all was going in favour of the invaders, an important group of militians from the Iron Column intervened and exchanged fire with the Assault Guards. When things were at the point of complete deterioration, García Oliver and the CNT National Committee stepped in and an agreement was reached: the plant would continue functioning under CNT control and the prisoners would be set free.

A short while later, in Vinalesa and Alfara, the campaign against the collectives peaked, which led to a clash between the peasants— duly assisted by the militians from the Iron Column—and the Assault Guards who were attempting to dismantle the collectives. Many were killed and wounded, as a result of which more than one hundred men,

2   Juan García Oliver, *El Eco de los Pasos*, 414.

mostly from the Iron Column—including Pedro Pellicer, who was in charge of recruitment—were imprisoned in the Las Salesas barracks.

On Sunday 21 March the Iron Column assembled to decide on its future. During the preceding weeks, the War Committee had been busy holding meetings with the defence agencies of the CNT and the FAI, from which we can draw the conclusion that the Iron Column was well aware of its dilemma: disintegration or militarisation. In the event of the latter, things had to be handled very carefully in order to keep the government from attacking the unit and dissolving it by means of amalgamating it with other units that were already organised.

The results of this grand assembly were as follows:

IRON COLUMN
Minutes of the Assembly Held in the Teatro Libertad on 21 March 1937 by the Comrades Belonging to this Column

The day's agenda:
1. Report from the War Committee
2. Financial Report
3. The Militarisation Issue
4. Initiatives and Proposals

The assembly begins with the naming of comrade Sanchís, the delegate from the Third Division, as chairman. He accepts the nomination and ascends the rostrum.

Comrade Daniel Martín, from the telephone section, asks what is going to happen to the prisoners. A dialogue with the chair takes place on this theme, but it is cut short by comrade Pellicer, who reads the following message sent by the prisoners to the assembly:

'The comrades imprisoned in Torres, in order to demonstrate their revolutionary spirit, salute you and wholeheartedly embrace the decisions you may adopt for the good of the social revolution. Hurrah for the CNT and the FAI! Long live anarchy! On behalf of the ninety-two prisoners from the Column, Furió, Pellicer and Guillermo Villarroya.'

That matter having been resolved, we proceed to the agenda, with comrade chairman giving the floor to comrade José Segarra to make his report on behalf of the War Committee.

1. Report from the War Committee

Comrade Segarra first explains in detail the measures taken by the Column's War Committee since the last assembly with the century delegates, at which it was agreed that the Column would go on leave. He then continues:

'All of the comrades in the Column know about the disagreements that have existed from the very beginning surrounding militarisation, but we must abide by the reality of the moment and see that all the columns adhering to confederal and anarchist norms—all of them—have accepted militarisation.

'We, seeing that most of the Column's members are included in the mobilisation and call-ups agreed to by the government, have decided that formation of a force (brigade)—for which the government gives us the four necessary battalions in addition to the commands—would be the best way for the Column to remain united, even though it would lose some of its libertarian content. However, in this way we would be able to ensure that its libertarian and anarchist essence would not be lost completely.

'It had been thought that, once this Column refused to accept militarisation, the comrades would return to their villages and be able to propagandise and engage in positive work there. But, concurrent with all the circumstances enumerated previously regarding the government's mobilisation and call-ups, it is more likely that these comrades—shortly after leaving our side—would be incorporated into one of the regular forces that the state is preparing. It is in view of all these circumstances that the War Committee is presenting this opinion in front of the assembly'

Comrade Segarra concludes by giving an account of the measures undertaken, the posts conceded to us by the government, and the probability of returning to the Teruel front.

Comrade Pellicer, from the War Committee, takes the floor in order to expand upon Segarra's report.

A debate begins, concerning the measures taken by the War Committee.

Guerra raises the matter of leave not being granted to militians but being enjoyed by members of the War Committee.

Martínez says that such a matter should not be discussed and that the measures taken by the War Committee need to be approved.

Ferrer asks that comrades keep their comments relevant to the matter being debated.

Pérez Blanco talks about the recent meeting involving the War Committee, the CNT National Committee and some militants from the organisation, about which he makes certain remarks to which the assembly takes exception.

Comrade Segarra intervenes to give a detailed account of what needs to be dealt with.

Benet agrees and asks that the measures taken by the War Committee be approved.

Mares says that it seems unbelievable that the matter of responsibility is under discussion when it should really be a requirement for all comrades, otherwise debates would go on for years. He adds that the measures taken by the War Committee should be approved.

Comrade chairman asks the assembly if it approves of the measures taken by the War Committee, and THE ASSEMBLY UNANIMOUSLY GIVES ITS APPROVAL.

2. Financial Report

Comrade Pellicer takes the floor on behalf of the War Committee in order to give an account of the sums in the Column's coffers and says that, due to the scarcity of time and the multitude of accounts that need to be examined, he is asking the assembly to designate a commission to proceed with the audit in conjunction with the War Committee.

He says that, at a meeting with the delegations, it was agreed to submit to the assembly the proposal that certain sums be set aside for those entities that do not have official recognition or are not receiving income assistance from any organisation. The distribution would be as follows: 100,000 pesetas for the CNT field hospitals, another 100,000 pesetas for the Orán trial, 100,000 pesetas for rationalist schools and the remainder—almost a million pesetas—for anarchist libraries, publishing and press.

The assembly approves the distribution made in principle by the delegations, and designates a commission composed of comrades Salcedo, Francisco López , Zamorano and Argente to audit the accounts.

3. The Militarisation Issue

Some comrades objected to the conduct of the chairman, and the assembly agreed to recall the designated comrade and name a substitute. Thus, comrade Mares promptly occupies the rostrum as the new chairman.

The debate on the militarisation issue begins with the chairman giving the floor to comrade Segarra, from the War Committee, to expand upon his report.

Segarra expands upon his assertions regarding the meaning of militarisation. He repeats that, while no one is more opposed to militarisation than he, reality demands it and we should accept it, as he does not want to see the Column disbanded.

Pellicer, also speaking on behalf of the War Committee, expands upon comrade Segarra's remarks. He explains the format of the mixed brigades and says that in the petition it was asked that the four brigade battalions be manned by our personnel, which request was agreed to. He adds that only the artillery unit would be manned by professional soldiers.

THE ASSEMBLY IS ASKED IF IT AGREES TO MILITARISATION, AND IT AGREES UNANIMOUSLY.

4. Initiatives and Proposals

Sanchez requests that, once the brigade is organised, it returns to the Teruel front, because we have someone to avenge there.

Arroyo also says that we should return to the Teruel front.

Heath services asks what its condition will be.

Comrade Segarra, speaking on behalf of the War Committee, answers by saying that health services—like the rest of the delegations—will be briefed on its situation by the delegates from the respective departments.

A comrade moved that comrade Segarra had clarified the matter and this was endorsed.

Salcedo requests that any experts incorporated into the brigade be soldiers who are well-known to us due to their having fought on the same front.

Falomir asks that women not be admitted to the newly organised Column, on the grounds that they are a source of disturbance and only there to look for a man.

After unanimous objection from the assembly, these remarks are retracted.

Comrade Pellicer clears up the situation of these female comrades by saying that any woman who wants to can come along as a *miliciana*, as long as she brings her rifle.

Comrade Segarra proposes that the assembly designates a commission to meet with the War Committee and present to the assembly the nominations for positions of command within the brigade.

The proposal is accepted and the following comrades are named to the commission: Martínez, De Gracia, Orea, Durá and Ferrer.

After the commission concludes its meeting, a list of the nominated comrades is read and, after two changes, it is approved.

Comrade Segarra briefs the assembly on the matter of uniforms and pay, as well as the question of salutes, and the assembly approves comrade Segarra's remarks.

As there are no more matters to attend to, the session is concluded at 1:15 p.m.

21 March 1937[3]

Immediately after this assembly, the press published a statement entitled 'To all Members of this Column,' which was signed by José Segarra on behalf of the War Committee:

---

3   *Nosotros* (24 March 1937).

You are hereby informed that, by agreement of our extraordinary general assembly held last Sunday, 21 March at the Teatro Libertad in Valencia, our Column is to become the Eighty-third Army Brigade. This being the case, you should remember that militarisation does not oblige you to enlist in any other military unit, and that only those of you who agree with militarisation should abide by the directions given to you by the comrades who you have freely chosen as representatives for this Brigade.[4]

At around the same time, another statement appeared in *Fragua Social* under the title 'Supply Department': 'Let it be known to all comrades belonging to this department that tomorrow, 24 March at 3:00 p.m., they are to report without fail to the supply delegation in La Puebla de Valverde in order to attend the assembly scheduled for that date and time.'

Roque Santamaría, who attended this assembly and was on the War Committee during the conversion of the Column into a brigade, gives the following commentary regarding militarisation:

It was a paradox, because the greatest opponents of militarisation later turned out to be the ones wearing the most scrambled egg: José Pellicer was Brigade commander, with the rank of major; José Segarra, the Column's strongest anti-militarist theorist, was Brigade commissar; Cortés, who now lives in Venezuela and whose temperament and character were the least suited to being a soldier, was captain of the General Staff; Rodilla, who the Nazis killed in France, was absolutely uncontrollable, but he was also a captain; Angel Gómez, another determined anti-militarist, was a captain as well...

At the end of April, in view of my physical deficiencies, I decided that I would not make a good soldier and I communicated the following to my comrades and friends: 'Once the Column is militarised, I'm out of here.' At the time I held the post of supply delegate within the Column, which would have likely given me the rank of quartermaster captain. But I had already rejected all that.

The CNT Defence Committee travelled to La Puebla de Valverde in order to see how the militarisation of the Column was

4   *Nosotros* (25 March 1937).

proceeding. It began to rain *sardinillas* (stripes) there, and each one put as many as he wanted on his sleeve. This was completely normal; it was simply not an issue. No one wanted it, but if it had to be then so be it. In the same way that they were century delegates before, they had now subjected themselves to a kind of moral obligation, and they had to play the game... And this was how the Eighty-third Brigade, formerly the Iron Column, was formed.[5]

---

5   Roque Santamaría, testimony cited above.

XVIII
The Testimony of an 'Uncontrollable'

Spread over its editions of 12, 13, 15, 16 and 17 March 1937, *Nosotros* (the organ of the FAI in Levante) published a long article signed by 'An "Uncontrollable" from the Iron Column.' We do not know who the author of this document was, but we do know—as Burnett Bolloten writes—that it represented a 'significant act,'[1] by which Bolloten means that it was a stratagem utilised by someone for the purpose of influencing the spirit of the militians with regard to the acceptance of militarisation. This is indeed a possibility.

But it is also possible that the author was one of the many members of the Column who had passionately experienced the revolutionary adventure and who had remained faithful to the spirit arising from 19 July; a spirit that bureaucracy and counterrevolution had transformed into a hierarchical column.

We prefer the latter possibility, and thus consider this text to be the best of the texts produced by the Column's men, largely because of the simple yet simultaneously profound manner in which it expresses enchantment and disenchantment, coupled with an optimistic note of human fraternity. Thus, we have no hesitation in considering this article from the 'uncontrollables of the Iron Column' as their political testament, and a lesson for generations to come.

It is followed by a more prescient and bitter article from *Línea de Fuego*.

THE IRON COLUMN, MILITARISATION AND THE REVOLUTIONARY FUTURE OF SPAIN
Received and Published

Comrades of the *Nosotros* editorial group: Greetings!

If you see any merit in the content of the little article I have sent you, then publish it. However, if after reading it you discover nothing within that is not already well-known to my own comrades-in-arms—or indeed to those who, though

---

1   Burnett Bolloten, *La Revolución Española*, 265.

not by my side, fight on other fronts or who are members of other columns—then tear it up.

Now then, I want to tell you something directly: what I am saying—I am no writer—has taken me three days to say, which means that I gave it a lot of thought. If it is not fit for publication, then take from it whatever there is of value and arrange it as you see fit, but say something about the Column. It is a sorrow that is vanishing; a sorrow and, possibly, a ruin.

Anarchist greetings to you,

An 'Uncontrolable' from the Iron Column

Editor's note: We are publishing this text in a slightly cleaned-up but undiluted form. It is shot through with a profound pain, a rebellious scream, and a noble sincerity that enchants us. We will publish it in its entirety over the course of two or three days.

The Iron Column and the Revolution

I am an escapee from San Miguel de los Reyes, a sinister penitentiary erected by the monarchy to bury alive those who, not being cowards, would never submit to the infamous laws which the mighty have dictated against the oppressed. I was taken there, as were many others, to wipe out an offence, for revolting against the humiliations visited upon an entire village, to be blunt, for killing a *cacique* [boss].

I was a young man then, and I am young now, for I was twenty three years old when I went to prison and I am out, because the anarchist comrades threw the gates open, at the age of thirty four. Eleven years prey to the torment of being, not a man, but a thing, a number!

Out with me came many who had suffered like me and were just as hurt by the ill treatment meted out to them since birth. Some, on reaching the streets, went off into the world; others of us joined our liberators who treated us like friends and loved us like brothers. With them, bit by bit, we formed the Iron Column; along with them, with quickening pace we stormed barracks and disarmed the terrible Civil Guards: with those arms we drove the fascists back as far as the peaks of the sierra, where you can find them now. Used to taking what we need, we seized provisions and rifles from the fascist as we pushed him back. And for a time we lived off what the peasants brought us, and we armed ourselves, for no one made us a present of a single gun. We wrested them from the rebels in battle. The rifle I am cradling, the one that has been with me ever since I quit that fateful penitentiary, is mine, my very own: like a man, I took it from the man who had it in his hands, just the way that virtually all of the guns that my comrades hold in their hands are our very own, we having captured them.

Neglect

No one, or practically no one, has ever given a thought to our needs. The stupor of the bourgeoisie when we walked out of the prison has been shared by all and sundry, up to now, and instead of our being heeded, helped and assisted, we have been labelled bandits and accused of being uncontrollables, just because we do not tailor our appetite for life and for living free to the silly whims of some who have obscenely and pompously imagined themselves to be the masters of men, just because they sit in some Ministry or on some committee, and because, in the villages through which we have passed, we have, after wresting them from the clutches of the fascist, changed their way of living, annihilating the fierce *caciques* who blighted the lives of the peasants, after robbing them, and we handed over their wealth to the only ones capable of creating wealth: to the workers.

Conduct

No one, I can assure you, no one could have behaved towards the destitute, the needy, towards those whose whole life has been blighted by robbery and persecution, better than we uncontrollables, bandits, escaped prisoners have. No one, no one—and I challenge anyone to prove otherwise—has displayed more affection and solicitude towards children, women and the aged: no one, absolutely nobody, can label this Column which, on its own and unaided, and even obstructed has been in the front lines from the very beginning, as anti-social, despotic, soft or irresolute in battle, or as indifferent towards the peasants, or as other than revolutionary, since dash and daring in battle have always been the norm with us, just as our law has been gentlemanly treatment of the vanquished, cordiality towards brothers our watchword, and kindness and respect the parameters within which we have lived our lives.

Blackened reputation

Why the dark legend peddled about us? Why this senseless obsession with discrediting us, when such discredit, not that it can be achieved, would only bring the revolutionary cause and the war itself into disrepute?

There is—and we prisoners who have suffered more than anyone else on earth, know it only too well—there is in the air, I hold, a tremendous growth of bourgeois attitudes. The bourgeois individual of body and soul, the very model of mediocrity and slavishness, quakes at the prospect of losing his comforts, his fat cigar and his coffee, his bullfights, his theatre and his whoring, and at the merest hint of the Column, this Iron Column, the Revolution's spearhead in the Levante region, or when he learned that the Column had announced its intention to travel down to Valencia, he trembled like a leaf at the thought of the Columnists snatching away his pampered and wretched existence. And the bourgeois—and bourgeois come in many varieties and are found in lots of places—tirelessly wove, with threads of calumny, this dark legend which has been tacked on to us, because the bourgeois alone has lost and stands to lose from our activities, our rebelliousness and these madly irrepressible yearnings in our hearts to be free as the eagles in the heavens or the lions in the deepest jungles.

Nosotros, 12 March 1937

Even our brothers...

Even our brothers, who suffered with us in field and workshop, who were foully exploited by the bourgeoisie, echoed the latter's terrible fears and began to believe, on the mere say so of a few would-be leaders, that we, the men fighting with the Iron Column, were brigands and thugs, and a hatred which has frequently spilled over into cruelty and fanatical murder, has strewn our path with stones, so that we might not make progress against the fascists.

On certain nights, those pitch dark nights when, with gun at the ready and ears cocked, I was trying to penetrate the depths of the countryside and plumb the mysteries of things, there was nothing for it but for me to jump up from the parapet as if in a nightmare, and not merely to stretch my numbed limbs, (which are like steel because they were tempered with pain), but rather to grip my rifle all the more furiously, itching to open fire, not just at the enemy cowering barely a hundred metres away, but rather at the one lurking beside me, pretending to be and calling me comrade, while foully selling me out, for there is no sell-out more craven than that fed by treachery. And I felt like weeping and laughing, like running across the fields screaming, and crushing throats in my iron grip, just like when I tore the throat out of that filthy cacique, and like blowing to smithereens this wretched world where it is so hard to find a loving hand to mop the sweat from your brow and staunch the blood from your wounds when you return, weary and wounded, from the battlefield.

Sadness and joy

How many were the nights when, huddled with the men in a huddle or a cluster, telling my anarchist comrades all about my sadnesses and sorrows, there, in the harshness of the sierra, facing an enemy just waiting to pounce, a friendly voice and loving arms made me love life again! And so all of the open wounds of my suffering, my whole past, all of the horrors and torments, I threw to the wind like relics from a bygone age, and I surrendered joyously to dreams of the future, my heated imagination seeing a world which had never existed but for which I had yearned: a world such as none of us had lived in but of which many of us had dreamt. And time just flew by, and my body felt no weariness, and my energy was redoubled and I became reckless and ventured out into the dawn across the open ground to seek out the enemy and… All of this for a complete change of life: because we men, myself included, could be brothers: because were joy to burst forth from our breasts just once, it would put down roots: because the Revolution, this Revolution which has been the Iron Column's pole star and device, could, at a time not far distant, become a reality.

My dreams evaporated like the white wisps crossing the sierra above our heads, and again I gazed upon the causes of my disillusionment, only to revert to my delights come nightfall. And so I lived my life, between sadness and joy, between anxiety and sobbing, joyful life in the midst of danger, compared with that life of darkness and misery I had known in that dark and miserable penitentiary.

But one day…

But one day—a dull and dismal day—over the crest of the sierra there floated a piece of news which cut us to the bone like a wintry blast: 'We have to militarise'. And this news struck at my vitals like a dagger's point, and I had a foretaste of the present anxiety. By night the news was relayed along the trenches: 'We have to militarise.'

Beside me, watchful while I rested, although I did not sleep, was my group's delegate, who would end up a lieutenant, and two steps further along, asleep on the ground, his head cradled by a pile of shells, lay the delegate from my century, who would finish up a captain or a colonel. I … would remain just as I was, a son of the soil, a rebel unto death. I did not then nor do I now want any crosses, stars or commands. I am what I am, a peasant who learned to read in prison, who has seen sorrow and death at close quarters, who was an anarchist but did not know it and who, knowing it now, am more of an anarchist now than back then when I killed in order to be free.

That day, the day that the dismal news arrived, sweeping down from the high sierra like an icy blast that clutched at my soul, will live on in memory, like so many others in my lifetime of sorrow. That day ... bah!

We have to militarise!

Nosotros, 13 March 1937

LIFE, BOOKS AND PRISON

Life has more to teach men than any theories, more than all the books in the world. Those wishing to put into practice what they have learned about others by drinking deeply of printed books will go astray: those who bring to the reading what they have learned along the winding path of life, may well create a master-piece. Reality and imagination are two different things. Dreams are all very well, because a dream is, almost always, a glimpse of what is to follow: but the ultimate is to make life beautiful, actually to turn life into a work of beauty.

I have lived life at an accelerated pace. Not for me the savouring of youth, which, from what I have read, means joy, sweetness and well-being. All I tasted in prison was sorrow. I may be young in years, but I am an old man in terms of all I have lived through, all the weeping I have done, all that I have suffered. In prison one scarcely ever laughs: in prison, there is always weeping, inside or out.

Learning from life

One day I read, I cannot recall where or who was the author, that a writer cannot have a proper picture of the earth until he has roamed around it and discovered it for himself. Such a claim struck me as laughable; but that sentence made such a deep impression on me that sometimes, talking to myself as I necessarily had to do in my lonely prison cell, I called it to mind. Until one day, as if I too had stumbled upon something wonderful that had previously lain hidden from other men, I rejoiced at discovering for myself that the world was round. And on that day, I, like the author of that axiom, roamed, measured and touched the planet, my imagination lit up with the 'sight' of Earth spinning in infinite space, an integral part of the universal order of the worlds. It is the same with pain. One has to weigh it, measure it, squeeze it, taste it, understand it and discover it, in order to form a clear mental picture of just what it is. Beside me, hauling along the cart on to which the others had climbed to sing and make merry, I have had men who, like myself, did the donkey work. And they did not suffer; and there came no rumblings of complaint from them; and they saw it as only fair and reasonable that these others, as gentlemen, held the reins and clutched the whip, and even found it logical and fair that the master should lash them across the face. They grunted like beasts, dug their feet into the dirt and set off at a gallop. Later—how ironic!—upon being unyoked, they licked the hand that beat them, like so many grovelling dogs.

Pain's bitterness

No one who has not known humiliation, vexation and ridicule; no one who has not felt like the most wretched creature on earth, and at the same time, like the noblest, kindest and most human, and all of these things simultaneously, and just when he felt his wretchedness and considered himself happy and strong, has felt the chill hand of the brute jailer upon his shoulders or on his face, without warning or cause, just for the simple pleasure of doing him down and humiliating him; nobody who has not seen himself dragged off to the punishment cells, and there been slapped and kicked around, heard his bones crack and his blood gush until he collapsed on the floor in a heap; no one who, having suffered torment at other men's hands, has not known that sense of powerlessness and cursed and blasphemed about it, as if that might somehow restore his power; no one who, having endured punishment and ill-treatment, has understood just how unfair that punishment and how infamous that ill-treatment were; and, so doing, has set his sights upon doing away with the privilege that affords to some this power to punish and mistreat; in short, no one, be he a prisoner in a jail or a prisoner in this world, who has understood the tragedy of the lives of men condemned to silent, blind obedience to orders received, can plumb the depths of the pain, the bitterness of the pain, the awful, indelible scar that pain leaves upon those who have drunk deeply of, felt and known the pain of silent obedience. Itching to speak but having to keep one's mouth closed; wanting to sing but making not a sound; wanting to laugh and being obliged to smother that laugh on one's lips; wanting to love, and yet condemned to wallow in the mire of hatred!

Barracks and prisons

I was in the barracks and it was there that I learned how to hate. I have been in prison and there, in the midst of the weeping and suffering, I learned that rarest of things, how to love and love intensely.

In those barracks I was on the very verge of losing my identity, such was the severity they displayed in their efforts to foist their inane discipline upon me. In prison, after a great struggle, I regained my identity, feeling increasingly refractory to all imposition. It was there that I learned how to hate all hierarchy, from top to bottom; in prison, surrounded by the most acute pain, I learned to love my brother wretches, while preserving the hatred of hierarchy which I had conceived in the barracks pure and unadulterated. Prisons and barracks, they all add up to the same thing; despotism and free rein for the malice of the few and the suffering of all. The barracks has nothing to teach that is not damaging to physical and mental well-being, any more than prison is a corrective.

With this outlook, on the basis of this experience—hard experience, in that my entire life has been spent wallowing in pain—when the word reached me from the mountains that the order for militarisation had gone out, I felt for a moment as if my world had collapsed, because I could plainly see that the bold guerilla fighter of the Revolution in me would perish, and the creature who had been pruned in barrack and in jail of every hint of personality would live on, only to fall again into the pit of obedience, into the animal sleepwalking to which the discipline of the barracks or the prison leads, for they are both the same. And angrily picking up my rifle, watching enemy and 'friend' from the parapet, scanning the forward positions and our rear, I spat a curse like the ones I used to spit in the days when my rebellious self was being hauled off to the punishment cell, and I shed an inner tear like the ones I used to shed, unseen by any eye, on sensing my powerlessness. And I made a note that the Pharisees who aim to turn the world into a barracks and a jail, are the same, the same ones, the very same people who, just yesterday, in the punishment cells, were cracking men's bones.

Barracks... Jails... what a contemptible and miserable life.

Nosotros, 15 March 1937

WIDESPREAD INCOMPREHENSION

They have failed to understand us and, not understanding us, have not loved us. We have fought—no need for false modesty now, for it does no good—as I say, we have fought like few others have fought. Our firing line has always been the furthest forward, since we were the only ones in our sector, right from the start.

For us, there was never any relief nor... worse still, a kind word. Fascists and antifascists alike and even—the shame of it!—our own people have treated us with indifference.

They have not understood us. Or, and this is an even greater tragedy in the midst of the tragedy in which we have been living, maybe we have failed to make ourselves understood, in that, having had showered upon our backs all of the contempt and severity of those who were life's hierarchs, we wanted, even in the midst of war, to live a libertarian life, whereas the rest, to their shame and ours, have remained yoked to the chariot of State.

Such incomprehension, which has wounded us deeply, blocked our path with calamities, and the fascists, to whom we mete out the treatment they deserve, were not alone in seeing us as a danger. So too have those who call themselves antifascists and shout their antifascism until they are hoarse. This hatred which has been woven around us, gave rise to painful clashes, the vileness of most of which filled our mouths with bile and made us clutch all the tighter to our rifles, and those clashes occurred in the middle of Valencia, when 'certain red antifascists' opened fire on us. Then... bah!... then we ought to have put paid right then to what the counter-revolution is now doing.

History will show

History, which records the good and the evil that men do, will have her say some day.

And that History will say that the Iron Column was, perhaps, the only one in Spain with a clear view of what our revolution should have been. She will say, too, that it was the one that put up the greatest resistance to militarisation. And also that, on account of its resistance, there were times when it was abandoned utterly to its fate, even on the battle-front as if six thousand men, battle-hardened and prepared for victory or death, should expose themselves to the enemy to be devoured.

How many, many things will History have to say, and how many, many figures who believe themselves glorious, will find themselves cursed and vilified!

Militarisation

Our resistance to militarisation was based on what we knew about the military. Our current resistance is based upon what we now know about the military.

Now and always, whether here or in Russia, the professional soldier has formed a caste. He is the one who gives the orders; all that remains for the rest of us is the duty of obedience. The professional soldier despises with all his being anyone that is a civilian, believing him to be his inferior.

I have seen—and I always look men in the eye—an officer quivering with fury or loathing whenever I used the familiar form of address to him, and I know of cases, now, right now, where the officers, having forgotten their humble beginnings, refuse to countenance—and there are horrific penalties for so doing—any militian's addressing him with familiarity.

The 'proletarian' army does not demand discipline which might be, at best, respect for military orders; it sets store by submissiveness, blind obedience and the eradication of a man's personality.

It is the same, the very same as when I used to be in the barracks. The same, the very same as when I spent time in prison later.

How we lived

We in the trenches lived a happy life. True, we saw the comrades with whom we had started this war fall at our sides; and we knew, too, that at a moment, a bullet might leave us prone upon the field—that is the reward that awaits the revolutionary—but our lives were happy ones; when rations were short, we fasted. And we were all content. How come? Because no one was superior to anybody else. We were all friends, all comrades, all guerillas of the Revolution. Our group or century delegate was not imposed on us, but chosen by us, and did not regard himself as a lieutenant or a captain, but as a comrade. The delegates from the Column Committees were never colonels or generals, but comrades. We ate together, we fought together, we laughed or cursed together. For a time we were paid nothing; nor were they. Later, we earned ten pesetas, and they earned and earn still their ten pesetas.

The only thing we recognise is their proven competence, which is why we elect them; and their bravery, similarly proven, which is another reason why they were our delegates. There was no hierarchy, no superiors, no severe orders; there was camaraderie, kindness, comradeship; a joyful life in the midst of war's calamities. And thus, as comrades, imagining that this fight had a point and a purpose, we made war with a ready heart and even embraced death readily. But when you are surrounded by officers, where it is all orders and ranks; when you can see in your hand the dismal soldier's pittance with which you can scarcely support your family in the rearguard, and you see your lieutenant, captain, major and colonel earning three, four, ten times more than you, although they are no more pugnacious, no more knowledgeable, no braver than you, life turns bitter, because you can see this is not Revolution, but exploitation, by a few, of a wretched situation which works only to the detriment of the people.

Nosotros, 16 March 1937

Now...

I don't know how we are going to live now. I don't know if we will be able to get used to abuse from the corporal, sergeant or lieutenant. I don't know if, having felt ourselves to be fully men, we can accept the feeling that we are domestic animals, for that is what discipline creates and what militarisation stands for.

We cannot now—it is going to prove utterly impossible—countenance despotic behaviour and bullying: for it is a sorry sort of a man who holds a gun in his hand and meekly submits to insult: but we have had worrying reports of comrades having submitted to militarisation and being subjected once again to the leaden weight of orders emanating from people who are frequently inept and always hostile.

We thought that we were working towards our own redemption, that we were saving ourselves and now we are falling into the very thing we are fighting against; into despotism, into caste rule, into the most brutal and arrogant authoritarianism.

Two routes

But these are grave times. Caught—by whom we do not know and if we do, we will not name them here—caught, as I say, in a trap, we have to scramble out of it and escape from it as best we can, for the countryside is strewn with snares.

The militarists, all the militarists—and there are rabid militarists even in our own ranks—have us surrounded. Yesterday, we were the masters of everything. Today, they are. The Popular Army, popular only in the sense that it is made up of the populace, and this was always the case, is not the people's army but the Government's, and it is the Government that commands, the Government that gives the orders. All that the people are allowed to do is obey and obedience is always required of them.

Caught in the militarists' net, we have two courses open to us; the first leads to disbandment of those of us who are, today, comrades in arms, through the dismantling of the Iron Column; the second leads on to militarisation.

Disbandment of the Column

The Column, our Column should not be disbanded. The homogeneity it has always boasted has been admirable—I am speaking for ourselves alone, comrades—the camaraderie among us will go down in the history of the Spanish revolution as exemplary; the courage displayed in a hundred encounters may have been matched in this heroic struggle, but never exceeded. From day one we were friends; more than friends, comrades; more than comrades, brothers. There is no way that we could part company, go away, not see one another again, not feel, as up to now, the urge to fight and to win.

The Column, this Iron Column which has set the bourgeois and the fascists quaking from Valencia to Teruel, must not be disbanded, but must carry on to the finish.

Who can make the case that, in the fray, because of their being militarised, they were stronger, sturdier, more generous in irrigating the fields of battle with their blood? We have fought as brothers in defence of a noble cause; like brothers sharing the same ideals we have dreamt in our trenches; like brothers yearning for a better world, we have been driven by our courage. Disband as a homogeneous whole? Never, comrades. For as long as a single century of us remains, to battle: for as long as a single one of us is left, on to victory.

Militarisation

A great evil it may be, but it will be a lesser evil for us to take orders from men not of our own choosing. But ... It is much the same to us whether we are a Column or a Battalion. What counts is that we get respect.

If the same individuals as now remain together, it won't matter to us whether we make up a column or a battalion. We won't need any encouragement to fight and when we rest we won't be needing anyone to bar us from resting, because we won't stand for that.

Either the corporal, sergeant, lieutenant and captain are ours, in which case we will all be comrades, or they are enemies, in which case they will have to be treated like enemies.

If we want, it will be all the same to us if we are a Column or a Battalion. Yesterday, today and tomorrow, we need no encouragement to fight; yesterday, today and tomorrow we will be warriors of the Revolution.

What becomes of us depends upon ourselves, upon what cohesion there is between us. Nobody is going to force us to dance to his tune; having minds of our own, we will set the pace for those around us.

Conclusion

Let's keep one thing in mind, comrades. This struggle requires that by no act or enthusiasm of ours should the war effort be hindered. In a column of our own, or in a Battalion of our own, in a division or in a battalion other than our own, we have to fight on.

If we disband the Column, if we disband, then, conscripted, we will have to serve, not with those whom we choose, but with those with whom we are ordered to serve. And as we are not and refuse to be domestic animals, we may well clash with those with whom we ought not to come into conflict; with those who, for good or ill, are our allies.

The Revolution, our Revolution, this proletarian and anarchistic Revolution, in which we have written pages of glory right from the first days, asks that we do not lay down our arms nor abandon the tight little unit which we have formed thus far, whether it be described as Column, Division or Battalion.

An 'Uncontrollable' from the Iron Column
Nosotros, 17 March 1937

THE CONDEMNED
by Arsenio Olcina

I

Crazy. He must have been crazy. Because the moon was full, he had wandered away from us all and had sat down on the peak overlooking the valley.

The Column had lots of crazies like him, poisoned by sentimentality. I already told you about the case of Dum Dum. But mentalities like that, like his or Claudio's, were not unique.

Román was also poisoned. One of the worst, perhaps. His nerves were on edge and he was overcome by enthusiasm. He would sit up in his trench all of a sudden and begin to shout and leap over the blackberry bushes. It seemed then as if he were trying to embrace the whole of nature: 'How lucky I am! How lucky I am to have the opportunity to live at this moment!'

At other times he would curl up as if he wanted to disappear, and retreat into an impregnable silence. Everything about him seemed to take on a bitter appearance.

The first battle that the Column fought against the fascists was a grandiose affair. Half-naked, almost weaponless, they threw themselves like a raging whirlwind upon the enemy, who fled in disorder, abandoning the bodies of the fallen in their rout:

'We're a horde of crazies,' was Román's comment.

II

Because the moon was full, he had sat down at the top of the peak.

Two sentry duty shifts have already finished and he continues to sit. Has he slept? It has been a while since I saw the little flame that enlivens his untiring pipe.

Culata is on the same parapet as Román, but three groups further along. Now he is on sentry duty. He watches the front, the motionless wave of hills that lead away from the enemy trenches. From time to time he looks behind, at the place where Roman is reclining with his back against the rocks. As soon as his shift ends, he will go over there, even though it disturbs Román's solitude. He wants to talk to Román... He needs to talk to Román.

Culata has a mentality and a physique that are also plentiful in the Column. Herculean. Fierce. Sweet. An overgrown child...

'Who goes there?'

'Libertad!'

It is the century delegate.

'What is it?'

'Nothing ... I'm off to take a rest.'

The centurion follows the parapet down to his hut. He is breathing heavily.

It must be midnight. Time for Culata to be relieved. He enters his billet. A jumble of bodies and blankets. Stuffy atmosphere... He gently shakes one of the bodies.

'Hey, you! Time for sentry duty... .'

III

Already outside, still half-sleeping, Culata's replacement clings to his rifle. He wraps his blanket around himself. It's cold. Every one of his limbs is shivering.

'I can't sleep ... I'm going over there to smoke a cigarette,' says Culata.

And off he wanders. His replacement stops to watch him for a moment. Then he turns his back and stands immobile, gazing into the night with his eyes fixed on the hills.

Román is not asleep. He has just lit his pipe. His head turns at the sound of footsteps. Culata approaches.

'What are you doing?'

'Smoking.'

Culata sits down beside him. There is a long silence. The pair seem preoccupied solely with encouraging the flames that consume their tobacco.

'You're a strange one...'

It is Culata who has spoken. Román has barely turned

his head. It seems as if he is going to speak. But he chooses instead to put his pipe between his lips.

'You're strange ... I like your nature. Although sometimes, I don't know... You're a good comrade to all of us. But one is always left with the sensation that you are holding something back. It seems as if you are always shielding something from prying eyes... Yes, that's it. I would like to be that way.'

Culata pauses for a moment, before adding:

'Look. This afternoon, when you were arguing with someone, I heard you say that once the revolution has triumphed, many revolutionaries will commit suicide. I'm not sure if that's what you intended to say... Is it... ?'

Román lifts his head a bit, as if trying to remember:

'Something like that,' he says.

Culata makes himself more comfortable on the rocks, satisfied:

'That made me think. I have thought the same thing you said this afternoon ... I just couldn't find the words to express it. But I have thought the same thing and... Yes. We will win the revolution. We must win it! But some of us, if we fall on the battlefield ... will have the advantage of dying with our dreams of victory intact; while those who remain ... of those who witness the administration of the victory, some—as you have said—will perhaps commit suicide ... out of disgust.'

Román makes an abrupt gesture. He seems startled by what he is hearing. In reality it is an interpretation of what he said that afternoon. A somewhat simplistic and shallow reading, perhaps. Through Culata's words, he sees that Culata is also drunk with scepticism. And he believes that he is obliged to lie:

'You have not understood what we were saying.'

Culata looks at him, dubiously.

Román continues:

'No. You have not understood.'

The other seems to agree:

'That could be ... I am dull-witted. I have read very little. But...'

He interrupts himself, only to continue by adding energetically:

'I have understood you! I don't know how to express myself, but I have understood you. What is happening is that you fear that this could spread and be harmful to the revolution. Why this fear? If the ball is already rolling, no one will be able to stop it! I... Look, I am one of those who expects nothing good from the triumph of the revolution. Once it is over, if I am still alive, the same comrades will kill me or I will kill myself. Yes... I have no reason to hide it. Everyone knows it. I am prison fodder. All my life I have done things that ... well, they just weren't right. But although I could not define what it was that I felt then, nor can I now ... I felt a yearning for rebellion ... I felt that injustice was gnawing away at my flesh. I was entirely revolted, and I screamed that this could not be right...'

A pause. He takes out a lighter. One click and the loose tobacco starts to glow. Down below in the valley, a shot rings out, like the crack of a whip. The bullet is heard; the path of the whistling projectile can be traced.

'Perhaps I have done some harm... But greater harm was done to me. My body has had to endure tremendous punishment. If it wasn't for my strength, my lungs would be worn out by now... Now the revolution has given me a chance to turn the tables. And turn them I have! Here and in the rearguard. I know that I am a wanted man back there. I know that yesterday's shameless enemies have today gained influence on the committees. They can always find someone to stick up for them. That doesn't matter to me. Anyone whom I knew for certain was an enemy, I have buried. I know that I will fall, that they will knock me down... But no matter how soon they do that, they will have been too late. These months of open fighting are worth a lifetime... And although you say the opposite, I believe I understand you. Your struggles, although distinct, are essentially the same as mine. You know, you suspect that the revolution will not go where you want it to go... You see, you are already seeing social climbers worming their way into positions from which they can administer

the victory. You have your problems, your dreams, your yearnings for improvement... I and many like me, prison fodder, am only accepted now as cannon fodder. Later on...'
Another silence.
'You, and we, even if we should triumph ... despite having contributed more than anyone to that very triumph! ... we are condemned...'
A lengthy silence. Culata waits for Román to speak. Seeing that he will not, he asks:
'What do you say?'
Román is on the verge of exclaiming: 'You're right!' But it seems to him that, if he did that, it would have a negative effect. And he tries to change the subject:
'Yes ... maybe so... But that is of no importance.'
And he tries a different tack:
'Listen, some of us have planned a raid on the fascists' position. Can we count on you?'
Culata jumps up:
'Sure! When?'
'At sunset tomorrow... It will be dangerous. Look...'
And he lowers his voice, explaining the details. The other listens, avidly, enthusiastically: 'You're on!'
And the two men stay on that peak for another sentry shift.
From across the way comes machine-gun fire. It sounds like a rifle gargling.
The night is bathed in the glow of its full moon...

Línea de Fuego, No. 68 (11 December 1936)

Epilogue

The adventures of the Iron Column did not end with its transformation into the Eighty-third Brigade. Information collected regarding the new military status of the former Iron Column tells us that at the very moment it was holding the assembly that would determine its fate, ninety-two of its fighters were in prison, Pedro Pellicer—the Column's delegate to Valencia—among them.

Until the arrival of the republican government in Valencia, everything had been going well. All the workers' forces and political parties were represented in the Executive Committee, which was the organ of peoples' power. Functions had been distributed among the members of this Committee, and for the CNT and UGT labour associations these were the functions most directly related to production, which were a logical fit for union control. The fields and the factories operated under workers' control and a collectivist system. There was no UGT supremacy over the CNT, nor vice-versa; both organisations had reached a point of agreement on the formation of joint unified bodies.

Such was the state of affairs until the month of November 1936, at which point the republican government took root in Valencia and—through its and the PCE's counterrevolutionary policies—created a situation marked by aggressiveness towards the workers' organisations, especially the CNT. The objective, according to the political opinion of the PCE, was 'to put an end to the workers' gains in order to return the country to the socio-political conditions of 18 July'; or in other words, to a regime that respected bourgeois property rights.

This bourgeois policy had already manifested itself clearly in the form of the October 1936 decree made by the Communist minister of agriculture, Vicente Uribe, a decree which was designed to destroy the agricultural collectives controlled by the peasants and to return their lands to their former proprietors. That decree failed in Levante thanks to the attitude jointly adopted by the UGT and the CNT. But the PCE did not accept defeat, and it created a peasant organisation into which it welcomed the former landowners, the aim being to pit them against the confederal and socialist farm hands. From that point on, clashes between the former owners—supported by the Assault Guards—and the workers' collectives took place in some villages in the region. The case of Burriana, previously cited, should be seen in this context.

To the socialist ministers, it was clear that the Burriana incident was a Communist provocation, to the extent that the minister of the interior, Galarza (a socialist), had not ordered the Assault Guards to intervene. But since the Communists' approach coincided with the government's reactionary policy, and since the government wanted to make the Popular Executive Committee of Valencia disappear, Galarza resorted to delaying tactics which effectively damaged the Burriana collective and the Iron Column, in that ninety-two members of the latter found themselves in prison. With this approach, the Largo Caballero government clearly demonstrated the natural tendency of power, as it could not tolerate the existence of another that diminished its authority.

Thus, in theory, the Iron Column, by deciding to militarise on 21 March 1937, did so under all kinds of pressure, including pressure exerted by the CNT's own National Committee.

Practically none of the Iron Column's members voluntarily agreed to its transformation into the Eighty-third Brigade, which, together with the Fifty-eighth and Fifty-ninth Brigades, formed part of the Forty-first Division under the command of Colonel Eixea.

Forty-four years after that era, Manuel Velasco Guardiola, who participated in the assembly of 21 March and later became a soldier in the Eighty-third Brigade, leaves a record of his memories and an assessment of his time with the Iron Column in the following writing:

> I enlisted in the Iron Column on 14 or 15 January 1937, at the Column's offices in the Plaza Castelar in Valencia. From there, and on that very same day, I and comrades Pascual Sánchez Salmerón, Francisco Balsalobre Bartolomé and Jesús Yuste Sánchez left for Sarrión, where we ate and slept that first night. In the morning we left for the next village, Puebla de Valverde, where the offices and the century delegations were based. There they handed me a rifle and, together with the other comrades, off we set that same morning for Puerto de Escandón. And

on the right flank—facing the Puerto halt and the mine's train tracks—we joined the line with the twenty-second century, 'Los Desperados' group, of whose delegate all I can remember is that he was called Sánchez. And there we were until they transferred us to Valencia, to Las Salesas, to deal with the militarisation of the Column.

I was present at the assembly that was eventually held, at which militarisation was agreed to. I saw opposition come from many comrades, even from some female comrades who had earlier—according to some comrades—shown such bravery by leading the way into battle. I saw women who wept from anger and fury upon being told that they would no longer be able to continue fighting with the Brigade, nor on any other front. Many who opposed militarisation explained their reasons, but it was worthless. I, eighteen years old and very inexperienced, knew very little about such matters and could say nothing... But later, especially in the light of what was happening to us, I came to believe that those who opposed militarisation had a very clear-sighted vision of the Column's struggle. They knew that—whether as a column before or as a brigade now, and composed of the same men, from which were drawn the commanders—things were always going to be different and that the Column would be made to disappear in one way or another due to its being formed by CNT members.

Upon the formation of the Eighty-third Mixed Brigade, I was assigned to the Third Battalion, First Company, Second Section, Third Platoon, at which point I was made a corporal. Our commanding officer was called Izquierdo and our captain was Mislatas.

On 9 May (1937) we left Valencia for Benicarló, where we remained for a period of training until we were deployed to relieve the España Libre Column, which had retreated from Albarracín. We dug in at the foot of the Montes Universales, in a village called Moscardó.

The Eighty-third Brigade was never equipped, because the government or the high command never had confidence in it. When we went to relieve the Sixty-third Brigade (España Libre), we did not have a single weapon with us and they had to hand us theirs. But since the Sixty-third had sustained many losses and was short of men, when they handed us their rifles there were not enough for all of us, who at that time comprised a complete brigade. Many comrades had to endure the enemy attack without rifles with which to defend themselves. That is what happened on that hill in Moscardó on 24 July 1937, where after holding out against a very heavy artillery bombardment that demolished the hill and took the lives of several comrades who, defenceless, had been waiting to be able to take a rifle from a fallen comrade. We were simultaneously attacked from behind by the Moors, who had advanced through the Montes Universales. That attack dealt the Brigade a mortal blow, and it had to be relieved—in a little village in Cuenca called Tejadillos—in order to be replenished. The recruits who joined us were from the recently mobilised draft of 1930 and from a battalion of naval infantry whose officers had attempted to mutiny. With our Brigade thus replenished, we later returned to the Teruel offensive at Christmas 1937. We attacked Teruel along the left flank, via the villages of Gea and San Blas, while other troops occupied Teruel.

Then came Franco's counterattack, which recaptured Teruel once again. At that point the nationalists began their Levante offensive, during which the Eighty-third Brigade always gave everything it had in response until, after holding the front near Morella, it had to break through the cordon stretched around it by the nationalists and march towards Castellón. However, some ten or twelve kilometres from that city, the nationalists cut the road and then it was every man for himself.

Since a group of us comrades had lost contact with the Brigade, we provisionally joined the Seventy-fourth with the hope of finding our own. During our time with the Seventy-fourth we were informed that our own Brigade was resting in the village of Libras, and we requested a discharge from the Seventy-fourth in order to rejoin the Eighty-third. But, while looking for the latter, we were arrested at a checkpoint and forcibly conscripted into the 220th Brigade, which was being organised for transfer to Extremadura. I remained on the Extremadura front, at the Sierra Trapera positions, until the end of the war. When the war was over, I was able to escape and reach Alcázar de San Juan via Almadén, and there I was terrified to witness the arrival of the nationalists and the way the Moors were rounding up all the republican soldiers and taking them to the bullring under the pretext of giving them something to eat there. But once inside the bullring there was no way out, and the only thing they received were rifle butts lashing out right and left. I was able to escape through the nearest door, and I made a break for the hills...

Thus, I am honoured to say that I belonged to the Iron Column, which was much maligned by everyone when in reality it was an authentic column made up of revolutionaries. I, like all the comrades with whom I have had occasion to speak before and afterwards, have always taken a pride in my membership of that Column of antifascist fighters, the sole objective of which was to transform society around the world by means of the social revolution.

Manuel Velasco Guardiola, Murcia, November 1980.

Appendices

Subtitle: Mouthpiece of the CNT-FAI Iron Column on the Teruel front.

Place of Publication: La Puebla de Valverde. Presses installed inside a bus.

Production Team: Printing workers from the CNT Graphic Arts Union in Valencia, who were also active fighters enlisted with the Iron Column.

Frequency: Daily, with occasional interruptions due to the war.

Publication: Date of first issue unknown.

Collection Consulted: From No. 29 (Sunday, 25 October 1936) to No. 72 (Tuesday, 15 December 1936).

Objective: Internal news bulletin of the Column. It was launched as a result of a collective need articulated by a general assembly of the combatants.

Number of Pages: Four.

Format: 22 x 30 centimetres.

Sections: 'Editorial,' usually with illustration; 'News from the Wire Services,' 'Literature,' 'Contributions' and 'Communiques.'

Editorial Staff and Contributors

Editorial Staff: Arsenio Olcina and R. Giménez Cuesta.

Contributors: Gregorio Falomir, Anielo, Antonio Lurbes, Vicente Ibáñez, Daniel Martín, Manuel Gimeno, 'Dietauro,' Juan Pérez, José Albiol, Doctor Astro, 'A Stoic,' Aurelio Tomás, Ernesto García, Fernandel, Francisco Carmona Pinedo, Francisco Cueva, Pascual Llopis, 'Trilita,' Ramón Sánchez, Gonzalo Vidal, Elías Manzanera, Ramón

Martín, F. Direteino, Rafael Herrero, Juan Martínez López, Rafael Llopis, Antonio Edo, 'Coblas,' etc.

Most Significant Articles

On the Everyday Life of the Column on the Front: 'The Vagrants: A Visit to the Front,' 'Cold Water,' 'Puerto de Escandón,' 'Sentimentality?,' 'Burst of the Day,' 'The Way to Fight Effectively,' 'The Sentry,' 'The Atmospheric Enemy,' 'Parapets of Iron,' 'Aldehuela, Capital of the Left Flank,' 'Malatesta, Governor of Mora,' 'One More Dirty Trick,' 'The Militian's Frame of Mind,' 'Responsibility,' 'Snapshots from La Puebla,' 'The Condemned,' 'Snow in the Line of Fire,' 'We Are.'

Revolutionary Critique: 'The Word, the Pen, and Action,' 'Friendly and Humanitarian Voices,' 'The Defence of the Revolution,' 'False Positions,' 'What Democracies Are,' 'We Have to Take a Stand,' 'Criticism of Performance,' 'Iron Column' (manifesto), 'The National Defence Council,' 'The Governmental CNT.'

Note: The bulletin's 'Literature' section carried short stories by French and Russian writers.

Issues 29–39, 42, 47, 50–62, and 65–72 can be found at the International Institute for Social History in Amsterdam. There are also a few issues at the Hemeroteca in Madrid.

Two Significant Articles from *Línea de Fuego*

FALSE POSITIONS
by Fausto and Mefistófeles

The Spanish revolution currently underway has had the surprising ability to effect a strange metamorphosis, the result of which has been the change of the positions and the rectification of the trajectories of a specific social ideology. We have encountered acts of maximum compromise in times of absolute intransigence, all in the name of some circumstances that—whilst they do obtain and have come about—do not carry the potency and importance given to them. Bases of support and the basic premises in which can be found the foundation of revolutionary anarchist tactics have been hushed up for the foreseeable future, or perhaps forever.

By voicing this critique, I am going to be accused of not living in reality, of spreading defeatism among those whose ideas are not sufficiently rooted, of using the arguments of a trite and out-of-place Platonism; in short, of a number of more or less well thought out epithets without any ideological basis but with an enormous abundance of sophistication.

In order to justify this ultra-radical change of action and behaviour, 'circumstances' are wielded and presented as the product of the current war. Now we have the everlasting argument of those who want to justify the unjustifiable! The eternal weapon of the turncoats! The new myth that they grasp in order to regain their balance on that slippery, crumbling ground upon which they are standing.

At first glance and upon superficial examination, it seems as if their behaviour has been consistent with and in response to the only things that could be achieved during these times. Nevertheless, once we delve beneath that surface, the false foundations upon which they base their arguments appear with all obviousness. Let me ask and I should like a plain answer to this: why has an apolitical organisation par excellence—one that had always insisted that no fact, no 'circumstance,' could bring about a deviation from the road it has always taken—given in to the stubbornness and blindness of a representative of a more or less proletarian government who, in his insistence on having his way, refused to consent to the petitions presented to him? It seems to me that this says nothing in favour of the numerical potential represented by that organisation or the moral and ideological personality of the organisation itself. The objection will be made that, were it not for this swallowing of our principles and this absolute lack of personality, we would have either seen ourselves engaged in a war between distinct proletarian sectors or displaced completely from the technical direction of the war. What a subtle and sophisticated piece of reasoning this is! What a way to deceive oneself and deceive everyone else as well!

Those who say such things don't realise that, upon their becoming functionaries of the country, these effects—thought to be a result of the maintenance of principles in all their integrity—would not only have vanished, but the efficiency they hope for in matters of war would have been equalled and even exceeded. Weaponry and manpower win wars, and those two things could have existed without any need for transgressions, changes in tactics, or the ideological failings which have come about and which they speak of.

Those who sustain the 'compromise' position are walled up in an ivory tower symbolised by the weaponry issue; weaponry which—it is said—cannot be procured without the collaboration and support of the government due to the complete absence of the funds required for their acquisition. Nevertheless, it seems to me that these affirmations contain a bit too much negligence and haste. Firstly, the funds with which to purchase the necessary weapons for the struggle exist and have always existed in the banks and as a result of the searches undertaken, and these funds were sufficient to acquire war material. Thus, the difficulty posed by the non-intervention 'boycott' could have easily been overcome. Are there no arms-producing countries that did not sign that pact? Are the arms factories of United States and Japan not eager to find customers for their products?

The issue that confronts us with regard to the war, in my judgement, could not have been that which drove us to the 'sacrifice' of participating in the responsibilities of a government.

As for the other argument—that this is being done in order to preclude what happened to the anarchists in Russia once the war was over—its puerility strikes me as beyond any doubt. Because with weapons in hand and a contingent of forces almost equal to the other segments of society who aim to impose their will, and based on the magnificent achievements readily visible to the people in those places where our economic and moral principles have been put into practice, we can be sure that no one—no one at all—will dare seek our elimination. On the contrary, our governmental position puts us in constant danger—and no one can deny it—that once times of peace and complete revolutionary achievement arrive, those at the top may well seek to impose social changes upon us from above, because they will have discovered that the real work of war and revolution should be done by the various organs of the state.

Thus, it is quite clear that this departure from long-sustained principles—even if only for a provisional period of time—does not benefit us. Rather, without making such ideological 'sacrifices' and without having to make such abrupt and dangerous 'ministerial' changes, it is only through tried and tested revolutionary methods that one reaches the objectives that originally induced us to climb to such lofty heights: heights which are endangering those who have reached them with an imminent case of vertigo.

Línea de Fuego, No. 36, 27 November 1936

CRITICISM OF PERFORMANCE
by A Stoic

The current circumstances, which are a result of the military uprising of 19 July, have created problems in Spain whose strict and necessarily social resolution had to be determined through appraisals and objectives consonant with the constructive and moral sense that should guide not only all revolutions, but also the most insignificant changes that can be made to the political or social order. Thus, accepting the primordial aims that a revolution must realise in order to be considered such, let us examine—quickly and without delving too deep—if the directions and courses through which the incipient Spanish revolution has been channelled have fulfilled those basic premises, without which no transformation of the social and economic order can even begin to take place.

With profound astonishment, we observe that not only have all those revolutionary principles required by circumstances not been fulfilled, but that—on the contrary—instead of removing all obstacles in order to clear the road to complete emancipation, those very obstacles have increased to the point that their obstruction becomes the factor that produces the very stagnation and paralysis of the march towards supreme liberation. Our claims are not based on whimsy, nor have they been dictated by inconsistency; rather, they are supported by and founded on the firmest realities. And since actions speak louder than words, we are going to explain them with all the clarity demanded by our desire that the revolution does not fail.

An immediate endorsement of what I have just been saying—and which allows us to explain things in a practical way—is the paradoxical fact that it exposes the conception of revolution put forth by those who claim to be its mentors, when it has been clearly demonstrated that the people in arms had nothing to fear with regard to the defence of their liberties and rights, which were conquered at the cost of their own blood. When this activity was visibly and clearly sanctioned in every Spanish locality during the first days of the fascist uprising, a pseudo-revolutionary civilian defence body was formed that was utterly at odds with what the people had achieved through practical application, and this immediately led to the appearance of more than two thousand parasites with nothing better to do than carry out the work entrusted in the old days to the gendarmes of the bourgeoisie. At the same time, and as a product of this type of approach, these individuals underwent such a radical metamorphosis that they were converted—not by magic, but by something more practical—from enraged revolutionaries and ardent enthusiasts of the radical suppression of all authoritarian institutions into stalwart defenders of neo-revolutionary authority.

These people talk tirelessly—precisely because they do not act—about sacrifices, about stockpiling and about the intensification of production. And in response to these laments—which are heard at every rally—we now have this inspired measure of the new authorities adding a completely useless expense to the, shall we say, revolutionary budget, while at the same time keeping of a number of able arms out of work: arms that would be much better employed holding a rifle on the front or assisting production in the fields than strolling through the peaceable, tranquil city streets with a pistol or baton.

The same negative result is achieved—and is being achieved—through what can be called, in technical terms, the epidemic of the 'committee-ocracy': that new bourgeoisie formed by the heat of this upheaval. The parasitism engendered by the work of the committees, many of which are useless, is also one of the factors impeding those on the committees from manning a plough or marching to the front. For, when all is said and done, these are virtually the only occupations in which all of us who truly aspire towards the complete disappearance of all fascism and all tyranny should be engaged.

I have spoken of two of the many points with which the current directors of the revolution can be critiqued. The bureaucratic committees and the new authorities will, in the last analysis—even if we do achieve victory over fascism in battle—be those who choke and impede all rebellious and liberatory intent that emerges from the people and that threatens to stray from the organisational forms and ways of life that they wish to impose on us. Fascism, in the broad and full sense of the word, does not just consist of insignias and the modes of operation of regimes that call themselves such. Rather, its theatre of operations and its training ground are much wider and extensive than that which is demarcated by the Hitlers, the Mussolinis or the Francos. It is authority in all its different forms and manifestations that generates and gives rise to fascism, whose means of conflict and methods of combat are used by all powers when those under their control attempt to rebel and emancipate themselves from such tutelage.

Thus, let us realise this evident truth and not allow our struggle to be taken advantage of by those who, once we have finished off fascism proper, will insert a new fascism that will impose its own orders and methods, thereby sterilising the virile and magnificent accomplishments realised by the people during the conquest of their liberty. Many feel that the social transformation should not begin until the fighting on the battlefields is over because, as they see it, we would be dawdling over matters of a social character while those matters pertaining to the war—which are the priority—would be relegated to a dangerous oblivion. Turning to this issue, at a rally described as one of unification—yet another tired theme—the problem was solved in a quite original way, leaving all the segments of society desirous of such unity entirely in agreement. The speaker showed the similarity between the current debate over whether or not the social question needs to be addressed at the same time that the war is being fought, and the famous Spanish classic in which a discussion arises surrounding the matter of whether fruit should be sold from a tree that had yet to be planted.

But my modest reply to those deploying this argument as a means of thwarting those social changes that need immediate implementation is that this is a debate about whether or not a tree intended to bear certain fruit has yet been planted; however, it has been amply demonstrated that not only has the tree been planted, but that its fruits are lying on the ground, and we run the risk that those fruits will rot if we do not gather them up quickly.

I have momentarily succumbed to metaphor in order to precisely show that the revolution—the transformation of every sphere of life—can indeed take place in unison with the war in the trenches, and that this delay which almost everyone believes is necessary, this recourse to temporary stratagems, will achieve nothing more than the introduction of an imminent danger: once the fighters return from fighting fascism in the line of fire, they will find here in the rearguard that another fascism has been formed whose methods will be identical to those of the fascism they have just defeated, even should it dress itself up in the garb of proletarian, trade-union society.

Línea de Fuego, No 35, 6 November 1936

Composition of the Iron Column (October–December 1936)[1]

General Headquarters of the Column in Valencia: Las Salesas.
Administrative Offices: Avenida Blasco Ibáñez, 4, principal.

War Commitee in La Puebla de Valverde (4 November 1936): Gómez, Montoya, Armando, Antonio Rodilla, Valentín Rufino, Jornet, José Pellicer and Pedro Pellicer (liaison with the War Department in Valencia).

Sections

General Supplies (Quartermaster): Elías Manzanera, Morell, Bartolomé Asensi, Enrique Mirabel Galarza.

Front-Line Rations: Gumbau, Isaías Sanchez (kitchens), Diego Navarro, Benito Blas (kitchens).

Intelligence and Liaison: José Segarra, José Cortés Pérez.

Administration: Jaime Serna, José Marín (switchboard).

Transport: Dolz, Ginés Montiel (driver), Alfonso Maciá (driver), Sirval (armoured car), Victoriano López Tello (tank no. 4), Antonio Vidal Vidal (tank no. 9).

Miscellaneous Trades Section: Joaquín Canet, Moisés Jarque (master builder, fortifications), Máxima Capillera (laundry), Mariano Capillera (laundry).

---

1   I have compiled this list of names from *Línea de Fuego, Fragua Social* (August 1936 to March 1937) and *Nosotros* (November 1936 to 1 March 1937).

Valverde-Sarrión Hospital: Ramón Sanchis (doctor), Mariano Palanca (orderly), Rafael Navarro Pellejaro (nurse), José Cortés Torrent (first aid post no. 5), Vicente Castellón González (first aid post no. 5), Vicente Cortés Pinilla (first aid post no. 5), Rafael Navarro (first aid post no. 1), José Martínez Bart (nurse), José Pradas (nurse), Angelita Molas (nurse), Francisco Marín (nurse), José Vicente Silvestre (nurse), Amadeo Alcántara (nurse). Barber Service: Manuel Aumenteros, Luis Ramos, Sebastián Iranzo, Jacinto Martínez.

Information, Press and Radio

Radio Station: José Segarra, José Cortés. *Línea de Fuego*: Arsenio Olcina, R. Giménez Cuesta (editors), Coblas, Antonio Edo, Rafael Llopis, Doctor Astro, Juan Martínez López, Rafael Herrero, Manuel Jimeno, Pascual Llopis, F. Dieretina, Tomás Aurelio, Ramón Martín, Elías Manzanera, Gonzalo Vidal, Ernesto García, Ramón Sánchez, Juan Pérez, 'Trilita,' Francisco Cueva, Francisco Carmona Pinedo, Fernandel, Vicente Ibáñez, Daniel Martín, 'A Stoic,' José Albiol, 'Dietauro,' 'Fausto and Mefistoféles,' Gregorio Falomir, Lurbes, Aniclo[2] (contributors).

List of Names by Century

The century (one-hundred strong) is divided into: eighty-one combatants, nine delegates per ten-man group, three delegates per thirty-man group, one century delegate, six stretcher-bearers, six ammunition- and water-carriers, four couriers.[3]

Century I: José Marcos Rodriguez, Lázaro Tadeo Rodrigo, Vicento Megino, Vicente Colomer, Agapito Castillejo Sanz, Alfredo Pla Sala, Isidro García Humada, Antonio Sánchez Valero, Antonio Giménez García, Antonio García Romero (native of Lebrija; 'Elche' Group), José Martínez, Manuel Gerardo, Ruiz Llera, Miguel Sánchez Argilés, José Cortés, Emilio Campello, Joaquín García, José

---

2   All of this data is taken from *Línea de Fuego*.
3   *Línea de Fuego* (13 December 1936).

Cuquerella, Benjamín Garcés, Pedro Radujo, Agustín Manex, Juan López, Francisco López Bocanegra (native of Olivera, Cadiz; 'Elche' Group), Ildefonso Segarra, Alfonso Torregrosa, Guillermo Cirela.

Century II: Francisco Escrich, López Medina, Emilio Sospedra, Manuel Muñoz, José Abad Izquierdo, Francisco López, Francisco García Lloró, Miguel Tomás Roda, Lucas González, Fidel Panizo Álvarez, Julio García, Manuel Perera, Mario Berruti, Domingo Díaz, Lázaro Ledesma, Manuel Quintana, Antonio Escamilla (his partner, Francisca Asín, fought in the Torres-Benedito Column, Second Division, Century II), Abel Fortea, Antonio Lara, Bautista Ibáñez, Antonio Carmona, Santiago Delgado, Guillermo Cerizola, Leopoldo Polo Herrero, García Domingo, Francisco Asensi, José Torres Soto, Emilio Val, Enrique Óscar Navarro, Ramón Belsaduch Arnau, Antonio Tormo, Jesús Senen, Vicente Sánchez.

Century III: Laurentino Calleriza, Ramón Navarro, Luis Obrero, José Torres, Manuel Paujada, José Mozón, Enrique Molla, Manuel Payá, José Ibáñez Nebot, Miguel Gil, Alfredo Benet ('Los Lobos del Mar' Group).

Century IV: Joaquín Canet, Ángel Cardona, Tortajada, Enrique Candal Ferrer, Juan Sanz Miralles, Bautista Fortes Marcos, José Gabriel, José Bernal, Vicente López, Miguel Roig, José Nostón Martínez, Vicente Martínez, Juan Día Deviá, Vicente López.

Century V: Marcelino Fombuena ('El Mando' machine-gun), José Gil, Enrique Fernández, José Grau, Alfredo Perca, Francisco Cortina, José Sabater, José Valles Martínez, Federico Gregoris, Francisco Bou, Higinio Cebrián, José Ruiz Martín, Francisco Lledó Sebastián, Ezequiel Cuñat, Josefa Torres, José Vicente Pastor, Manuel Gómez.

Century VI: Justo Rubio, Juan Sánchez, Francisco Sáez ('Los Saltamontes' Group), Enrique Moliner Osca ('Star' Group), José Torres Torrents, Juan Sansols, Francisco García Mirón, Francisco Pons Cases, Esteban Rodríguez, Miguel Andreu Torrecillas.

Century VII: Bautista Belda Ruiz, José Baixauli, Jesús Cejalbo ('El Vidrio' Group), Vicente Martínez, Miguel Mudano, Ramón González, Manuel Cadete, Bartolomé Martínez Montfort, Vicente Ordaz, Manuel Sanchis, Luis Berenguer.

Century VIII: Eloy Agrasar Fabeiro, Juan Sánchez Sánchez, Enrique Carrascosa, Amadeo Aguas, Francisco Usedo Muñoz,

Salvador Iborra Martínez, José Romaguera Chauzá, Juan Villar, Bautista Guillén, Juan Billán, Alfredo Benet, Julián Malmeda, Emilio Nal, Juan Martínez, Juan Vilar Viñals, Pascual Marín Marín, Agustín Guardiola, Manuel Vindel, Miguel Llin García, Francisco Noguera, José Espert, Jesús da Costa López, Juan Villar, Francisco Sanchis, Avelino Salgado, Manuel Duarte, Vicente Veimunt, Luis Conejos Reig, Pascual Muñoz Romero.

Century IX: Casto Bolufer Saiz, Nicolás López Grumer, José Morón, Benjamín Creus, Manuel Soriano, Francisco Guillermón Meseguer, Francisco Tordera, José Briz, Ernesto Gómez (tank no. 9), Emilio López , Francisco Juan Marcos, Vicente Colomer, Francisco Mejina, Luis Mengual, Agustín Salas, Rafael Amón, Benito Vicente, Pedro Llagues, Juan Borrás Salinas, Manuel Granero. Pascual Rosales Gimeno, Miguel Farga Zapata, José Esteve Antequera, Miguel Marcos Mestres, Juan Antonio Montfort, José Catalá Mas, José Arlandis Arnau, Antonio Gómez , Baltasar Morera, Alfonso Alfaro.

Century X: Vicente Górriz, Manuel Muñoz, Joaquín Pérez, Francisco Llopis, Victoriano Giner, Francisco Campany, José Tades, Ricardo Ramírez, Manuel Muñoz, Vicente Villar Segur, Julián Pérez, Manuel Ibáñez.

Century XI: Vicente Benavent Peris, Ricardo Soler Muñoz, Gervasio Martín, Jesús Alarcón, Francisco García, José Cobo, Juan José, Gonzalo Domínguez.

Century XII: José Sánchez Gómez, Antonio Vizcaíno, Vicente Navarro, Dolores Calatayud, Bernardino Jiménez, Antonio García García.

Century XIII: Maximino Pallás, Francisco Valera, Antonio Soler.

Century XIV: Francisco Gómez, Manuel Pérez, Rafael Pérez Gil ('Star' Group), Fernando Sevilla ('Star' Group), Matías Martínez, Ignacio Sánchez, Eusebio Pérez , Clemente Montero.

Century XV: Manuel Fora, Adolfo Cano Ruiz, Rafael Soler Aguilar, Ángel Ballester Castillo, Vicente Miralles Castelló.

Century XVI: Daniel Grifo Igual, Ignacio Bou López, Joaquín López, Juan Valverde Sánchez, Ramón González, Vicente López, Andrés Fitó, Domingo Cervera, Gerónimo Gigas, Manuel Carrasco, Manuel Ros, José Sola, José Agustín.

Century XVII: Vicente Montserrat Alemany, Vicente Guillén, Antonio Costa, Manuel Vera Ripollés, Miguel Martínez Abril,

Salvador Boronat (century delegate), José Pastor, Mariano Soler Selma, José Moliner Corral, Alejandro Gómez Salvat, Antonio López ('Metalúrgico' Group), Antonio Garcerán, Gregorio Andrés Pi, Francisco Fluixà, Antonio Ortolà, Antonio Salas, Antonio Fabra, José Furió Molina, Sebastián López, Avelino Millán, Basilio Aparicio, Alberto Herrero.

Century XVIII: Julio López Asunción, Bautista García, Roberto Fuster, José Alaport, Domingo Úbeda, Arturo Ortiz, Hilario García, José Panblanco, Francisco Montoro.

Century XIX.

Century XX: Manuel Catalá, Francisco Biosca, Matías Martínez, Jaime Bensi, Juan Pat, Antonio Moreno Fernández, José Cerezo García, Ramón Sánchez, Juan García Alcaraz, Isidoro López Crespo.

Century XXI: Mariano Fernández, José Ríos Ríos, Antonio Sallueca, Vicente Ros, Mariano Aguilar, José Martínez, Constantino Vicente, Constantino Úbeda.

Century XXII: Francisco Saturnino, Pedro Alvarado Ros, Onofre Palazón, Hospicio Sáez.

Century XXIII: Luis Navarro, Luis García, José Roca, Pascual Peñalba, Jesús Lérida, Félix Lara, José Montserrat, Francisco Sánchez Galiana.

Century XXIV: José Covina Cereveró.

Century XXV: Salvador Albiach Camps, Joaquín Giménez Palomares (from La Vall de Tavernes; declared a deserter from the Column on 18 February 1937), Vicente Visedo Perós (from Corbera de Alzira; declared a deserter on 19 February 1937), Antonio Hernández Plaza (native of Requena; declared a deserter on 19 February 1937), José Bataller Raymundo (from La Pobla de Vallbona; declared a deserter on 19 February 1937), Antonio Rodilla, Juan Díaz, Antonio Sala Bou (serves on the Column's right flank), Fernando Fuentes, Modesto Yuste, Francisco Sáez Sánchez, Manuel Ferrer.

Century XXVI: Francisco Gimeno, José Simbor, Justo Cádiz Senilles, Enrique Ramón, Antonio Moreno Fernández ('Los Vagos' Group; see the report in *Línea de Fuego*, No. 36, 4 November 1936), Antonio Briones ('Los Vagos' Group), Silviano Planet, José Alcañiz.

Century XXVII: José Puchades Vidal, Emilio Isabel.

Century XXVIII: Gonzalo Asensi, Gonzalo Pérez José (killed by shrapnel), José Herrero.

Century XXIX: Eduardo Ruiz, Antonio Moreno, José Cambas, Casto Sáiz, Pedro Serrano.

Century XXX.

Century XXXI: José Molina, José Zanón.

Century XXXII.

Century XXXIII: Juan Sancho, Sebastián López García (Construction Union), José Esteve, Carlos Vendrell.

Century XXXIV: Vicente Solvella, Salvador Tomás, Andrés Ibor, Vicente Miralles, Tomás Salvador.

Attached to the Column

Engineers' Regiment: Vicente García, Enrique Ruiz, Antonio García, José Argente.

Infantry Regiment No. 10: Benito Viano, Blas Cuevas, Bartolomé Guandala, Francisco Muñoz, Fernando Hernández, Antonio Vidal Requena, Salvador Fructuoso, José Juanes, Sebastián Montaner, José Moreno, Fernán Ferrus, José Picó Pérez (Machine-gun Company), Eugenio Montaña García.

Infantry Regiment No. 9: José Caballero, Vicente Escuder Roig, Francisco Pérez, Francisco Padula, Domingo Romeo, José Sanchís, Joaquín Romaní, Francisco Font Villarreal, Vicente Martínez, Miguel Fernández (Machine-gun Company).

List of Column Members Not Identified by Combat Unit

Manuel Aladí Ferrer, Vicente Aladí Pérez, [Manuel Aladí Pérez], Gerónimo Alonso ('Vila' Group), Gregorio Andrés, Francisco Aragó Martín, Arcas, Gabriel Aspal, José Avilés Salmerón, Diego Ayola, Jaime Biyerri Singnes ('Vila' Group), Alfredo Benet, Francisco Beril Piñol (Metalworkers' Union, Valencia),[4] Salvador Boluda Sánchez, (from Mislata) Vicente Burgos Lozano, Juan Cañizares, Tomás Castelló Jarasó (from Cullera), Helenio Catalá, Juan Cayetano Bono (Amalgamated Trades Union, Millars), Bernardo Cogollos Palanca (Amalgamated Trades Union, Alzira), Vicente Colomar, Domingo Crespo Malbuena, Faustino Domingo la Huerta, José Esculia García (Peasants' Union, Alginet), José Escrihuela (Amalgamated Trades

---

4 All unions—unless otherwise mentioned—are CNT-affiliated.

Union, La Vall de Tavernes), Rafael Fernández Saura ('Albacete' Group), Gabriel Fernández (Construction Union, Valencia), Francisco Ferrer Borrás (Amalgamated Trades Union, Bétera), Ramón Fragua Rodríguez (Maritime Transport Union, La Coruña), Ricardo Fuster, Manuel Galiano Socorro, Joaquín Galera Juan (Amalgamated Trades Union, La Vall de Tavernes), Vicente García, Adolfo García (Construction Union, Valencia), Enrique García Amor (Metalworkers' Union, Valencia), Miguel García García (Construction Union, Valencia), José García García (Glassworkers' Union, Valencia), Miguel Gómez, Avelino Granados, Federico Gramofell Agustín ('Albacete' Group), José Grau Juan ('Albacete' Group), Agustín Guardiola (from Mira, Cuenca), Rafael Herrero Aix, Blas Hernández Gabarda, Luciano Igualada (Foodstuffs Union, Valencia), José Gimeno (member of 'Nosotros'), Gregorio Jaén (member of 'Nosotros'), Eleuterio López Borrás (Construction Union, Valencia), Rosendo López Navarro ('Albacete' Group), Antonio López Piqueras, Isidoro Limada, Antonio Lázaro Benajas, Emilio López Asensio, Francisco Mejino, Mateo Messeguer, Vicente Muñoz Manrique (Painters' Union, Alcoy), Miguel Moya Doménech (Public Entertainments Union, Valencia), Rafael Martín (alias 'Pancho Villa'; member of the Column's first War Committee; killed in action in Puerto de Escandón on 20 August 1936), José Montaño Oro (married *miliciana* María Pérez Blanco on 30 October 1936 in front of witnesses José Ballester and José Nador), Bartolomé Martínez, Martín Mestres, Francisco Márquez, Bautista Moya Casanova, Antonio Moreno Fernández, José Mateo Raugel, Juan Bautista Molina Bas, Agapito Mezquita Selvi, Delfín Montaña, Rafael Martínez (Alcoy century), José Martín, Aniceto Nuevo Gómez, José Orhiced, Benjamín Olmedo, Gerónimo Ortiz, Bautista Pérez Escrivá, Silvestre Picó, Silvio Planell, Francisco Peñalver Pérez, Sebastián Pérez Sánchez, Tomás Peris, Antonio Pérez ('Ferrioviario' Group), Vicente Palomares, Fernando Prieto, José Quijal Gascón, Antonio Queral Amor, Manuel Rodríguez, Domingo Rodríguez, Gómez Rufino, Roque Santamaría (Barbers' Union, Valencia), Maritón Segovia Pérez, Ricardo Sales, Miguel Sancho Pérez (UGT Amalgamated Trades Union, La Pobla de Vallbona), José María Solano Mañofel (Amalgamated Trades Union, Torrevieja), Sebastián 'Palete,' Joaquín Sendra López, Alfonso Salcedo González, José Sanchís, Tronchoni (member of the War Committee during September and October

1936), Jaime Sabater Rosario ('Albacete' Group), Ramón Sánchez ('Valencia-Madrid' Group), Miguel Sánchez Pérez, Juan Serrano Campos, Aurelio Tomás, Amadeo Tortosa Mollá, Eugenio Victoriano Pérez, Manuel Vindel (from Mira, Cuenca), Valera, Modesto Yuste (from Mira, Cuenca), Francisco Blanes 'El Gato' (Alcoy century), Espí, Peñarrocha, Quiles, Mares (all four were War Committee delegates during December 1936), Tiburcio Ariza González (murdered by 'La Guapa' [GPA]), Dimas, Armando (both killed in the Plaza Roja).

THE COUNTERREVOLUTION IN LEVANTE AND THE MILITIAS

One cannot understand either the events in the republican rearguard or the drama confronted by the revolutionaries in the autumn of 1936 unless we uncover the mysteries of the counterrevolution that began to grow.

The reconstruction of the machinery of the state and the reestablishment of government authority begun by Largo Caballero had to bypass those organisations that possessed almost all the social power: the revolutionary committees. This would not be an easy task, because the local committees were armed and often supported by militians returning from the front on leave.

The Iron Column's fighters wasted no time in recognising this, and an article written in Puerto de Escandón and significantly titled 'CAREFUL WITH THE REARGUARD!' could be read in the pages of *Línea de Fuego* and *Fragua Social* (11 October 1936). The article contained sentences like: 'Things are not going to remain as they were before July ... we have not come to the front in order to defend a bourgeois-democratic republic. If that were the case, then the spilling of so much blood would not be worth the trouble ... we are living in the epoch of the proletariat ... those of us who are on front lines—on all of the fronts—will crush fascism, but we will not allow any move by what perished on 18 July. Careful with the rearguard!'

It is in this sense that one must interpret the forays of Iron Column members and others into the rearguard, with or without the permission of the War Committee. At all costs, they wanted to stop a return to the past.

In order to implement his plans in the rearguard, Largo Caballero needed strength; in other words, a well-armed and loyal police force. Thus, the Assault Guards, the Carabineers, and even the re-named Civil Guards were reinforced. In addition, in order to counterbalance the control militias, the Popular Executive Committee had established another corps known as 'la Guapa' (GPA). All of these were instruments for disarming the revolution.

Once the dissolution of the control militias in the rearguard—which were dependent on the labour organisations—was decreed, many militians were going to be disarmed, including those who carried weapons permits (*Fragua Social*, 13 October 1936). Assault Guards and 'Guapos,' sent by the civil governor, had attempted to occupy the collectivised villages of Carcaixent, Foios, Gandía and Albalat dels Sorells, but they were repelled by a general mobilisation of the collectivists. Revolutionaries were still able to make their voices heard, and this is what they said:

> We placed two crates of bombs in the bell-tower, we occupied the houses at the entrance to the village—making sure we were sufficiently equipped—and we sent word to the commissar for public order and the governor, telling them: 'We are waiting for your forces to prevent the burning of the town hall archives, and we only hope that you—imbecile governor of Valencia—come to the front as well.' (*Fragua Social*, 20 November 1936)

The process of suppression of the revolutionary organs was enormously accelerated with the transfer of the government to Valencia and the CNT's acceptance of the dissolution of the rearguard militias and committees. In Castellón, villages that did not dissolve their committees were either not supplied with provisions or had their provisions requisitioned, and this sparked confrontations with the Assault Guards in Sant Mateu, Cálig, Canet and Torreblanca.

But the worst thing of all was the addition of the counterrevolutionary work of the PCE to the counterrevolutionary work of the government. The PCE was looking to pit the landlords and the rural middle classes against the revolutionary peasants in order to neutralise the latter as a class while simultaneously establishing PCE supremacy in the countryside. In October, the Federación Provincial Campesina (Provincial Peasant Federation—FPC) was formed for the expressly recognised purpose of defending the landlords and tenants 'from the excesses of collectivisation.' The 'Campesina' became a refuge for peasants who supported the disbanded Catholic organisations and the DRV (Derecha Regional Valenciana), for *caciques*, informers, landowners and people who had previously distinguished themselves by persecuting the workers; in short, all those harmed by the revolution.

In December there were problems with landlords in Llombay, Alginet and Altea. An Iron Column detachment defended Altea and prevented it from being attacked. In January, the FPC set the landlords of Segorbe against the town's Revolutionary Committee; shots were fired and there were injuries. But the hardest blow was directed against the foundation of the Valencian agrarian economy: the export of oranges, which was in the hands of the CLUEA, a joint UGT-CNT organisation. A definitive strike was aimed at the most important export centres, like Gandía, Sueca, Cullera and Carcaixent. On 3 February, Assault Guards attacked Cullera, resulting in two deaths and many wounded. An appeal to the surrounding local federations and to the militias on leave from the Teruel front put the area on a war footing. The resistance lasted for four days, until the arrival of the CNT National Committee interrupted the fighting. Weapons were returned and prisoners released. The same thing happened shortly thereafter in Burriana, in connection with a munitions factory being run by the CNT. The Iron Column intervened again, tipping the scales of battle in favour of the revolutionaries.

All these events turned the question of law and order into a fundamental issue for the state. In a climate of high tension, leading collectivists were continually detained for improbable offences, provisions were taken away and all kinds of pressures were being applied to the collectives. Then, the occupation of a workers' centre in Vinalesa by Assault Guards on 8 March 1937 triggered an outbreak of violence. The district was immediately mobilised following the arrival of numerous Assault Guards and Carabineers along with an artillery section complete with armoured cars and machine-guns. The Iron Column sent two battalions from Segorbe, and there was fighting in Vinalesa, Alfara, Tabernas Blancas and Moncada until the arrival of García Oliver and the National Committee. Four *cenetistas* and eleven Assault Guards were killed. As a result of the fighting, the minister of the interior ordered the occupation of the district and imprisoned more than two hundred libertarians—ninety-two of them from the Iron Column—in Valencia's medieval Torres de Quart prison.

After these events, the government published a statement in which it attributed responsibility for the conflicts to agents provocateurs within the CNT. The surprising thing was that the CNT's own National Committee used the same language, and instead of confronting the campaign that was being orchestrated around the confrontations, it dared to threaten its own militants in a declaration that said the following:

1. No one but the responsible committees—with full knowledge of the course of events—may issue orders, decide on mobilisations or call for action.

2. Regarding the political problem, it is for this Committee alone to indicate the appropriate course of action.

3. Under no circumstances should those serving on the fronts be mobilised without the express authorisation of their military commanders and political commissars.

4. Industrial federations and committees representing a branch of production are hereby stripped of their authority to issue orders, as these only compete with the CNT's organs of general administration: the Regional Committees.

5. Anyone who does not act in accordance with these guidelines, which are rules based on organisational accords, WILL BE PUBLICLY EXPELLED FROM THE ORGANISATION … (*Fragua Social*, 11 March 1937)

Following this declaration was another that was identical to the order for the withdrawal of rifles issued by Galarza in *La Gaceta de la República*:

CNT. NATIONAL COMMITTEE. RIFLES ARE TO BE
IMMEDIATELY HANDED OVER FOR DELIVERY TO
THE FRONTS... We are making all CNT comrades, unions
and committees aware that all rifles must be handed over within
forty-eight hours ... those comrades who do not want to give
up their weapons should immediately place themselves and their
rifles at the disposal of the defence sections in order to be mobilised upon incorporation into the brigades of the People's Army.
Anyone ignoring this warning will have to face the consequences
of disarmament...

And what were these consequences? According to the 13 March
1937 edition of *La Gaceta de la República*, they consisted of searches
of suspected secret arms caches, followed by arrests and court
appearances.

At the Peasant Plenum of the Levante CNT, which took place
on 15 March, the National Committee was accused of sabotaging the
revolution, and it provoked angry protests when it attempted to deny
responsibility for the jailings by in turn accusing some supposed provocateurs from Vinalesa. The Plenum's board concluded the debate
over the abuse dealt out by the Assault Guards in Vinalesa and other
villages by making the following proposal, which was unanimously
approved:

1. That all CNT and UGT members arrested during the recent
events be released immediately, excluding those who are openly
considered to be agents provocateurs, as these will be brought
to trial.

2. That the government be lobbied regarding the necessity of
mobilising all the Assault Guards for the front so that the peasants can proceed to intensify production with certainty, secure
in the knowledge that they will not be abused on the basis of
information given by *caciques*.

3. That a commission composed of CNT and UGT personnel be seconded to the government in order to intervene in and
positively resolve potentially violent peasant conflicts.

4. That weapons taken from comrades who are known to be
reliable militants be returned to them.

So energetic was the demand for the release of the prisoners that the National Committee resorted to moral blackmail:

> [The National Committee] says that it is unable to comprehend exactly how it could occur to anyone to propose strike action in these circumstances when thousands of comrades are losing their lives on the parapets, always waiting for the products that we send them, which they cannot be without under any pretext, as it is they who have the greatest right to be assisted. Thus, if a strike is called, it will have negative repercussions on the fighting comrades.

But it seems that this misrepresentation of the prisoners issue convinced no one, and the next item up for discussion was the matter of weapons: 'The National Committee says that in order for the government to send arms to the front, the weapons in the hands of the unions must also go to the front.' Regarding aggression on the part of the security forces, 'it is resolved that the agreements concluded between the armed forces and the CNT must be honoured.' (*Fragua Social*, 16–20 March 1937.)

The National Committee's fire-fighting attitude and the types of arguments wielded by it during the Peasant Plenum disappointed the militants, and verified to them that their own organisation was handing them over, unarmed, to the enemy. The results favoured the repression, and soon after the congress the Carcaixent, Benaguacil, Cullera, Catarroja and Utiel collectives were attacked in a foretaste of an all-out drive against collectives that would reach every village—without exception—by the end of the year. It was the end of the revolution.

The prisoners were not released as promptly as the Plenum was told they would be by the commission that met with the government authorities. The second Regional Congress of the CNT in Levante, which took place in Alicante during the month of July, declared that the Vinalesa events were already resolved. But at its opening session, a communique from the prisoners at Valencia's Modelo prison was read:

> Upon learning of the Plenum, the prisoners wish to remind the comrades in attendance of the motives behind their

incarceration, and they also want to remind those gathered there that their sessions should be as concrete as possible so that their agreements can be put into practice without delay. In addition, they ask that not only economic issues be addressed, but also moral issues and demands.

Next, a list of the imprisoned comrades is read, among which are found the comrades from the Real de Montroy collective in Llombay, as well as members of various FAI groups and the Iron Column. (*Liberación*, 16 July 1937.)

Ironically, the proposal that was to be put into effect without delay—as agreed to by the Plenum—amounted to the categorical recognition of the necessity of intervening in politics and in all the agencies of the state, including, of course, the prisons.

The assaults on the collectives and the persecution of those libertarian militants prominent within them thus represented the other face of militarisation.

As for the columns, the Torres-Benedito and the Iberia Columns comprised the Eighty-first Mixed Brigade. Together with the Eighty-third Brigade formed by the Iron Column, these were made part of the Forty-first Division commanded by the pro-Communist Colonel Eixea. The Ruesca-Taino Battalion, which was a column of anarcho-syndicalists from Alcoy commanded by Camilo Bito, had come to the front between December and February at the request of the Iron Column's War Committee. It was amalgamated with the dissidents from the First Division of the Iron Column—who had accepted militarisation along with Rufino Rodríguez and Hermosillo—and with a POUM battalion to form the Eighty-second Mixed Brigade of the Fortieth Division. The Courage and Rebelliousness Column, which was formed by anarchists from Valencia in December before being added to the Iron Column, was split into two battalions: one was sent to the Jarama front, where it was dissolved after rejecting militarisation; the other, together with the former Peire Column, formed the Eighty-fourth Mixed Brigade of the Fortieth Division under the command of another pro-Communist. In all likelihood, CNT Column Thirteen did not form its own brigade. Its leader, Santiago Tronchoni, was named major of militias and sent to Ciudad Libre in order to assume command of the 215th Brigade, which was formed by a conscription of reservists.

These four Brigades participated in the battle for Teruel. During the first Francoist counter-attacks in December 1937, a disorganised Eighty-first was defeated while defending Campillo, southwest of Teruel. The Eighty-fourth, after exhausting itself in combat, was sent to the front lines instead of being relieved. Its soldiers mutinied. At the time (20 January 1938), its Communist commander, Major Nieto, ordered the shooting of forty-six of them and the summary trial of a further hundred. The Brigade was disbanded. The Eighty-second was completely annihilated in the battle for Alfambra during January and February 1938.

The Eighty-third Mixed Brigade had its share of ups and downs throughout the war. After militarisation, it was disarmed and transferred to Vinaroz for training. Personnel under the age of twenty or over the age of thirty-five were discharged. At least four hundred members were jailed for opposing their transfer to other units. In addition, twenty men from the Column were arrested in Villahermosa and imprisoned in Castellón in June.

This was all part of the policy of the Communists, who were then dominant within the army. They looked for easy victories that they could exploit politically, and they used forces adhering to other ideologies as cannon-fodder. During the battle of Albarracin, the Eighty-third was sent to the front without any artillery or aerial support, yet it still captured Torres in July 1937 before it was exposed on its left flank and had to retreat to Terriente.

The Communist commanders of the army ordered that the Eighty-third be disarmed and disbanded, but in the end it was transferred to the Sixty-fourth Division commanded by the Communist Martínez Carton, and it fought in the battle for Teruel. There it participated in strategic manoeuvres designed to surround Teruel, and it conquered positions in Primer Vallejo, Campillo and Los Morrones before linking up with the Twenty-second Army Corps and digging in to defend those positions. It fought with such courage that it was congratulated by the General Staff and the Commissariat. Battalion commissars Lorenzo Robles and Pedro Pellicer were applauded for their 'energy and valour.'

In January 1938, the Brigade returned to barracks in the rearguard, joining the Forty-first Division—this time with anarchist commanders—in April. During the nationalists' attack on Levante, it defended the sector between Ares del Maestre and Llamas in the province of Castellón, sustaining heavy losses in the process. Reorganised in August, it was added to the Seventy-third Division. In March 1939 it was on reserve duty in Valencia but went to Madrid in order to assist Mera and Casado in suffocating the Communist insurrection. It fought inside the city and was later posted to Alcalá de Henares. Which is where it was overtaken by the ending of the war. Its last commander was Francesc Mares, who was shot in Barcelona in 1939.

THE PLENUM OF CONFEDERAL AND ANARCHIST COLUMNS

Present with the appropriate credentials are delegations from the Tierra y Libertad, Durruti, Andalucía and Extremadura Columns, Valdepeñas and Manzanares Sectors, Francisco Ascaso, Iberia and Iron Columns. These are joined by delegations without credentials from the confederal militias of the centre: the Ortiz Column, the Courage and Rebelliousness Column and CNT Column Thirteen. (p. 1)

The Plenum opens at 10:30 a.m. and comrade Pellicer from the Iron Column starts the proceedings: 'As you will have read in the circular, in Valencia there was meeting of the Levante columns along with the Maroto Column, and in view of the need for a general exchange of impressions, the idea emerged of holding this Plenum for the purpose of liaising with those who were unable to attend [the Valencia meeting].' (p. 3)

[Extracts from the circular]: We are only emphasising the fact that, in these times of heroism and tragedy on the front and frivolity and nonchalance in the rearguard, an enormous number of agreements have been reached by all types of committees, organisations and parties. These agreements were probably reached with revolutionary effectiveness in mind, but they suffer from a great defect: it never occurred to anyone to ask the *opinion of the fighters.*

This is unforgivable; even more so when we who are actually defending Iberian soil do so with the more or less defined intention, in each column, of creating a new way of life. It is clear that we belong to organisations that have countless delegates assigned to every imaginable committee. But there is one overwhelming and indisputable reality: *in the rearguard at this time, revolutionary consciousness seems to have been forgotten...*

We are not going to present an extensive agenda. Once we are gathered together and each column has explained its problems, those problems that are considered important can be discussed. Thus, we offer only two points for your consideration:

1. The attitude of the columns towards the mobilisation decree.
2. Liaison amongst the columns...

We look forward to your fraternal attendance.

On behalf of the Committee,

The Iron Column (pp. 6–8)

Pellicer, from the Iron Column, says: 'We are not going to retell the history of what has happened to us and what is happening to everyone, as we believe that would be unnecessary. We believe that the state's boycott must end, and we should express our disagreement with the fact that the CNT and FAI columns not being properly attended to on any front.

'We were briefed by some comrades who went to Cartagena— and it was about time—on the enormous quantity of weapons being unloaded at that port, while some months later there are still columns fighting with shotguns in Andalusia.

'The state is surrounding itself and consolidating itself with forces magnificently equipped with arms and uniforms, both of which we lack.

'We should accuse the responsible organisations as well as ourselves, since it is our fault that our best elements are at the front while social climbers are left to sit comfortably on the organisational committees and work against the progress of those very organisations. We told and repeated all this to the organisation—which did not do anything— to the point that we were almost convinced that we were isolated. But upon hearing from comrades in other columns who found themselves in the same situation, we harbour the hope that the feeling that has always underpinned our actions in the CNT and the FAI may yet flood back, and all the standards of freedom prevail. (p. 9)

'There has been a lot of talk about militarisation, with the argument being made that the militias are running away [from battle]. Those who make this argument should not forget that whenever our militias run away from some front, the soldiers with all their commanders and officers already have a three kilometre head start.

'It is also repeated too insistently that there is an intolerable lack of technical personnel and iron discipline, both of which would compel the militians to conduct themselves more courageously.

'We are not stubborn enemies of technique, but those who make such boasts should know that in Spain the soldiers who have not mutinied have failed to do so out of either cowardice or simple lack of opportunity. This is true in the majority of cases. Of course, let us not forget that there are cases of military comrades whose more or less liberal education attracted them to our side during the first days of fighting, and let no one dispute this, for there were some in our column.

'But do you know what the High Command did with them? When it saw that they sympathised too much with certain comrades, it replaced them and forced them into bureaucratic positions, just as it has done with us. And in light of this mere affirmation of a lack of technical personnel, are we going to swallow the so-called expertise of trumped-up officers fabricated wholesale over a couple of weeks in some military academy?

'We cannot deceive ourselves, for it is clear to all of us all that the lowliest of our century delegates knows more about war than the cleverest of these officers.

'And let us talk about discipline, upon the absence of which it looks as if everybody has agreed to preach to all and sundry. To compare our militians to the fascists, on the grounds that the latter coax their men at gunpoint, is to choose to ignore things as important as the ideas and the courage by which our men are driven, and which the others have none of.

'Furthermore, let us make a categorical statement: if our success in the war is contingent upon every seven or eight comrades having a pistol at their backs, then we can say right now that we have lost the war...

'The political parties have always hated us and propagandised against us. But we were the ones who—in defiance of the CNT—destroyed the property register, burned the files, disarmed the Civil Guard and forced the Assault Guards and Security Guards to go to the front.

'Our aim was always to cleanse the rearguard of filth. The government knows that those in the Iron Column are the only ones capable of cleaning up Levante, and this is why it denies us arms. (pp. 10–11)

'With regard to Levante, the CNT has played a dirty game, trifling with the committees, and it was these committees that voted for militarisation even though the last Regional Plenum of Unions voted the other way.

'We are not bad-mouthing our CNT, which we cherish as much as anyone else. We are speaking out against the committees that are ruining its reputation.' (p. 12)

[Ascaso Column delegate]: 'The Ascaso Column has experienced what all the confederal columns have experienced. Most of the issues that the Iron Column has raised also apply to us.

'We put it directly to the Catalonia Regional Committee, the CNT Defence Committee and the specific organisations that we have been sabotaged. No one today can doubt this. [They did not supply us] with anything we needed for winning the war, and things have taken such a turn that I even suspect there are those among us who purposefully cause us trouble every time we are at the front...

'We are being sabotaged. The Ascaso Division is just now discovering this fact, yet things are the same as ever: much intervention by Russian military officers who take meddle in the practicalities of war. But with regard to this, I must repeat a phrase I uttered just a few days ago: "Many Russians, but very little gear from Russia." (p. 15)

'The war must be won before the revolution. We needed to prepare ourselves for that fact, but we still did not have sufficient forces at the time. We should have been thinking about whether we were making the revolution on our own or with the collaboration of others. We were under-resourced and we agreed to collaboration in order to defeat fascism, and that is what is fundamental in the first place, so that we can make revolution later.' (p. 16)

[Ortiz Column delegate]: 'Our failure to achieve more victories is not due to a lack of discipline. Rather, it is because we faced no serious enemies until we reached Belchite, and we therefore stopped to rest on our laurels, because Aragón is the only place where we have not lost ground and where we are not currently losing ground...

'We should do the impossible in order to break out of their encirclement and ensure that this victory is a genuine one. Let us look for our own weapons, because I have already lost hope that Russia or anyone else will supply them to us.

'Either we of the CNT-FAI will win, or those antifascists who are seemingly waging the war together with us will win. If any of the others win, then they will immediately lash out at us. We have to build up our strength on all fronts and never abandon those fronts.' (p. 17)

The delegate from CNT Column Thirteen takes the floor: 'Our Column has chosen reorganisation and militarisation because we have learned from experience that one cannot play at making war on the front lines. We have observed—though it pains us to say so—that when the time comes to face enemy fire, a hundred or so cowards get sick and give a thousand excuses for turning back, and no ideological factor has made the slightest difference to this.

'In view of such conduct, I issue the passes myself for their return, and in huge capital letters I write "SICK FROM PANIC," and they shamelessly display these passes on their journey back. Now we must look for a way to ensure that nobody turns back under any pretext. It is no longer voluntary: we either throw ourselves into the war or we allow ourselves to be defeated by the war.

'During the attack on Teruel, CNT Column Thirteen failed to achieve its objective—just like the Del Rosal Column—for the reasons cited: because every volunteer did what he wanted to do. We all moan about the number of cowards and jumped-up types in the rearguard, and the responsibility for this lies with us.

'We must create a climate in which every man goes to the front to do his duty and no one shirks danger.

'It is for these reasons that we have accepted militarisation: so that we can be sure that if a thousand of us go to the front, a thousand of us will be obliged to do our duty.' (pp. 17–18)

[Iberia Column delegate]: 'We accept a sole command, we accept iron discipline and we will shoot anyone who abandons the front. But we do not accept someone who sits behind a desk and wants to direct us from there without putting himself in danger...

'I agree that our Moors and those who are strutting about the place be required to go to the front lines.[5] And the requirement should not come from the government, but from ourselves, forcing them to go, because one must fight or work if one wants to eat, yet these people do neither.' (pp. 19–20)

The delegate from the National Committee takes the floor and protests that the National Committee was not notified of the meeting. Comrade chairman Pellicer replied that that did not alter the fact that there had been no intention of the meeting's proceeding without him.

The delegate from the National Committee goes on to say: 'It is easy to condemn the Committee. When the Committee accepted militarisation, it was not imposed on anybody. Let that be well understood.

'It [accepted militarisation] in accordance with a Plenum of Regional Committees.

'If an agreement has been reached, then it should be made public. The fault lies with those who exceeded their mandate and gave their approval to something by attending a National Plenum on flimsy authority.

'I must say that yours truly petitioned the minister of war for weapons. We have done everything possible in order to obtain arms, and Largo Caballero has said loud and clear: "*How can I give you machine-guns when I know you won't return them?*"

'The CNT has no other weapons besides those taken from the barracks at the very beginning, and García Oliver himself tendered his resignation from the War Council because he disagrees with Largo Caballero's sabotaging of our forces, especially in Catalonia.

'But the government refuses to take this on board, or is not competent to procure them for itself.

'Militarisation is an accord stemming from a National Plenum of

---

5 "Franco employed Moroccans—"moros"—as shock troops. These men had no choice in the matter they were 'colonials' and therefore expendable cannon fodder. I do not know if it was Garcia Oliver, or Peiro, an anarchist minister at the time (for whatever that is worth!) who declared that the CNT-FAI had suffered too many losses and would, therefore, have to fall back on the *moros* or nonpoliticised in the Republican sector (those who had not volunteered for the militias), but certainly Mera protested vigorously against this anti-anarchist mentality." Frank Mintz, *Cienfuegos Press Anarchist Review* 2, p37 in a review of *Guerra, exilio y carcel de un anarcosyndicalista* by Cipriano Mera. [KSL]

Regionals. It was agreed to because we saw that columns with Communists in positions of command were superbly equipped, while our equipment was deteriorating with every day that passed.

'I personally asked Largo Caballero why this was so, and he responded that it was because the confederal forces did not want to be organised into brigades and that the government had lost confidence in the militias. "The state's arms are for the state's forces," he told me, "and if you do not want to join us, then let your own organisations give you weapons."

'There was no other recourse but to storm the site where the arms were stored. But reflect upon the implications of such an action; reflect upon the effect it might have had, and how it could have given rise to fascism finding in our troubles the perfect moment to take advantage of our weakness and secure its victory.

'We accept militarisation, but let the record show that we will not accept Communists and socialists in positions of command, as these positions should be occupied by our militants.

'What is lacking are *Moors*. They must be pressed into service, and let us not argue over whether we should or should not accept this or that type.' (pp. 21–22)

The delegate from the militias of the centre says: 'There have been lots of expressions backing up my earlier wish that this gathering should have had official status.

'I would have liked that so I could have shamed [the National Committee] over its flight from Madrid, its lack of virility and the current political chaos it has caused, since it fled Madrid even before the government.

'There were no more than two or three hundred CNT militants who stopped fascism in Madrid, and our National Committee offered no other solution besides flight. [Its members were] fearful that bombs might fall on them and kill them, as if their lives were more precious than the life any other militant.

'Allow me to also tell you that we should not call a section of our people "MOORS," as we have no right to do so. We ourselves would have censured such talk had it not come from the mouth of a CNT minister, for which reason we all now use the word.

'But I repeat that calling some brothers of ours "Moors" is contrary to our principles.

'Experience has taught me that if we militias continue to fight as we have been, the result would be a huge failure, because we no longer have the self-discipline we had at the beginning of the war. The instinct of self-preservation is stronger than we are.

'The dangers of war overwhelm the individual, and self-discipline is reduced to zero. Militants of action, upon seeing the cruelty of real war, complained about it and lost all fighting spirit. In light of all these considerations, the centre region believed that the time was right to take a new approach to the structure of the confederal forces, given the failure of the militias.'

The delegate concludes by invoking comrade Durruti's words about the cruelty of war and the need to have weaponry equal to or superior to the enemy's.

Comrade Mera then explains the necessity of iron discipline; remarks to which Durruti once replied: '*Perhaps you are right. Let us talk about that soon.*'

Mera describes the incidents that occurred at the Clinical Hospital and talks about the circumstances that led certain comrades to accept strong discipline in an organisational sense, rather than in a barracks sense. He says that discipline should begin in the committees, and that it is unacceptable that discipline is only expected of the militian while the committees do what they like without consulting the comrades concerned.

By way of an example, he talks about an offer from the commissar-general, which he rejected on the grounds that it did not go through the proper channels. He concludes by reiterating that it is up to the committees to set an example in terms of discipline. (pp. 23–24)

The delegate from the Tierra y Libertad Column says: 'At the beginning we accepted militarisation. But today, in light of events, we are going to have to go back on our word because the facts do not correspond to what we were offered by the Catalan Regional.

'In order to thoroughly address this matter, we convened an assembly of our Column, and the general feeling among the comrades was against militarisation. This was proven by the fact that half of our complement of men—more than 143 of them—said that the comrade who is overwhelmed by panic would still be overwhelmed whether he was called a soldier or a militian.' (p. 26)

Comrade Collado from the Durruti Column takes the floor. He begins by recalling some words spoken by comrade Mera regarding the National Committee's transfer from Madrid to Valencia, before continuing: 'The Durruti Column left Barcelona for Aragón in a truck carrying just thirty-seven comrades, yet we were able to defeat the fascists all the way from Barcelona to Pina, at which point we encountered an airplane that made us retreat forty-eight kilometres. Had we been experienced in warfare, that would not have happened, nor would five of our most beloved comrades have been killed by the shelling.

'We are not going to accept militarisation, for in the army you would never see the corporals, sergeants, lieutenants and captains being appointed by the men who compose said army. Yet we do that. Consequently, the issue is not militarisation, but rather a military-style structure. We do not accept the assignment of ranks to those who would take pleasure in commanding, though we do accept company and battalion delegates...

'If we were to give those who oppose militarisation the stars of which they are so critical, I am certain that—with very few exceptions—they would not abandon the front no matter how much militarisation the militias were subjected to.' (pp. 27–28)

Raquel Castro takes the floor: 'In reference to the first air raid mentioned by the comrade who spoke before me—a raid in which we members of the Durruti Column were the victims—I must say that lack of battle experience did not play a part. On the contrary, the fault lay with Farrás, who was our drunken military consultant at the time.'

Collado protests the remark. (p. 29)

The comrade chairman says: 'Since a Plenum of Regionals is scheduled for tomorrow, it would make sense to keep that Plenum informed by sending it the minutes of this Plenum of Columns. Therefore, I propose that the Plenum of Regionals be rescheduled for the day after tomorrow.'

Comrade Mera expresses his disagreement on the grounds that assuredly not all of the delegations were in attendance yet.

The comrade chairman insists on his proposal due to the indisputable significance of the current meeting...

Comrade Mera takes great pains to ask that the record reflect his request that the Regional Committee meeting be held tomorrow. (pp. 31–32)

Third session: The proceedings open at 10:40 p.m. under the chairmanship of comrade Val. During a visit to the Plenum of Regionals, comrade Val had arranged for the Plenum of Regionals to appoint a delegate commission to come to us instead of a delegation from the Plenum of Columns going to them, and that delegation is now present...

The Iron Column delegate makes some comments to the effect that the poor delegation sent by the Plenum of Regionals is inadequate for the discussion of such a momentous issue at a meeting that could be called HISTORIC, and upon which depends the future vitality of the anarchist columns.

The representative from the Plenum of Regionals asks that note be taken of his objection to the use of the description 'poor,' at which comrade Pellicer—from the very same Iron Column—elaborates: 'Adjectives should be taken in the spirit in which they were intended. There can be no doubt—and all will have understood this—that when my comrade delegate used the word "poor" he was not referring to any deficiency on the part of the comrades in the delegation, but was rather referring to the small size of said delegation, given the understanding that all the Regionals should be attending a plenum like ours.'

The delegation from the Plenum of Regionals declares that the plenum has assumed that it was empowered to pass resolutions and intervene in the matter offered for discussion, despite the gathering's being unlawful.

Comrade Pellicer says: 'The least that can be asked of the delegation from the Plenum of Regionals is that it not make comments of that nature, keeping in mind that the CNT has not taken care of the columns at all for quite some time, and therefore we have had to call upon ourselves to put an end to such an abnormal situation.'

The delegate from the Ortiz Column says: 'Let the record reflect my protest at what the delegation from the Plenum of Regionals is saying. Having not been consulted, the columns have a duty to protest any militarisation implemented without prior discussion, the aim of which militarisation is to negate the strength that the columns could or should have at the front.' (pp. 33–34)

The National Committee delegate intervenes: 'I wish to put things in their proper perspective. It is not possible to go to such extremes, and it is the duty of all to realise the organisational forms that correspond to our aspirations. Instead of creating discrepancies amongst ourselves, we must make such discrepancies disappear. This meeting should never have taken place, for it is completely abnormal and irregular, and I want to stress those descriptions as they apply to this meeting…

'You have given the impression that the CNT is divided. The controversies were created by the Iron Column when it issued a circular from the periphery of the CNT and without the authorisation of the CNT. I ask that the record reflect this.

'I want to harmonise all of our interests. If I had my way, the National Committee would stand in for the combatants on the various fronts, and that would not be a novelty for me, as I was on those fronts and I plan to return to them. We thus accept this irregular *fait accompli*, which was provoked by the Iron Column's use of a procedure that has very little honour about it.' (pp. 34–35)

Comrade Jover says: 'To me it is an insult that the entire Plenum of Regionals is not in attendance, and this can only be remedied if the National Committee invites us to a new plenum. Otherwise, let us withdraw and break with our organisations, as thus far—for whatever reasons—they have utterly neglected us, and this negligence should deprive them of the right to come listen to us.' (p. 35)

[Roda, from the Durruti Column]: 'We attended this meeting in the belief that it was sanctioned by our organisation, and we believe that this discrepancy—given the effect it could have—should not go beyond these walls, and that the disputes should be smoothed over.' (p. 36)

[Pellicer, from the Iron Column]: 'We cannot consent to the conduct of these committees. According to their criteria, the Column would have to be dissolved and we would be obliged to impose ideas about militarisation that clash completely with our own ideology. When we revealed ourselves to be against militarisation, the solution imposed on us with the option of surrendering our arms and being relieved, which we felt was out of order. Our Column believed in the right to defend itself from a situation created by other political columns. We repeat: voluntarily or not, the National Committee has played the state's game…

'In addition, we are being compelled to give up weapons that we captured first from the barracks and later on the front lines, at the cost of much blood spilled and the sight of our best comrades cut down forever. We would find it natural if it was the state that was attempting this, but for our own organisation to suicidally destroy its own forces seems barbaric to us. We have tried to make the National Committee see the error of its ways in departing from its confederal principles. We thought it displayed reluctance or (worse still) indifference that we were called here to be briefed on what was happening and thus to come away with a rough impression.

'In addition to our being Confederation members, we—as columnists with our own personalities—want to make it very clear that we are neither below nor above the committees. But we will not be overwhelmed by the trick of majority agreement used by these committees. We do not want to hear personal justifications given in a pathetic, weepy tone. We simply want a certain committee to explain itself and to stop insisting that the Iron Column embrace representation that it does not respect.' (pp. 38–40)

Comrade Mera, from the confederal militias delegation, says: 'When the delegations from the centre were summoned, we had taken it for granted that this was a Plenum convened by the Iron Column.

'Upon leaving our locale in order to come to Valencia with the delegation, I remember my comrades and I commenting on whether the Iron Column had the good sense to invite the National Committee and the Regional Committees.

'Yesterday we saw that this was not the case, and for that reason we said that their absence was tantamount to a conspiracy, as it was our understanding that we had to resolve our problems together with our organisations.

'I say this as a delegate, but now I will speak in a personal capacity—as comrade Mera—and ask the Committee if it thought to consult the comrades on the front in a confederal way, as it should have; not just with regard to the serious problem of militarisation, but also with regard to its own ministers entering the government, and other problems.

'In view of all this, and since it has not taken even the slightest account of us, the National Committee has no right to say that this meeting is abnormal or irregular or anything of the sort. If what has not been done has not been done thus far, then it is imperative that it gets done. The Committee has behaved in an anticonfederal manner by not discussing problems with the unions and by imposing its accords on the front-line comrades in a dictatorial way, without any consultation; accords that they resolve internally among themselves like friends, in what we could call a casual way. If the youngest son, as a minor, does not have the right to meet with his brother without the father's permission, then the father should first take an interest in how his sons are doing in the trenches.

'The National Committee and the Regional Committees are thinking in ways that are strangling the revolution, and this should not be hidden from the combatants.

'Let us accept what we might call 'AUDACITY' and acknowledge militarisation. But we object to the organisation making us swallow something just because a minister wants it, and I will say it clearly: I could not care less about the organisation in this case. This I say as Mera.'

The delegate from the National Plenum says:

'I have listened to you with the greatest bitterness, and watched as you heaped all your criticism upon us, and I tell you frankly that if the solution to the entire problem posed by the Plenum is to shoot the National Committee, then shoot it, even if this position could be called maudlin by some.

'Let the record show that I did not use, nor did it occur to me to use, the description "illegal meeting." The words used were "abnormal" and "irregular." What the Committee does not want to consent to is the division currently taking place.

'The National Committee issued a confidential circular to the Regionals and to the comrades at the front in order to glean their opinions, and within twenty-four hours a copy of that confidential circular was in the hands of Largo Caballero. How could it have come into his possession? This is just one of the fifty thousand problems that the organisation has to deal with.

'The confederal family should at all times be in harmony, because that is how we will defeat the enemy. But if we are divided, then I do not even want to think about what might happen. I accept the possibility that errors have been committed, but at times like this one should remember that the enemy is on the front and in the rearguard, and he is creating constant difficulties for us.' (pp. 40–42)

[Extremadura-Andalucía Column delegate]: 'These acts of provocation, which began with several actions directed against Carlos Zimmerman, were brought to the attention of the military authorities, since we—despite advising our men to be prudent—would not have been able to respond if at any time our men mutinied in the face of such unacceptable acts.

'A telegram was sent in which we inquired if there was some grudge against us and in which we asked for instructions on how to avoid a mutiny. Comrade González Inestal responded that there was no grudge against us, and his proposed solution to our problem was that we leave the jurisdiction, which only led to more abuse directed against us.

'The National Committee's response was that it had assumed its functions on 20 November last and had no knowledge of the two communiques being referred to, which communiques surely would have reached the previous National Committee. It also emphasised that it was taking over from a Committee that had been completely disorganised, with no archives or anything of the sort.' (pp. 47–48)

The delegate from the Del Rosal Column asks if the brigades would be completely our own or whether, on the contrary, they would be mixed. The National Committee delegate replies that this point still has not been clarified, but that it is clear to the National Committee that if we form brigades, they will be absolutely ours.

Comrade Mera says: 'On the first point, militarisation, we are agreed. But we should militarise along fully confederal lines. We should militarise ourselves through our organisation into homogenous, confederated militias. A battalion of ours among other Marxist battalions, with a Marxist commander, would spell the death of the CNT. Likewise, two battalions of ours and two Marxist battalions, with the same commander, would also spell the death of the CNT, as we can see in practice. (p. 50)

'Everything that was said yesterday is being repeated today. I say that if those who are in Aragón were in Madrid, they would change their opinion. We see that we lack the discipline required to achieve good results from the war; discipline that would oblige the militian to remain at his post rather than abandon it at a decisive moment due to the self-preservation instinct.

'None of us here can demonstrate the disciplined deployment of his personnel. If we must wage war, then we must wage it with military discipline. One does not argue with one's commander, but there also should be no argument when that commander is guilty of mismanagement: two bullets should do the trick. There is no room for sentiment in war.' (p. 55)

Comrade Raquel Castro asks whether the National Committee would be able to guarantee the delivery of arms if militarisation is accepted, and whether it would be able to guarantee that what happened elsewhere—no arms forthcoming after the acceptance of militarisation—would not happen again. The National Committee replies: 'Our duty is to our organisation and we cannot guarantee anything, but we assure you that we would make every effort to achieve the desired results.' (p. 58)

[CNT-FAI, *Acta Del Pleno de Columnas Confederales y Anarquistas* (Valencia, 5–8 February 1937, 63 pages—page numbers reference placement in original document) as reprinted in Frank Mintz, *La Autogestión en la España Revolucionaria* (Madrid: Ediciones La Piqueta, 1977), 295–308.]

Dossier on Gino Bibbi

Gino Bibbi was born in Carrara, Italy, in 1903. He studied aeronaval engineering at the University of Milan, where he came into direct contact with anarchist militants, and at that point his activity as a militant within the Italian anarchist movement began.

Following Mussolini's coup d'état in 1922, Bibbi was jailed in 1923 for distributing antifascist leaflets. But he managed to escape from prison, and after various ups and downs he took refuge in France, where he joined a group of Italian anarchists who were continuing their struggle against fascism from that country.

In 1931, upon the proclamation of the Republic in Spain, Bibbi travelled there in order to support the activities being undertaken by the CNT and the FAI.

In the FAI there was an anarchist group that was planning to liberate Malatesta from Mussolini's clutches. The plan was to smuggle Malatesta out of the coastal district where he was confined, and thus a launch with a high-speed engine was required. Gino Bibbi undertook to build such an engine. While he was working on this project, a leak reached the ears of one of Mussolini's police agents, which resulted in Malatesta being relocated to Rome. This put paid to the escape plan, and was perhaps one of the factors that hastened the death of the veteran Italian anarchist in 1932.

Once the military uprising happened in Spain, Gino Bibbi placed himself at the disposal of the Comité Central de Milicias de Cataluña (Central Militias Committee of Catalonia—CCMC), where he worked alongside García Oliver, who was then serving as the secretary of the Committee's War Department. Bibbi played an effective role in organising the war industry launched by the CNT under the auspices of the CCMC.

He used his aero-naval engineering knowledge to create a remote-controlled rocket-launching apparatus, the initial trials of which achieved a range of twenty kilometres. With the dissolution of the CCMC on 1 October 1936, Gino Bibbi's work was interrupted, but that did not stop the Durruti Column from using a prototype of the device to bombard the Francoist lines.

Facing the government's boycott of the confederal columns, especially the Iron Column, the latter organised several raids on jewellery shops in the city of Valencia for the purpose of amassing a war chest with which to acquire war material and raw materials for the collectives. Gino Bibbi was entrusted with the task of purchasing from abroad the sorely needed materials for the war as well as for industry.

While engaged in this work in January 1937, he was arrested by the Stalinist police, who charged him with currency smuggling. In order to hinder this Communist intrigue and free Gino Bibbi from prison, Minister of Justice García Oliver—who represented the CNT in the Caballero government—had to intervene. The dossier that was compiled in order to clarify the matter of the charges brought against Gino Bibbi contained the letters and documents that we reprint below.

At the end of the war in Spain, Bibbi became one of the half-million exiles in France, where he was interned in the Gurs concentration camp until the outbreak of the Second World War in 1939. He escaped from the camp and wandered around France until the German occupation. Then he joined the French resistance and, much later, was able to enter Italy in order to fight the Nazis. He was one of the partisans who liberated Carrara. Later on, he continued his militancy by participating in different anarchist activities throughout his country.

Statement of Gino Bibbi

I, Gino Bibbi, declare and confirm that (in the presence of Enrique Maciá) in Paris, I received from Pablo Rada the sum of two-and-a-half million francs in several instalments, as follows:

On the first occasion, I received five-hundred thousand francs, which I placed at the disposal of the Gandía District Committee in Paris for the purchase of items unknown to me.

The second sum totalled one million francs, which I handed over in the presence of Maciá and Pablo Rada to Paul Jouhaux for the purchase of arms, which could not be made due to Jouhaux's arrest at the Franco-Belgian border.

Much later I received another instalment of five-hundred thousand francs, which I delivered to a number of distinct entities for the purchase of agricultural and food products.

And lastly I received yet another five-hundred thousand francs, which I handed over to Giopp for the realisation of the maritime explosives project. I am unaware of the uses to which said sum may have been put to date.

Likewise, I declare that I have had no recent contact with Facchinetti.

Valencia, 23 March 1937
Signed: Gino Bibbi

Levante Regional Peasant Federation (CNT-AIT)

Valencia

This Levante Regional Peasant Federation hereby confirms that it received foodstuffs and other commodities from Paris valued at five-hundred thousand francs, which was delivered to us by comrade Gino Bibbi.

Everything received has been handed over to the columns operating on the front and used for social assistance purposes.
Valencia, 30 March 1937
On behalf of the Committee: (signature illegible)

Gandía District Committee (CNT-AIT-FAI)

Gandía, 31 March 1937
Head Office: Plaza de la Revolución
War material from Paris was sent to this District Committee through some comrades to whom comrade GINO BIBBI delivered five-hundred thousand francs.

This District Committee, as it was receiving the material, passed it on to the columns operating on the front. We are attaching to this note a copy of the receipts in our possession from the IRON COLUMN and the CONFEDERAL COLUMN.

We hope that this note serves to clarify the sum that comrade BIBBI claimed he delivered for this purpose.

On behalf of the District Committee: Bernardo Merino

Gandía District Committee (CNT-AIT-FAI)

Gandía, 31 March 1937
Head Office: Plaza de la Revolución

LIST OF WAR MATERIAL DELIVERED BY THIS DISTRICT COMMITTEE TO THE 'CONFEDERAL COLUMN'
500 Lafitte bombs
6000 detonators
50 trench mirrors
3 field range finders
7 field telephones
40 field telegraphs
40 field lamps
20 batteries for telegraphs
2000 bullets; various calibres

1 mortar; 7.5 calibre
20 rifles; various makes
150 standard rifles
3 machine-guns
2 automatic rifles
2 antitank guns
2000 rifle cartridges
300 grenades

> On behalf of the District Committee: Bernardo Merino

Gandía District Committee (CNT-AIT-FAI)

Gandía, 31 March 1937
Head Office: Plaza de la Revolución
On 24 December this District Committee handed over to the IRON COLUMN the material listed below, which was received by this District Committee from Paris and acquired with funds delivered for this purpose by comrade GINO BIBBI. The sum amounted to five-hundred thousand francs.

LIST OF WAR MATERIAL
180 rifles
30 hunting rifles
6 carbines
5 automatic rifles
3 machine-guns
12,000 rifle cartridges
500 shock grenades
400 Lafitte bombs
7,000 detonators
1 mortar; .50 calibre
12 pistols; various calibres
300 pistol cartridges
10 field telephones
3 kilometres of telephone wire

> Bernardo Merino

Cooperative Nationale de Reboisement

The undersigned, Paul Jouhaux, acknowledges having received one million French francs from comrade Gino Bibbi, who is a member of the CNT-FAI's Gandía District Committee.

This sum was destined for the purchase of war materials and for the cause of the government of the Spanish Republic.

This declaration has been made at the behest of comrade Giobbe Giopp, who came from Valencia to declare that the Valencia government's minister of justice, comrade García Oliver, required such record of receipt in order to confirm comrade Bibbi's statement.

Issued on this 8 April 1937 in Paris.

Paris, 9 April 1937

I hereby declare having received, on behalf of the Antifascist Republican Action Committee, the sum of five-hundred thousand francs from the Committee represented by Messrs. Raa, Meziat and Bibbi. The sum has been sent and entrusted to me in order to be used, under my supervision, for actions in support of the republican cause in Spain.

This confidential declaration has been labelled as personal information and addressed by me to Mr. García Oliver, minister within the Spanish government.

Cipriano Facchinetti

Paris, 10 April 1937

Mr. García OLIVER
Minister of Justice
Valencia
Mr. Minister,

Please find enclosed the two declarations that confirm Gino BIBBI's statement, in accordance with the declaration made to me in Barcelona by Mr. Salvado, secretary of the Levante Peasant Federation, following his talk with you.

With my most distinguished regards, Mr. Minister,

Eng. Giobbe Giopp

NATIONAL CONFEDERATION OF LABOUR (FAI)

Foreign Propaganda Office
Barcelona, 10 April 1937
I HEREBY DECLARE:
That in the month of January 1937, comrade Gino Bibbi entrusted me with the sum of HALF A MILLION FRENCH FRANCS in Paris for delivery to the Italian Revolutionary Committee, which delivery I made at the same time as I disclosed the purpose of said sum, which was for the defence of antifascist Spain.

Camillo Berneri

In Memory of José Pellicer

José Pellicer Gandía was born in Valencia on 28 April 1912 and was executed in Paterna on 8 June 1942. He was a typist by trade, and he joined the CNT in 1932.

The two documents that follow, while radically different in nature, are of equal interest to the extent that each one bears witness in its own way to the dignity, intransigence and obstinacy of a CNT militant who was one of the leading figures in the Iron Column.

The verdict of the fascist court martial is, in terms of its terrible brutality and the stilted language of state justice (in this case military-fascist), an unwittingly authentic tribute to a libertarian revolutionary who never gave up.

The letter from José Escrig Ivars testifies—as if it were needed—to the seriousness and determination of all those libertarian militants who knew, without ambiguity, what they wanted: the collective, egalitarian management of all aspects of social and economic life. And they attempted to provide themselves with the necessary means to that end. Enthusiastically and methodically, they threw themselves into the construction of a new world in opposition to its traditional owners, but also in opposition to all the 'republican' parties, who were above all anxious to suffocate the revolution. José Escrig Ivars was assuredly on the latter side of the fence, but his testimony cannot be regarded as simply circumstantial, and it becomes all the more precious when one realises that within it we find the remarks of a militant of a decidedly Leninist persuasion.

Extract from the verdict of the court martial

Don Manuel Romero Bueno, a lieutenant in the Corps of Engineers and the clerk of Standing Court Martial No. 1 in this jurisdiction, where the examining magistrate is Infantry Major Don Pedro de Tomás Giménez, hereby certifies that Court Report No. 6981-V-39 contains the fragments reproduced word-for-word below, which state the following:

Ruling:

In the Valencia military jurisdiction, on 26 May 1942, Special War Council No. 2 met in order to examine and make a pronouncement regarding Case No. 6981-V, which was handled by exceptional proceeding and brought against the accused José Pellicer Gandía ... of punishable age and having other characteristics contained within the report. Having understood the list of charges read by the clerk, the indictment by the prosecutor, the arguments of the defence and the statements of those of the accused present in the court, let it be shown that the accused José Pellicer Gandía—thirty years of age, a native and resident of Valencia, married, a typist, the son of Pedro and Virginia, well-educated and with no criminal record—is admonished for the following:

Prior to the glorious National Movement, he was a member of the CNT since 1932. During the days following the start of said National Movement, given that he lived in Valencia, he presented himself as a volunteer in order to join a column organised by the CNT Defence Committee. Said column had been formed by Pérez Feliu, one Mariano from the construction sector, one Sánchez from the woodworkers' sector and Castillo Virumbrales from Zaragoza. This column was initially known as the 'CNT Defence Group' and was commanded by Rafael Martí, aka 'Pancho Villa,' who died in late August on the Teruel front. After the death of 'Pancho Villa,' the column was reorganised and led by a Committee on which the accused served as war delegate alongside Antonio López Lahiguera, both of whom played prominent roles within the military command assumed by Pérez Salas. This was the Committee to which the Iron Column was answerable, and the Column carried out instructions that emanated from said Committee. The Column had delegates in many villages, such as Mora de Rubielos, where it appointed as its delegate one Eliado, alias 'Málaga.'

In late October, on the pretext that one of its militias had been murdered in Valencia, the Column abandoned the front with weapons in hand and launched an attack on the Communists in Valencia's Plaza de Tetuán, during which attack the accused was wounded. In March 1937, the Iron Column disbanded and became the Eighty-third Mixed Brigade, in which the accused was appointed commander with the rank of major before being wounded again on the Albarracín front. On the grounds that he had failed to explain the use of some automobile tyres, the accused was arrested by the red Servicio de Información Militar (Military Information Service—SIM) and transported to Barcelona, where he was jailed until 31 August of that same year. He was restored to the aforementioned position of command before travelling from Barcelona to Valencia by plane, due to the fact that the lines of communication between the two cities had been severed. In October of that same year he was appointed commander of the 4th Battalion of the 109th Mixed Brigade. At the beginning of the uprising, acting on orders from the Popular Front and from the CNT, the Column's Committee, on which the accused was serving as war delegate, ordered that one or two centuries be attacked—I beg your pardon—that one or two centuries be assigned to set fire to the archives of the city's Modelo prison and release the prisoners being held there. Moreover, another two centuries, commanded in turn by the accused José Segarra and Ricardo Cortés, attacked...

Decree Law of 10 January 1937
Whereas:
The aforementioned articles are generally applicable, but section nine of the addenda to the decree of 25 January 1940 is inapplicable to the case under consideration because, prior to and during the glorious National Movement, the damage and harm caused to the state and to individuals were extremely serious. In addition, the contribution made by the accused to the national cause was non-existent. If the persons named in the report were indeed saved thanks to the accused, their number had little weight compared to the ravages and murders committed by the Iron Column under the command of the first two accused. A significant portion of the persons rescued were so saved not because the accused wanted to help, but rather because they were trying to satisfy intermediaries who had intervened, as set out in earlier documents... And since the conduct of the two accused falls within the domain of application of articles four, eight, nine, fifteen and seventeen in the case of the first of the accused, and articles four, five, eight and twelve in the case of the second, all of which articles pertain to section one of the ordinances that appear in the addendum to the decree of 25 January 1940 ... we hereby determine that we must and do find the accused José Pellicer Gandía ... guilty of the proven offence of adherence to the rebellion, with extremely significant aggravating circumstances: to wit, that he displayed enormous perversity and caused significant damage to the state and to individuals, which circumstances are described in article seventy-three of the Code of Military Justice as warranting the death penalty or, in the event of clemency, withdrawal of all citizenship rights and absolute legal incapacitation... Furthermore, as a result of their civil liability, the three accused are sentenced to pay a yet-to-be-determined sum as compensation.

Addendum:

The War Council, which reaffirms the obedience and respect that it owes Your Excellency, esteems that, given the nature of the verdict pronounced against the first two accused, pertaining as it does to section one of the ordinances that appear in the addendum to the decree of 25 January 1940, it is not appropriate in this instance for the two accused to be offered the possibility of clemency mentioned in the verdict. Nevertheless, that is a decision to be made by Your Excellency.

(There follow five illegible signatures.)

The sentence concerning José Pellicer Gandía was carried out in Paterna on 8 June 1942...

(Document delivered to Mrs Coral Pellicer Veloso on 27 March 1980, at her request, by the Valencia Military Court)

A handwritten comment by Coral Pellicer follows:

'My mother secured clemency (she then moved away to Madrid). But the Falangists wanted to do away with the Pellicers. The clemency order was stored in a box and handed over to my mother after the sentence was carried out.'

Letter from José Escrig Ivars to Coral Pellicer

Mrs. Coral Pellicer
Elche
5 March 1986
Señora,

You will probably be surprised to receive my letter. I myself am surprised to find myself writing to someone whom I have not had the pleasure of knowing, apart from things I have heard.

In truth, my aim is to honour a promise I made in Chile to your aunt Lolita—who is an old friend of mine—when I was about to embark on my trip back to Spain. I last saw her in Santiago, where I had spent three months for family reasons.

Your aunt asked me to visit you or write to you—on my return to Madrid, it proved impossible to satisfy that first wish, which is why I am honouring the second—in order to accommodate your burning desire to have news and details from her regarding your father's personality, with which you did not have time to become acquainted. From contrasting vantage points—Pepe Pellicer's was apolitical while mine was political—that proved compatible despite our both being of the left and among the workers, we expressed our differences on numerous occasions, and we also clashed. But despite the harshness of such confrontations, we never lost our regard and respect for each other. It is precisely for this reason that I can now speak of him without being partisan.

Pepe was above all a man of firmly rooted ideas. Secure in his generosity, he never hesitated to risk everything for the sake of those ideas. He was not a theorist, but rather a man of action who was always on the move. He did not share the point of view of those within the anarcho-syndicalist movement whose only objective was to enlarge the CNT in order to build an active trade union force capable of confronting the employers.

He was one of those who clearly saw that the trade union organisation was extremely important for rallying the workers and increasing their strength, but that on the other hand it was also necessary for the organisation to have the determination to radically alter the foundations of society. This is the reason why he believed that the trade unions should be led by militants who were conscious of the necessity of those objectives and of the actions to be carried out by the specific groups of the Iberian Anarchist Federation (FAI).

Thus, he was always the first to participate in direct actions in support of strikes and in the expropriation of the economic machinery of the property-owners; never for his own benefit, but rather in order to place such machinery at the service of collective needs: in other words, the needs of the organisation to which he belonged.

This resulted in his imprisonment at the Modelo de Mislata (Valencia) on more than one occasion. Once, he displayed great audacity by refusing to escape in the company of a number of other inmates through a tunnel dug beneath one of the courtyards.

At the time of the military coup d'état, he was one of those who—from the very beginning—devoted themselves to the organisation of the Iron Column, together with the volunteers who left to fight on the Teruel front. In this capacity he played a role of the first order.

After the war, when he was imprisoned again in Mislata together with Peiró—who had been a minister representing the CNT in the

Popular Front government—it was proposed that they collaborate with the new regime's vertical trade unions in exchange for their release. They both declined the offer. Later on, they were tried and shot.

There you have, as far as I can remember, the principal features of your father's personality, of which you can be proud no matter what your current beliefs are.

For my part, even though my positions may have been different, I will always consider myself his friend and admirer.

José Escrig Ivars

Eye-witness in Barcelona

I.

Much has already been written about the May riots in Barcelona, and the major events have been carefully tabulated in Fenner Brockway's pamphlet, *The Truth About Barcelona*, which so far as my own knowledge goes is entirely accurate. I think, therefore, that the most useful thing I can do here, in my capacity as eye-witness, is to add a few footnotes upon several of the most-disputed points.

First of all, as to the purpose, if any, of the so-called rising. It has been asserted in the Communist press that the whole thing was a Carefully-prepared effort to overthrow the Government and even to hand Catalonia over to the Fascists by provoking foreign intervention in Barcelona. The second part of this suggestion is almost too ridiculous to need refuting. If the P.O.U.M. and the left-wing Anarchists were really in league with the Fascists, why did not the militias at the front walk out and leave a hole in the line? And why did the C.N.T. transport-workers, in spite of the strike, continue sending supplies to the front? I cannot, however, say with certainly that a definite revolutionary intention was not in the minds of a few extremists, especially the Bolshevik Leninists (usually called Trotskyists) whose pamphlets were handed round the barricades. What I can say is that the ordinary rank and file behind the barricades never for an instant thought of themselves as taking part in a revolution. We thought, all of us, that we were simply defending ourselves against an attempted coup d'état by the Civil Guards, who had forcibly seized the Telephone Exchange and might seize some more of the workers' buildings if we did not show ourselves willing to fight. My reading of the situation, derived from what people were actually doing and saying at the time, is this:—

The workers came into the streets in a spontaneous defensive movement, and they only consciously wanted two things: the handing-back of the Telephone Exchange and the disarming of the hated Civil Guards. In addition there was the resentment caused by the growing poverty in Barcelona and the luxurious life lived by the bourgeoisie. But it is probable that the opportunity to overthrow the Catalan Government existed if there had been a leader to take advantage of it. It seems to be widely agreed that on the third day the workers were in a position to take control of the city; certainly the Civil Guards were greatly demoralised and were surrendering in large numbers. And though the Valencia Government could send fresh troops to crush the workers (they did send 6,000 Assault Guards when the fighting was over), they could not maintain those troops in Barcelona if the transport-workers chose not to supply them. But in fact no resolute revolutionary leadership existed. The Anarchist leaders disowned the whole thing and said "Go back to work," and the P.O.U.M. leaders took an uncertain line. The orders sent to us at the P.O.U.M. barricades, direct from the P.O.U.M. leadership, were to stand by the C.N.T., but not to fire unless we were fired on ourselves or our buildings attacked. (I personally was fired at a number of times, but never fired back.) Consequently, as food ran short, the workers began to trickle back to work; and, of course, once they were safely dispersed, the reprisals began. Whether the revolutionary opportunity *ought* to have been taken advantage of is another question. Speaking solely for myself, I should answer "No." To begin with it is doubtful whether the workers could have maintained power for more than a few weeks; and, secondly, it might well have meant losing the war against Franco. On the other hand the essentially defensive action taken by the workers was perfectly correct; war or no war, they had a right to defend what they had won in July, 1936. It may be, of course, that the revolution was finally lost in those few days in May. But I still think it was a little better, though only a very little, to lose the revolution than to lose the war.

Secondly, as to the people involved. The Communist press took the line, almost from the start, of pretending that the "rising" was wholly or almost wholly the work of the P.O.U.M. (aided by "a few irresponsible hooligans," according to the New York *Daily Worker*). Anyone who was in Barcelona at the time knows that this is an absurdity. The enormous majority of the people behind the barricades were ordinary C.N.T. workers. And this point is of importance, for it was as a scapegoat for the May riots that the P.O.U.M. was recently suppressed; the four hundred or more P.O.U.M. supporters who are in the filthy, verminous Barcelona jails at this moment, are there ostensibly for their share in the May riots. It is worth pointing, therefore, to two good reasons why the P.O.U.M. were not and could not have been the prime movers. In the first place, the P.O.U.M. was a very small party. If one throws in Party members, militiamen on leave, and helpers and sympathisers of all kinds, the number of P.O.U.M. supporters on the streets could not have been anywhere near ten thousand—probably not five thousand; but the disturbances manifestly involved scores of thousands of people. Secondly, there was a general or nearly general strike for several days; But the P.O.U.M., as such, had no power to call a strike, and the strike could not have happened if the rank and file of the C.N.T. had not wanted it. As to those involved on the other side, the London *Daily Worker* had the impudence to suggest in one issue that the "rising" was suppressed by the Popular Army. Everyone in Barcelona knew, and the Daily Worker must have known as well, that the Popular Army remained neutral and the troops stayed in their barracks throughout the disturbances. A few soldiers, however, did take part as individuals; I saw a couple at one of the P.O.U.M.. barricades.

Thirdly, as to the stores of arms which the P.O.U.M. are supposed to have been hoarding in Barcelona. This story has been repeated so often that even a normally critical observer like H. N. Brailsford accepts it without any investigation and speaks of the "tanks and guns" Which the P.O.U.M. had "stolen from Government arsenals" (*New Statesman*, May 22). As a matter of fact the P.O.U.M. possessed pitifully few weapons, either at the front or in the rear. During the street-fighting I was at all three of the principal strongholds of the P.O.U.M., the Executive Building, the Comité Local and the Hotel Falcón. It is worth recording in detail what armaments these buildings contained. There were in all about 80 rifles, some of them defective, besides a few obsolete guns of various patterns, all useless because there were no cartridges for them. Of rifle ammunition there was about 50 rounds for each weapon. There were no machineguns, no pistols and no pistol ammunition. There were a few cases of hand-grenades, but these were sent to us by the C.N.T. after the fighting started. A highly-placed militia officer afterwards gave me his opinion that in the whole of Barcelona the P.O.U.M. possessed about a hundred and fifty rifles and *one* machine-gun. This, it will be seen, was barely sufficient for the armed guards which at that time all parties, P.S.U.C., P.O.U.M., and C.N.T.-F.A.I. alike, placed on their principal buildings. Possibly it may be said that even in the May riots the P.O.U.M. were still hiding their weapons. But in that case what becomes of the claim that the May riots were a P.O.U.M. rising intended to overthrow the Government?

In reality, by far the worst offenders in this matter of keeping weapons from the front, were the Government themselves. The infantry on the Aragon front were far worse-armed than an English public school O.T.C., but the rear-line troops, the Civil Guards, Assault Guards and Carabineros, who were not intended for the front, but were used to "preserve order" (i.e., overawe the workers) in the rear, were armed to the teeth. The troops on the Aragon front had worn-out Mauser rifles, which usually jammed after five shots, approximately one machine-gun to fifty men, and one pistol or revolver to about thirty men. These weapons, so necessary in trench warfare, were not issued by the Government and could only be bought illegally and with the greatest difficulty. The Assault Guards were armed with brand-new Russian rifles; in addition, every man was issued with an automatic pistol, and there was one sub-machine-gun between ten or a dozen men. These facts speak for themselves. A Government which sends boys of fifteen to the front with rifles forty years old, and keeps its biggest men and newest weapons in the rear, is manifestly more afraid of the revolution than of the Fascists. Hence the feeble war-policy of the past six months, and hence the compromise with which the war will almost certainly end.

II.

When the P.O.U.M., the Left Opposition (so-called Trotskyist) off-shoot of Spanish Communism, was suppressed on June 16–17, the fact in itself surprised nobody. Ever since May, or even since February, it had been obvious that the P.O.U.M. would be "liquidated" if the Communists could bring it about. Nevertheless, the suddenness of the suppressive action, and the mixture of treachery and brutality with which it was carried out, took everyone, even the leaders, completely unaware.

Ostensibly the Party was suppressed on the charge, which has been repeated for months in the Communist press though not taken seriously by anyone inside Spain, that the P.O.U.M. leaders were in the pay of the Fascists. On June 16 Andrés Nin, the leader of the Party, was arrested in his office. The same night, before any proclamation had been made, the police raided the Hotel Falcón, a sort of boarding-house maintained by the P.O.U.M. and used chiefly by militiamen on leave, and arrested everybody in it on no particular charge. Next morning the P.O.U.M. was declared illegal and all P.O.U.M. buildings, not only offices, bookstalls, etc., but even libraries and sanatoriums for wounded men, were seized by the police. Within a few days all or almost all of the forty members of the Executive Committee were under arrest. One or two who succeeded in going into hiding were made to give themselves up by the device, borrowed from the Fascists, of seizing their wives as hostages. Nin was transferred to Valencia and thence to Madrid, and put on trial for selling military information to the enemy. Needless to say the usual "Confessions," mysterious letters written in invisible ink, and other "evidence" were forthcoming in such profusion as to make it reasonably likely that they had been prepared beforehand. As early as June 19 the news reached Barcelona, via Valencia, that Nin had been shot. This report was, we hope, untrue, but it hardly needs pointing out that the Valencia Government will be obliged to shoot a number, perhaps a dozen, of the P.O.U.M. leaders if it expects its charges to be taken seriously.

Meanwhile, the rank and file of the Party, not merely party members, but soldiers in the P.O.U.M. militia and sympathisers and helpers of all kinds, were being thrown into prison as fast as the police could lay hands on them. Probably it would be impossible to get hold of accurate figures, but there is reason to think that during the first week there were 400 arrests in Barcelona alone; certainly the jails were so full that large numbers of prisoners had to be confined in shops and other temporary dumps. So far as I could discover, no discrimination was made in the arrests between those who had been concerned in the May riots and those who had not. In effect, the outlawry of the P.O.U.M. was made retrospective; the P.O.U.M. was now illegal, and therefore one was breaking the law by having ever belonged to it. The police even went to the length of arresting the wounded men in the sanatoriums. Among the prisoners in one of the jails I saw, for instance, two men of my acquaintance with amputated legs; also a child of not more than twelve years of age.

One has got to remember, too, just what imprisonment means in Spain at this moment. Apart from the frightful overcrowding of the temporary jails, the insanitary conditions, the lack of light and air and the filthy food, there is the complete absence of anything that we should regard as legality. There is, for instance, no nonsense about Habeas Corpus. According to the present law, or at any rate the present practice, you can be imprisoned for an indefinite time not merely without being tried but even without being charged; and until you have been charged the authorities can, if they choose, keep you "incommunicado"—that is, without the right to communicate with a lawyer or anyone else in the outside world. It is easy to see how much the "confessions" obtained in such circumstances are worth. The situation is all the worse for the poorer prisoners because the P.O.U.M. Red Aid, which normally furnishes prisoners with legal advice, has been suppressed along with the other P.O.U.M. institutions.

But perhaps the most odious feature of the whole business was the fact that all news of what had happened was deliberately concealed, certainly for five days, and I believe for longer, from the troops on the Aragon front. As it happened, I was at the front from June 15 to 20. I had got to see a medical board and in doing so to visit various towns behind the front line, Siétamo, Barbastro, Monzón, etc. In all these places the P.O.U.M. militia headquarters, Red Aid centres and the like were functioning normally, and as far down the line as Lérida (only about 100 miles from Barcelona) and as late as June 20, not a soul had heard that the P.O.U.M. had been suppressed. All word of it had been kept out of the Barcelona papers, although, of course, the Valencia papers (which do not get to the Aragon front) were flaming with the story of Nin's "treachery." Together with a number of others I had the disagreeable experience of getting back to Barcelona to find that the P.O.U.M. had been suppressed in my absence. Luckily I was warned just in time and managed to make myself scarce, but other[s] were not so fortunate. Every P.O.U.M. militiaman who came down the line at this period had the choice of going straight into hiding or into jail—a really pleasant reception after three or four months in the front line. The motive for all this is obvious: the attack on Huesca was just beginning, and presumably the Government feared that if the P.O.U.M. militia knew what was happening they might refuse to march. I do not, as a matter of fact, believe that the loyalty of the militia would have been affected; still, they had a right to know the truth. There is something unspeakably ugly in sending men into battle (when I left Siétamo the fight was beginning and the first wounded were jolting in the ambulances down the abominable roads) and at the same time concealing from them that behind their back their party was being suppressed, their leaders denounced as traitors and their friends and relatives thrown into prison.

The P.O.U.M. was by far the smallest of the revolutionary parties, and its suppression affects relatively few people. In all probability the sum total of punishments will be a score or so of people shot or sentenced to long terms of imprisonment, a few hundreds ruined and a few thousands temporarily persecuted. Nevertheless, its suppression is symptomatically important. To begin with it should make clear to the outside world, what was already obvious to many observers in Spain, that the present Government has more points of resemblance to Fascism than points of difference. (This does not mean that it is not worth fighting for as against the more naked Fascism of Franco and Hitler. I myself had grasped by May the Fascist tendency of the Government, but I was willing to go back to the front and in fact did so.) Secondly, the elimination of the P.O.U.M. gives warning of the impending attack upon the Anarchists. These are the real enemy whom the Communists fear as they never feared the numerically insignificant P.O.U.M. The Anarchist leaders have now had a demonstration of the methods likely to be used against them; the only hope for the revolution, and probably for victory in the war, is that they will profit by the lesson and get ready to defend themselves in time.

George Orwell

(From *Controversy: The Socialist Forum*, v.1, n.11, August 1937.)

Bibliography

Andrade, J. *La Revolución Española, Día a Día*. Barcelona: Ed. Nueva Era, 1979.

Bahamonde y Sánchez de Castro, Antonio. *Un Año con Queipo*. Barcelona: Ediciones Españolas, 1938.

Bernecker, L. Walther. *Colectividades y Revolución Social*. Barcelona: Ed. Grijalbo, 1982.

Bolloten, Burnett. *La Revolución Española*. Mexico: Editorial Jus, S.A., 1962.

Bosch Sánchez, A. *Ugetistas y Libertarios*. Valencia: Publicaciones Alfonso el Magnánimo, 1983.

Buenacasa, Manuel. *El Movimiento Obrero Español*. Paris: Edición 'Amigos del Autor,' 1966; Gijón: Júcar, 1977.

CNT. *Los Sucesos de Barcelona*. Ediciones Ebro, 1937.

———. *De Julio a Julio, un Año de Lucha*. Barcelona: Editorial Tierra y Libertad, 1937.

Claudín, Fernando. *La Crisis del Movimiento Comunista*, Vol. I. Paris: Ediciones Ruedo Ibérico, 1970.

Cruells, Manuel. *El Separatisme Català Durant la Guerra Civil*. Barcelona: Ediciones Dopesa, 1975.

———. *Els Fets de Maig*. Barcelona: 1970.

Díaz, José. *Tres Años de Lucha*. Buscarets: Ediciones Ebro, 1970.

Durán, Gustavo. *Una Enseñanza de la Guerra Española*. Madrid: Ed. Júcar, 1980.

García Oliver, Juan. *El Eco de los Pasos*. Barcelona: Editorial Ruedo Ibérico, 1978.

Grossi, Manuel. *L'Insurrection des Asturies*. Ed. Edi-París, 1972.

Guillén, Abraham. *El Error Militar de las 'Izquierdas.'* Barcelona: Ed. Hacer, 1980.

Guzmán, Eduardo. *Madrid Rojo y Negro*. Caracas: Ed. Vértice, 1972.

Hernández, Jesús. *La Grande Trahison*. Paris: Ed. Fasquelle, 1953.

Koltzov, M. *Diario de la Guerra de España*. Paris: Editorial Ruedo Ibérico, 1963.

Krivitsky, W.G. *La Mano de Stalin Sobre España*. Toulouse: Ediciones Claridad, 1946.

Largo Caballero, Francisco. *Mis Recuerdos*. Mexico: Editores Unidos, S.A., 1954.

Leval, Gaston. *Espagne Libertaire (1936–1939)*. Paris: Ed. de la Tête de Feuilles, 1971.

Manzanera, Elías. *Documento Histórico*. Barcelona: 1981.

Martínez Bande, José Manuel. *La Invasión de Aragón y el Desembarco en Mallorca*. Madrid: Ediciones San Martín, 1970.

Mehring, Franz. *Carlos Marx*. Mexico: Ed. Grijalbo, 1957.

Mera, Cipriano. *Guerra, Exilio y Cárcel de un Anarcosindicalista*. Paris: Ed. Ruedo Ibérico, 1976.

Modesto, Juan. *Soy del Quinto Regimiento*. Paris: Ediciones Ebro, 1969.

Nettlau, Max. *Miguel Bakunin, la Internacional y la Alianza en España*. Madrid: Ediciones de la Piqueta, 1977.

Orwell, George. *Cataluña 1937*. Buenos Aires: Ed. Proyección, 1963.

——. *Homenaje a Cataluña*. Barcelona: Ed. Virus, 2000.

Paniagua, Xavier. *La Sociedad Libertaria*. Barceona: Ed. Grijalbo, 1982.

Paz, Abel. *Durruti, el Proletariado en Armas*. Barcelona: Ed. Brugera, 1978.

——. *Durruti en la Revolución Española*. Madrid: Fundación Anselmo Lorenzo, 1996.

——. *Paradigma de una Revolución*. Toulouse: Ed. A.I. de los T., 1967.

Peirats, José. *La CNT en la Revolución Española*. Toulouse: Ed. CNT, 1952.

Prieto, Indalecio. *Convulsiones de España*. Mexico: Ed. Oasis, 1968.

Ramos, Vicente. *La Guerra Civil*. Provincia de Alicante. Alicante: Ediciones Biblioteca Alicantina, 1974.

Rezzete, Robert. *Les Partits Politiques Marrocaines*. Paris: Ed. Armand Colin, 1955.

Richards, Vernon. *Enseñanzas de la Revolución Española*. Paris: Ed. Belibaste/La Hormiga, 1971.

Rieger, Max. *Espionaje en España*. Barcelona: Ed. Unidad, 1938.

Riera, Germán. *Habla un Vencido*. Barcelona: Distribuciones Catalonia, 1979.

Roig, Montserrat. *Rafael Vidiella, l'Aventura de la Revolució*. Barcelona: Ed. Laia, 1976.

Rojo, Vicente. *Así Fue la Defensa de Madrid*. Mexico: Ed. Era, 1967.

——. *España Heroica*. Mexico: Ed. Era, 1967.

Salas Larrazábal, R. *Historia del Ejército Popular de la República*. Madrid: Editora Nacional, 1973.

Santillán, Diego Abad de. *Por Qué Perdimos la Guerra*. Buenos Aires: Ed. Imán, 1940.

Smyth, Terence M. *La CNT al País Valencià 1936–1937*. Valencia: Tres i Quatre, 1977.

Thalmann, Pavel and Clara. *Combats pour la Liberté*. Paris: Ed. la Digitale, 1983.

Tolgliatti, Palmiro. *Escritos sobre la Guerra en España*. Barcelona: Ed. Grijalbo, 1980.

Torralba Coronas, P. *De Ayerbe a la Roja y Negra*. Barcelona: Creaciones Gráficas, 1980.

Toryho, Jacinto. *No Éramos Tan Malos*. Madrid: Ed. del Toro, 1975.

Other sources (for the period 19 July 1936 to August 1937): Oral testimony.

Press: *CNT*, *El Combate* (CNT-FAI Second Column, Valencia), *El Frente* (Durruti Column), *El Luchador* (Republican daily, Alicante), *Fragua Social*, *Frente Libertario* (CNT-FAI militias, Madrid), *La Correspondencia de Valencia*, *Liberación* (FAI, Alicante), *Línea de Fuego* (CNT-FAI Iron Column, Teruel), *Mundo Obrero*, *Nosotros*, *Solidaridad Obrera*, *Victoria* (Torres-Benedito Column).

Index

The **KATE SHARPLEY LIBRARY** exists to preserve and promote anarchist history. We preserve the output of the anarchist movement, mainly in the form of books, pamphlets, newspaper, leaflets and manuscripts but also badges, recordings, photographs etc. We also have the work of historians and other writers on the anarchist movement.

We promote the history of anarchism by publishing studies based on those materials—or reprints of original documents taken from our collection. These appear in our quarterly bulletin or regularly published pamphlets. We have also provided manuscripts to other anarchist publishers. People come and research in the library, or we can send out photocopies.

We don't say one strand of class-struggle anarchism has all the answers. We don't think anarchism can be understood by looking at 'thinkers' in isolation. We do think that what previous generations thought and did, what they wanted and how they tried to get it, is relevant today. We encourage the anarchist movement to think about its own history—not to live on past glories but to get an extra perspective on current and future dangers and opportunities.

Everything at the Kate Sharpley Library—acquisitions, cataloguing, preservation work, publishing, answering inquiries is done by volunteers: we get no money from governments or the business community. All our running costs are met by donations (from members of the collective or our subscribers and supporters) or by the small income we make through publishing.

Please consider donating or subscribing to our bulletin: www.katesharpleylibrary.net

Bulletin of the
Kate Sharpley Library

Support AK Press!

AK Press is one of the world's largest and most productive

anarchist publishing houses. We're entirely worker-run and democratically managed. We operate without a corporate structure—no boss, no managers, no bullshit. We publish close to twenty books every year, and distribute thousands of other titles published by other like-minded independent presses from around the globe.

The Friends of AK program is a way that you can directly contribute to the continued existence of AK Press, and ensure that we're able to keep publishing great books just like this one! Friends pay a minimum of $25 per month, for a minimum three month period, into our publishing account. In return, Friends automatically receive (for the duration of their membership), as they appear, one free copy of every new AK Press title. They're also entitled to a 20% discount on everything featured in the AK Press Distribution catalog and on the website, on any and every order. You or your organization can even sponsor an entire book if you should so choose!

There's great stuff in the works—so sign up now to become a Friend of AK Press, and let the presses roll!

Won't you be our friend? Email friendsofak@akpress.org for more info, or visit the Friends of AK Press website: http://www.akpress.org/programs/friendsofak